NEWFOUNDLANDS
TODAY

Hedd & Del Richards

Howell Book House

HOWELL
BOOK
HOUSE

New York

HOWELL BOOK HOUSE
A Simon & Schuster / Macmillan Company
1633 Broadway
New York, NY 10019

MACMILLAN is a registered trademark of Macmillan, Inc.

Library of Congress Cataloging-in-Publication Data

Richards, Hedd.
    Newfoundlands today / Hedd & Del Richards.
            p.   cm.
        ISBN 0–87605–248–4
        1. Newfoundland dog.   I. Richards, Del. II. Title
    SF429.N4R535 1998
    636.73--dc21   97–34518
                                                                        CIP

Manufactured in Singapore

10 9 8 7 6 5 4 3 2 1

CONTENTS

To all our dogs – past and present.

*A*CKNOWLEDGEMENTS

Many thanks to the following:

Judy Oriani, with whom the chapter on Grooming was co-written; Alan Farrar, who contributed the chapter on Water Work; Gareth B. Williams, author of the chapter on Draught Work; Nigel Gregory, our vet, for checking the contents of the chapter on Health and Ailments; Fay Greer (Canada) for her help with the chapter on North America; Donna Overman for her detective work in tracing breeders; Lou Lomax, who became a good friend through her tireless work contacting US kennels.

In the Worldwide chapter, grateful thanks are due to a number of correspondents and co-authors including: Joan Wilkins (South Africa); Lee Wales (Australia); Anne Rogers (NZ) who also provided many of the photographs; Søren Wesseltoft (Denmark); Knut Berglie (Norway); our friend Lena Pettersson (Sweden); Eric Prunier (France); Karin Bronnecke (Germany); Beatrice Schiatti (Italy); and our nephew, Christopher Meyrick, for his help with the translations.

Finally, we thank Viv Rainsbury for her excellent line drawings, Richard Firstbrook, Christine Foley, Di Sellers, Chris and Paul Tedder, and all those who have contributed towards this book.

1 AN INTRODUCTION TO THE NEWFOUNDLAND

The origins of the Newfoundland are somewhat indistinct. The breed may have descended from the Bear Dogs brought over by Leif Ericson in 1,000 AD, or it is possible that the Tibetan Mastiff, on its eventual journey over the Asian continent, had a part in the Newfoundland's development.

It is, however, generally agreed that the Newfoundland as we know it today probably did not originate on the island of the same name. Records show that the first known dogs on the island were smaller and of a Spitz type, with pointed ears and curled tails. Explorers and traders with Newfoundland are likely to have brought ships' dogs with them and, by crossing with the native dogs, caused a different type of breed to evolve. Many breeds have been suggested as being responsible for the varying traits displayed in the Newfoundland – Portuguese Water Dogs, Pyrenean Mountain Dogs, Collies, Setters and Spaniels are all mentioned. As there is no certain way of knowing, it may be as well to keep an open mind. Several breeds could have been used by the indigenous Beothuk Indians to assist them with fishing and hauling.

It is an amusing fact that anyone interested in any other large breed can quote the origins of the Newfoundland, while those who are involved in the breed itself, recognise its obscure history and are often unable to decide which version to accept.

In the 1600s, a breed of dog whose description bears great resemblance to the Newfoundland was being traded in North America. The breed's popularity grew until, in the late 1800s, it was considered an emblem of affluence at many large country houses.

Around this time, the Newfoundland appeared in Britain in a similar role, although there is some evidence to suggest that the breed had already been imported prior to that date. As well as being the children's guard dog and companion at wealthy homes, the breed was also used by traders who harnessed the dogs to carts. The dogs were expected to carry a variety of supplies for long distances, and there is no doubt that many of them suffered greatly and even died from exhaustion before a law was passed forbidding their use in this way.

The late 1800s also saw the Newfoundland's debut in the show ring. The first champion Newfoundland in Britain is recorded as being a landseer called Ch. Dick, owned by a Mr Evans. Breeders and exhibitors of the day strove to produce dogs that retained the retrieving and swimming instincts of the original dog of

The Newfoundland is admired worldwide. The multi BIS winner NZ Grand Ch. Wellfont Ironside, owned by the Sealcove kennel in New Zealand.

Newfoundland. As is to be expected, disagreements occurred when some owners aimed for a very tall dog and in doing so lost some of the desired bulk and power – an argument that is still valid today!

FAMOUS NAMES IN BRITAIN

By the beginning of the 20th century, the breed had gained a stronghold in Britain, but was possibly undergoing a slight decline in North America. Some notable British dogs of this time were Mrs Wetwan's Ch. Shelton Viking and his illustrious son Ch. Gipsy Duke, who became the breed record holder with twenty-two CCs (a record which held from 1910 until 1986, when it was surpassed by Ch. and Irish Ch. Wellfont Admiral). Another of Mrs Wetwan's dogs, Ch. Shelton King, was the sire of Ch. Siki who became of the greatest importance to Newfoundland history. Siki sired a great many Champions including Can. Ch. Shelton Cabin Boy, Can. Ch. Shelton Baron and Am. Ch. Harlingen Neptune. These three, exported to North America, were vital new bloodlines for the existing stock which had become weakened following World War Two. (It is said that, during the 1950s, every champion bred in America could be traced back to these three imports.) Descendants of these dogs, crossed with American

bloodlines, later returned to Britain in the shape of Harlingen Waseeka's Ocean Spray (landseer) and Harlingen Waseeka's Black Gold. This happened just prior to and after the Second World War, when British Newfoundlands were in need of new blood.

The Harlingen kennel of May Roberts in England was acknowledged by Newfoundland breeders throughout the world, with many champions (blacks and landseers) being produced. Black Gold's valuable contribution to the breed meant that, in the late 1940s, she was the dam of the only champion Newfoundlands in Britain, namely Ch. H. Brigantine and Ch. H. Pirate. Many imports to and exports from the Harlingen kennel ensured that the breed remained constant at a difficult time.

Another important British kennel during this period was the Fairwater affix of Mr and Mrs Handley who produced champions not only from their own stock but also via their stud dogs for other devotees of the breed. It is hard for today's breeders, who order their dog food in bulk and demand specific contents, to imagine the sight of Mr Handley who, we are told, cycled miles during the hostilities of the Second World War in order to collect left-over meat for his dogs. And this at the end of a full day's work!

The Newfoundland is still trained in water work – the task it was originally bred for.

Newfoundland annual registrations are now high enough to cause a twinge of concern but, in 1950 for example, there were only thirty-eight in England. Seventeen of those held the Perryhow affix of Mona Bennett, another breeder who concentrated her efforts on restoring the breed to its former popularity. Mrs Bennett's exports and imports from Holland ensured a varied gene pool. (The on-going importations gave rise to the situation where Mrs Bennett's landseer, Aurora of Perryhow, was one of only two English-bred Newfies alive at this time. She was reputed never to have been beaten in the show ring, although there were no Challenge Certificates awarded during this era.)

Later in the 1950s, when CCs were re-allocated to Newfoundlands, Mr and Mrs Aberdeen (Sparry), another couple dedicated to the breed, produced a total of fifty-nine puppies during a two-year period in order to keep the necessary quota of show awards in continuance. They were certainly rewarded three years later when every CC won over a period of eighteen months went to Sparry-bred males. Several Sparry bitches also took the top awards!

Since then many kennels have been founded, and assorted importations made from countries as varied as North America, Finland, Holland and Germany. From the 1960s onwards, kennel names such as Bachalaos, Barlight, Bonnybay, Clywoods,

Esmeduna, Harratons (well-known for its beautifully marked landseers), Laphroaig, Littlecreek, Littlegrange, Mapleopal, Orovales, Ragtime, Roydsrook, Sigroc, Sukiln, Tarnhill and Uskrail emerged and between them produced over fifty champions. There were others, but many of the above-named, although not actively breeding now, still own a Newfoundland and maintain considerable interest in the breed. Those interested in Newfoundland history can do no better than read *The Newfoundland,* edited by Carol Cooper.

IMPORTANT AMERICAN NEWFOUNDLANDS

In the USA, an important name is that of Elizabeth Power's Waseeka kennels. Starting in 1928, Mrs Power built up a valuable combination of bloodlines from imported dogs, which resulted in thirty Waseeka champions by 1940. Mrs Power's association with the Newfoundland Club of America Specialty is legendary, Waseeka dogs winning either BOB or BOS six times during the first ten years it was held. With nearly a decade of Waseeka dogs winning BOB at Westminster, it is hardly surprising that her skill as a breeder was recognised and she was invited to judge at the 1959 Specialty.

The well-known Dryad kennels, also founded in the late 1920s, had tremendous influence within the breed and were a starting point for other notable kennels such as Coastwise, Edenglen, Oquaga and Seawards. Major and Mrs Godsol (Coastwise), who owned the first Newfoundland to win a Best in Show, also became respected judges and , between them, officiated a total of four times at the NCA Specialty.

Bill and Helena Linn's Edenglen line was hugely successful for them, but even more important in founding other great kennels. Some, such as Britannia, Newton-Ark, Pooh Bear, Riptide, Shadybrook and Tuckamore, are still active today. As well as being acknowledged for Edenglen dogs, Bill Linn is fondly remembered by Newfoundland lovers all over the world.

Theodora and Clifford Hartz (Oquaga) spent nearly forty years breeding Newfoundlands and were themselves responsible for starting off a number of acclaimed kennels.

The Seawards kennel was another that spanned more than one human generation – starting with Elinor Ayers Jameson and passing on to her daughter Nell Ayers. Imported stock was also useful to this kennel, the best-known probably being the English-bred landseer Ch. Eaglebay Domino.

From the 1940s to the end of the 60s, dozens more illustrious names such as Bandom, Ganshlom, Harobed, Hilvigs, Indigo, Kuhaia, Little Bear, Minnemato, Nine Mile, Sojowase and Tranquilus appeared, and all made individual contributions to the breed.

CHARACTERISTICS

The Newfoundland can be described as the 'jack-of-all-trades' of the canine world – not as quick and agile as some Collies, but able and willing to do their work whether it falls into the category of herding livestock or competing in obedience and agility; lacking the aloof and watchful nature of a guard dog, but protective of his owner's children, should the need arise; without the versatility

The Newfoundland should be loving and reliable in temperament.

and zest of a gundog, but equally endowed with a soft mouth and retrieving skills. Most Newfoundlands are happy to attempt any task to please their owners and, although they may not excel, the effort made is a delight to watch. The hallmark of the breed, though, should be a loving and reliable temperament.

Despite their all-round abilities, Newfoundlands have very definite quirks of their own. 'Smiling' was once very common in the breed and, even today, many display this submissive grin, showing their teeth and gums, especially when they are in disgrace. (Inexperienced owners can sometimes mistake this for aggressive behaviour.)

The retrieving and pulling instinct can sometimes manifest itself in gently holding

Despite their size, the Newfoundland makes a wonderful family companion.

and tugging their owner's hands. Some people interested in water training occasionally encourage this behaviour, but it is another action which can be misinterpreted.

A Newfoundland who wants attention will, quite blatantly, paw (and claw!) the person next to him. Walking through two rows of benches at a championship show can be like passing under a bizarre 'Newfie Guard of Honour' while numerous paws swipe through the air in an attempt to catch the eye of a passerby!

There are very few Newfoundlands who do not have an instinctive love of water. Even those raised without ever seeing a lake or ocean can sometimes surprise their

owners with their response when they do. Rainwater, too, can be a treat and many owners will be familiar with having to call in their dogs when it rains. (First-time owners can become very concerned at the sight of their pet lying stretched out in a torrential downpour!)

Newfoundlands have no perception of their size. The look of surprise and 'How did it spot me?' is priceless if and when a Newfie tiptoes up behind a cat which promptly runs away as soon as it is overtaken by a large, black shadow. The look of hurt is unmistakable when a Newfie climbs on to the owner's lap amid screams of pain and cries of 'Get off me!'. Small cat or dog baskets meant for other pets in the household command no respect from a Newfie, who will happily lie in one like an overgrown soufflé convincing himself that he is comfortable.

Newfoundlands recognize their own breed (even if they are the only dog in their owner's household) and are generally not quarrelsome – a reason, perhaps, why so many Newfie lovers own more than one at a time. A Newfoundland's favourite companion, though, will be his owner and, on account of this preference, it is not surprising how many people have credited their pets with almost anthropomorphic qualities. This is no recent trend of present-day sentimentalists, but occurs throughout the Newfoundland's history. Those interested in collecting Newfoundland memorabilia are almost spoilt for choice in the range of items available. Since Sir Edwin Landseer's famous painting of *The Distinguished Member of the Humane Society* there have been numerous tributes to the breed in the form of portraits, memorials, poems and stories. Particularly meaningful to us is the plaque which says "Erected to the memory of Swansea Jack", who saved twenty-seven people from drowning in 1937 at Swansea, South Wales, and inspired our involvement with the breed.

LORD BYRON'S 'BOATSWAIN'

No book about the Newfoundland would be complete without a mention of Lord Byron whose companion dog, Boatswain, moved the poet to write the most touching of epitaphs when he died at the age of five. Boatswain was buried in the family vault at Newstead Abbey and a suitable memorial was raised, inscribed with both the epitaph and a poem depicting Byron's anguish.

Inscription on the Monument of a Newfoundland Dog.

Newstead Abbey, 1808.

When some proud son of man returns to earth
Unknown to glory, but upheld by birth,
The sculptor's art exhausts the art of woe,
And storied urns record who rest below;
When all is done, upon the tomb is seen,
Not what he was, but what he should have been;
But the poor Dog, in life the firmest friend,
The first to welcome, foremost to defend;
Whose honest heart is still his master's own,
Who labours, fights, lives, breathes for him alone,
Unhonour'd falls, unnoticed all his worth,
Denied in Heaven the soul he held on earth;
While man, vain insect! hopes to be forgiven,
And claims himself a sole exclusive Heaven!
Oh man! thou feeble tenant of an hour,
Debas'd by slavery, or corrupt by power,
Who knows thee well, must quit thee with disgust,
Degraded mass of animated dust!
Thy love is lust, thy friendship all a cheat,
Thy smiles hypocrisy, thy words deceit!
By nature vile, ennobled but by name,
Each kindred brute might bid thee blush for shame.
Ye! who, perchance, behold this single Urn
Pass on – it honours none you wish to mourn:
To mark a Friend's remains these stones arise,
I never knew but one, and here he lies.

Such is the Newfoundland character that the poem must strike a note of empathy with Newfie lovers everywhere.

2 TAKING ON A PUPPY

So you want a Newfoundland... You have just seen your first Newfie, a huge, magnificent creature who was well-behaved, immaculately groomed and gave you his paw within seconds of meeting you. To add to the overall appeal, this gentle giant was carrying his teddy bear in his mouth. You don't just want a Newfoundland – you want one *yesterday!*

You may be surprised to learn that this is the scene that inspires most people to telephone around to find a breeder with puppies for sale. You will certainly be surprised to hear that the great majority of them *never* get a dog because, by the time a responsible breeder has given them the true picture, warts and all, they realise that what they saw is only part of owning a Newfoundland.

Wonderful though they are, a Newfoundland is not for everyone. Even so, mistakes are made and, in Britain, out of every eight puppies reared, at least one will be discarded by the owner at some time during his life. It therefore makes sense to ensure that the dog is 100 per cent wanted by all members of the household before a purchase is made.

ARE YOU A SUITABLE OWNER?

Although responsible breeders thoroughly investigate prospective owners before allowing them to buy a puppy, nothing can really prepare you for the effect a Newfoundland will have on your life.

The addition of any dog to the household immediately curtails normal family life. In many respects, it is similar to having a child.

The Newfoundland is a most endearing breed – but think seriously before you take on a puppy.

You cannot suddenly decide to spend a night away from home, or take advantage of a last-minute holiday abroad.

As well as the cost of purchasing a puppy, there is the ongoing expense of feeding, vet's bills, boarding-kennel fees and necessary extras such as collars, pet blankets and the trademark of every Newfie owner, an estate car or station wagon! These are all items that will cost you more than if you had chosen to own a Chihuahua or Pomeranian.

Are you house-proud? If so, there is nothing more likely to plummet you into the depths of despair – for even clean and dry Newfies constantly shed their coats. Hair-less meals are a novelty in a Newfie household, and you will be perpetually amazed at how well-travelled a Newfie hair can be! Often, you will open a boiled egg to find that it is garnished by a single, black hair. You will be forced to dress only in dark-coloured clothes, so that the dog hair does not show up as easily (the only exception will be owners of landseers, who might as well go around naked, as there are no colours which disguise both black and white Newfie hairs).

Similarly, carpets and furnishings will need to be chosen with dog hair in mind, and the washing machine and vacuum cleaner filters will have to be changed more often. And that is just the good news! A wet or muddy Newfoundland can be enough to drive you over the edge. A dog who has been out in the rain carries a lot of water on such a large surface area, as you will see when he swiftly transfers it to the walls and furniture while shaking after coming indoors. Those webbed feet act like spoons when your Newfie has walked through puddles, and you will find it incredible how thoroughly four paws can wet an entire floor.

If you are already making a mental note not to go out on rainy days, remember that this scenario can be a daily occurrence. Most Newfoundlands love water and will actively seek it out on their walks. To a Newfie, a walk is not worth doing if he has not been

Children and dogs can make a good match, but make sure you have the time to devote to a giant breed.

through a puddle at least once. If he cannot find water outside, he will compromise by tipping his water bowl indoors and lie happily in the soggy mess!

Many Newfoundlands slobber, especially in hot weather. Taking a drink of water only adds volume to the saliva and your dog will have a permanently wet and slimy chest. Strings of slobber hanging from the dog's jaw are a common sight – until he shakes his head sending gooey bits on to ceilings, walls, people and anything else which happens to be in the room, including your dinner.

As stated earlier, Newfies have a considerable appetite and are expensive to feed (especially when they are still growing).

13

Consequently, a big dog who eats a lot will be even harder work to clean up from a toileting point of view and, unless done twice a day, your garden will soon become a minefield. You will also need to spend considerable time grooming your dog to keep him sweet-smelling and tangle-free.

Most importantly, your Newfie will need to be part of your family and cannot be left for ten hours a day while everyone is at work or school. It would be a never-ending task to attempt to house-train a puppy who was left for long periods. Similarly, a puppy or older dog who had no human companionship would soon become bored and, in an attempt to amuse himself, would switch his attention to chewing chair legs, doors or carpets.

Do you have the time to exercise and train a large dog? A healthy Newfie often enjoys his walks even more than his food and, although not be as fretful as some breeds if a walk is missed, the time spent with his owner investigating new scents and meeting new people and dogs will be important to him. A degree of basic training will also be needed if you are to avoid being hauled around by a dog who possibly weighs more than you do and who causes a nuisance everywhere he goes.

Do you have a young family? Many potential first-time dog owners are newlyweds whose next step into domesticity is to 'get a dog'. Not surprisingly, a subsequent move is to start a family and the combination of a boisterous teenage dog and a young baby or toddler is a major factor in dog re-homing statistics. Most Newfoundlands love children – they are, after all, nearer to the dog's mental age. Not all children, though, love Newfoundlands, and it is hardly fair to subject them to constant slobbering and being knocked over by a creature who is, to them, the size of a horse. Waiting just a few years can ensure a happier relationship for all concerned.

Maybe you have owned a Newfoundland in the past and, having now got over the loss of your old companion, are looking for a puppy. Both breeders and purchasers should take a step back in these circumstances. It is easy to believe that, having once shared your life with a Newfie, you are now prepared for another. If you have lost a ten or twelve-year-old dog, your memories of the last few years will be of a placid, undemanding dog who understood your routine and never put a foot wrong. Advancing years may mean that you will be unprepared for the hard work and hooliganism that often comes with young dogs. In these cases, taking on an older or rescued dog might be a better option.

Do you live in a high-rise flat or apartment? Even if you do, you may still be able to give your dog the love and attention he needs, but it is unlikely that he would be as happy as a Newfie with free access to a shady garden. And talking of that garden... Is yours a delight of manicured lawns and flower beds? If so, take a photograph and get it framed, for you will never see it again. A hot Newfie digs holes to find cooler earth. Even more fun is finding a bush or plant which bears his owner's scent. This will be dutifully uprooted and delivered indoors. To add to the game, the owner then re-plants the bush (re-inforcing the human scent) and a few days later the plant is retrieved again. So much more entertaining than a frisbee!

Even sensible older dogs can cause mayhem. Try speaking kindly to a mature dog who has just entered the room – then watch the devastation as his wagging tail sweeps ornaments off shelves and cups off coffee tables!

If you are still reading this book, and have not gone in search of a pet hamster to buy instead, congratulations! You have just crossed the first hurdle. Now you have only to convince a breeder that you are a suitable, prospective owner. Bearing in mind that responsible breeders have interrogation techniques that would put the FBI to shame, your greatest task is yet to come.

WHERE TO BUY

Never be tempted into buying a Newfie puppy from a pet shop, commercial dealer or puppy farm. They are only concerned with maximum profit for minimum effort. In other words, your puppy's parents will probably not have been screened for health defects. Lack of socialisation at commercial kennels often means that little is known about temperament. You will be paying a similar purchase price wherever you go, therefore it makes sense to deal with those breeders who have tried their best to produce a healthy, well-adjusted Newfoundland.

Similarly, do not rush off to buy a puppy from the first advertisement you see. Responsible breeders rarely need to advertise and usually have a waiting list for their puppies. Even if they have no puppies available, they may be able to recommend another, maybe slightly less well-known breeder, who has used their stud dog.

The most effective way of finding puppies for sale will be via the secretary of a breed club (your national Kennel Club will have contact numbers for those clubs). If you are simply looking for a pet (and this is the role in which a Newfoundland excels), you may want to restrict your contact to those breeders on the secretary's list who are nearest to your home. If you are looking for a particular bloodline for the show ring or working events, you may have to travel further.

Whatever your requirements, now is the time to decide on what colour, sex and quality of dog you want. Your Newfoundland will hopefully be with you for the next twelve years, so do not hurry into buying the first one you see just because it is available. Ideally, you will have made contact with a breeder before they have mated their bitch. The earlier you can book a puppy

from a breeder, the better chance you will have of being high on their list of potential purchasers. For someone who eventually wants to show a Newfie, it is obviously more sensible to be the second person to pick a puppy from the litter than the eighth! Quite often, the breeder and stud dog owner will choose first and second puppies, leaving third choice onwards to everyone else. Do not let this fact discourage you. Choosing puppies is not an exact science and, in the absence of a crystal ball, you could end up with the best or the worst in the litter. If the puppies are well-bred and fairly similar, even the 'worst' puppy can be a high-quality animal. If you have stated an intention to show your dog, an honest breeder with a good reputation will not deliberately sell you a puppy with an obvious fault. It does them no good in the long run if an inferior dog of their breeding is regularly seen at shows.

However, some people say they want a pet when in fact they intend to show, believing that they will get a puppy more cheaply. This is unfair to all concerned. To counteract this, many breeders now charge the same price for *all* their puppies, regardless of their 'show potential' or lack of it.

It is sometimes possible to have a puppy on 'breeding terms'. This is when a bitch puppy is given free of charge to the owner with the proviso that the breeder has the whole, or part of, her subsequent litter in due course. This is rarely an ideal situation and, even with a written contract, leaves many unanswered questions. While 'breeding terms' is a useful option in some circumstances, we feel it is not one that should be entered into lightly.

CHOOSING A PUPPY

You have passed all the tests, answered all the questions and are ready for your puppy. You are now approaching the big day when you choose your Newfoundland. In all probability, you have been waiting for this day since your breeder told you that the

NEWFOUNDLAND COLOURS

ABOVE: Black – the most common colour. Ch. Topsy's Oliver Twist winning BIS at the Working Breeds Association of Wales.   *Photo: Soren Wesseltoft.*

BOTTOM RIGHT: Brown – the shade is a matter of personal preference.
Ch. Merrybear Q'pid of Truesparta.

BOTTOM LEFT: Landseer – a white dog with black markings.
Int. and It. Ch. Geminorum Gomeisa, who has also won Ch. titles in Germany, Finland, Switzerland, Luxembourg and the USA.

puppies were born. It is very likely that you have been regularly going to see the litter since they were two weeks old, and have, mentally, already made your choice. Many puppy purchasers are impatient to select 'their' Newfie, and fail to see why breeders keep them waiting until the last moment.

From our own experience, we find that choosing a puppy has as much to do with luck as anything else, but the older the puppy the better the chance of assessing what he or she will be like when mature. For this reason, we are unwilling to make a choice before the puppy is six weeks old. Even when we go to view a litter of puppies bred by someone else, or sired by one of our stud dogs, we prefer to see them at about seven weeks of age. This is not always practical, but we have noticed a great difference in puppies who are just under six weeks old and those who are only a few days older.

Many breeders, like ourselves, have the litter checked by a vet at six weeks, and it would be extremely upsetting for a potential owner to be told that a chosen puppy had to be euthanised due to a severe heart problem. So, be patient when the breeder keeps you waiting for a few weeks – it may well be to your benefit.

WHAT TO LOOK FOR

Once again, it has to be remembered that the type of puppy you choose depends on your future plans for the dog. If you want an out-and-out pet, then you would choose a confident, but not pushy, puppy. In the event of several being equally confident, you can indulge yourself by choosing the one you think has the cutest face, a big white mark on the chest, or any other personal preference.

If you are intending to train your dog to work, you may wish to be guided by the results of the Puppy Aptitude Tests (where the breeder has had these carried out).

If you plan to show your Newfie, you will want a puppy that matches the Breed Standard as closely as possible. To achieve this, you will need to assess the puppy, point for point, first on a grooming table and then on the floor to check his movement. Someone once told us that "puppies are born as near to perfection as they will ever be – it is only as they grow that their faults grow with them!"

While the puppy stands on a grooming table, look for a square, cobby body. The whole puppy should look balanced, that is, without exaggerations such as too small a head, or being too long in the leg. The puppy's head should be fairly square and deep, right through to the muzzle. A shallow or pointed muzzle will only become more shallow and pointed as he gets older. Even breeds like German Shepherds have squarish muzzles as babies, so go for a puppy that has a blunt look to his head.

The ears should look slightly too big, but avoid pendulous, Cocker Spaniel-type appendages as they will always remain too big. Eye colour, at this stage, will be blue (or hazel in brown puppies), but it is fairly simple to predict the eventual colour because dark blue always turns to dark brown, while light blue becomes yellow or light brown. As a dark brown eye is the desired shade, you will do better to choose a darker blue. The eye rim should fit neatly around the eyeball, with no slackness or 'haw' showing. 'Loose' eyes are a common fault in the show ring and often detract from a dog's expression, so avoid any puppy displaying more than a minute pink triangle in the middle of the lower eyelid.

You will also need to look at the puppy's teeth to assess his bite. It is better to ask the breeder to show you the teeth, rather than struggle with the puppy and risk creating some sort of future phobia. There is nothing more likely to turn a mild-mannered breeder into a very 'protective parent' than to see his or her precious babies being handled roughly or incorrectly!

The puppies should look clean and well-cared for. Photo: Keith Allison.

The teeth should meet in a 'scissor' bite – that is, the top jaw tightly overlapping the bottom. There are many breeds that can be 'undershot' (the bottom front teeth protruding beyond the top) as puppies, but later 'grow right'. However, Newfies are not one of them. If the puppy is undershot at this stage, the condition will not improve as he grows, nor when the second teeth come through. Similarly, if the puppy is 'overshot' (top jaw protruding well over the bottom and creating a gap between the two sets of front teeth when the mouth is closed), then it is unlikely to be good enough for the show ring.

In order that a Newfie can cover a lot of ground when moving, it is essential that he has well-angulated front and hindquarters. Again, this can easily be assessed by putting a forefinger on the top of the shoulder (this will have a pointed feel and will be located at the withers near the bottom of the neck). Follow the rigid line of the bone down and slightly forward, until you find the next pointed bone (which will be the tip of the shoulder blade). From there, follow the line of the bone down and backwards, towards the puppy's elbow (which will be yet another pointed 'landmark' at the top of the front leg). By now, you should be mentally picturing a chevron shape. The angle created by the 'chevron' is known as the front angulation. The sharper the angle at the tip

of the shoulder blade, the better angulated the dog will be. Puppies tend to be better angulated as babies, but straighten out as they grow, so once again, it is best to opt for good, rather than moderate, angulation. Ideally, as well as the angle of the shoulder, the 'layback' (withers to tip of shoulder) should match in length the 'upper arm' (elbow to tip of shoulder), and this, too, can easily be checked.

The hind angulation also creates a similar chevron pattern. Starting at the hip, the bone runs down and forward towards the stifle joint (where the belly ends), and continues down and slightly backwards towards the hock joint. As the thigh bone cannot be felt as easily as the shoulder, a more effective way of judging hind angulation is to place the back leg with the hock and lower leg at right angles to the ground. The upper part of the leg (from hock to stifle) should then be lying obliquely, and pointing rather more forward than upwards when viewed from the side.

If the front edge of the leg gives an illusion of straightness from stifle to foot with a hardly discernible 'kink' at the hock, then the puppy will have poor angulation and will not cover as much ground as his well-angulated brother.

View the puppy's topline from the side. You should avoid any weak toplines that sag like an elderly horse. In our own line, we have noticed that a 'hump-backed' puppy at this age usually means an adult with a beautifully level topline, while those who are level have a tendency to 'give' a little as they get older.

The ribcage should feel well-barrelled, bearing in mind that it will straighten somewhat as the puppy grows. A narrow, 'slab-sided' Newfoundland is a great disappointment in the show ring, as he often looks quite impressive in outline, but is no more substantial than a cardboard cut-out when the judge has a closer look.

Most importantly, feel the girth of the front legs. A Newfoundland should have heavy, thickly-boned legs and huge feet. To allow for refinement occurring with maturity, look for a puppy whose feet and legs seem much too big for him.

Feel along the length of the tail. It should reach the hock and be free from kinks (which will feel like a knuckle or a break). Needless to say, if you are buying a male puppy, you will want to ensure that he has two descended testicles, as he will not be able to be shown if he is lacking in this department.

Next, place the puppy on the floor and watch as he moves around naturally (if he sits down he may have to be enticed by a toy on a string). He should move easily, although his feet may look a little heavy. He should be stepping out a wide rather than a narrow track. Watch how far apart his hind pads are. A puppy who moves closely now will be almost rubbing his legs together like a cricket by the time he is fully grown! Movement which is a little ungainly can be forgiven at this age, but any persistent lameness should not be ignored.

Give the puppy a toy to carry, and watch how high he carries his tail. Most puppies carry their tails gaily when playing, but the root of the tail should be set slightly lower than the back line. While the puppy carries his toy, a poorly-set tail will be easy to spot as it will point skywards. A well-set tail will

Check the temperament of the mother – this is a good indication of how a puppy may turn out.
Photo: Keith Allison.

curve firstly down and then upwards while the puppy is playing.

Observe the puppy's feet every time he stops. Are they pointing forward (as they should) or are they turning outwards? Look also at the elbows; they should be fitting snugly at the side of the ribcage, not jutting outwards leaving a noticeable gap. However, if they are sitting too closely under the ribs, he will be too narrow in front with hardly any space between the two front legs.

Finally, look for a puppy with a good temperament. While you are assessing the puppies, they may be bored, tired, playful or even a little hungry, and will make their feelings known by either falling asleep or attempting to 'beat up' their brothers and sisters. All this is normal behaviour for a Newfie puppy, but do not be tempted by a puppy who is nervous of being handled and who runs back to his bed to hide at every opportunity. However magnificent he looks, if he does not have a good temperament then you are not getting a true Newfoundland.

The breeder will help you to evaluate the puppies if you are looking for show potential.
                        Photo: Keith Allison.

REARING THE PUPPY

While you are carrying home the subdued little bundle who, more often than not, will have been sick in your lap, remember that you are taking home a puppy who has been reared to the best of his breeder's ability. Promise yourself that you will not undo years of experience by ignoring feeding and exercise instructions. There are several things that can go wrong with your puppy which are genetic and therefore unavoidable. Do not add to potential problems by disregarding the good advice your breeder has given (and in most cases, will have written down!)

ARRIVING HOME

As soon as you arrive home, you will be teaching your puppy some basic rules. Firstly, you will want to show him an area that he can use as a toilet. The fact that he will need to relieve himself is an absolute certainty, so the garden will be your first stop. Do not carry him to a distant spot 20 metres away; he will need an easily accessible area near to your back door. Summer puppies are particularly easy to house-train as the door to the garden can be left open all day. Do not forget to put newspapers on the floor indoors; most puppies are reared on newspaper, so this will be a familiar toilet to them until they learn to always go outdoors. All new puppies will soil the carpet or floor in their new home. How often it happens depends on how vigilant you are. Remember to take the puppy outside every time he wakes up, and after each meal or drink of water. If each trip outside is accompanied by an associated word, such as "Busy" or "Be clean", followed by verbal praise when the puppy obliges, then house-training should not take long. There will still be the occasional 'accident' at night time, as it is not reasonable to expect the puppy to last for seven hours or so without emptying his bladder.

The first few nights may be somewhat trying as the puppy will probably wail pitifully once everyone has gone to bed. Rushing to his side every time he whines is not the recommended action, as he will grow up into a dog who can never be left alone. Upsetting though it is, remember that your Newfie will grow out of this behaviour once he learns that everyone always comes back in the morning, and that he has not been abandoned!

FEEDING

Choose an area where the puppy will be fed, and leave a bowl of water permanently in this spot. Re-filling the bowl will eventually become second nature to you as the puppy

Give the pup a chance to explore the garden, giving him lots of reassurance.

Photo: Keith Allison.

either tips it or tries to climb into it. An anti-tip plastic bowl is best, because the heavy ceramic ones are easily broken on floor tiles as soon as your puppy learns to 'flip' it with his foot.

There are very few puppies who eat all their food when they go to their new homes, and this is a subject that causes more worried telephone calls to breeders than almost anything else. The most important thing to remember is that your puppy will not starve himself! It is very likely that you will have been advised by your breeder to take the puppy to your own vet within 24 hours of arriving home. It is best to follow this advice. Once you have been assured that your puppy is not suffering from something dreadful, you can safely ignore the starvation phase.

It is understandable that a puppy refuses to eat on the first day in his new home. He will be missing his litter-mates, and his routine will have changed. Offer meals at the same time as he is used to, but ensure that he is not over-tired from playing before giving the food. The most common problem is that the puppy eats normally four times a day for about the first week, then misses a meal or two on a regular basis. This could be due to being offered food when he is too tired (puppies need plenty of rest), meals not

sufficiently spaced out, or too great a quantity at the previous meal. Unless he is genuinely sick, your puppy will not refuse food unless he does not need it. Even greedy puppies have to stop somewhere!

Any fault usually lies with the owner who, in an effort to produce a *big* Newfoundland, gives the puppy too large a meal, reasoning that "if 6 ozs of feed makes him grow, then 8 ozs will make him grow bigger."

Quite often the puppy is also given tidbits between meals and this makes him less hungry. We always advise our puppy owners not to feed tidbits until a regular feeding pattern has been established. A small cube of his puppy meal can be used for teaching him to come when called and other basic training.

The type of food you give your puppy will depend greatly on your breeder's advice. If a certain brand name has been recommended, then it is best to stick to it. Some breeders prefer the old-fashioned method of feeding meat and biscuit, with various additives to make a balanced meal. If this is the case, you will need to be meticulous about the quantities you use. A pinch of this and a dash of that will not be accurate enough to provide your puppy's nutrition. The older breeders knew exactly how much of each ingredient to add. They also had the sense to realise that too much in the way of additives could be as harmful as none at all, and very few had the sort of canine health problems that we see today.

Some owners prefer to feed meat and biscuit simply because the dog prefers it, but, unfortunately, this can dwindle down to mostly meat. A diet of meat alone will not be adequate feeding for your dog. Children prefer the taste of burgers or chocolate alone, but this is hardly the best reason for pandering to their whims and not giving them a balanced diet!

However, feeding methods are a matter of personal choice and, for us, like a growing number of dog people, the complete meal does the trick as there is a grade of food to suit each stage of the dog's life. Dog food companies have become very advanced over recent years and it is possible to find at least one decent brand which suits your dog. Each one has a feeding guide printed on the bag so, with a helping of common sense, it is difficult to get it wrong. Any good-quality complete food will be adequate nutrition for your Newfie, although we personally steer away from anything that looks like muesli, as it can sometimes ferment in the stomach (see Gastric Dilation-Volvulus, Health and Ailments, Chapter Nine.)

Your puppy should have four meals a day until he is twelve weeks old or so, reducing to three meals until about six months of age. The subsequent two meals a day can be a permanent routine or, if you prefer, reduced to one a day after eighteen months of age. Most importantly, do not let your young Newfie get fat. You would be horrified if you saw someone putting a fully-laden backpack on a puppy and leaving it there permanently. However, you are doing equal damage to a puppy who is overweight and forced to carry around those needless extra pounds.

A number of complete dog foods are fed soaked in water. Even those intended to be fed dry to an adult dog will need to be soaked for your puppy. Remember that, as

he gets older, he will need something firmer to chew on and this can be in the form of dry, complete meal or a hard biscuit at bedtime.

Bones can provide hours of chewing activity for a Newfie provided they are large, raw marrow-bones, which should not be given too often as they cause constipation. Never be tempted to give any small, cooked bones as they cannot always be digested and may result in a blockage in the stomach. Newfoundlands, however, do not subscribe to this theory and will readily devour cooked bones of any kind, so take care to dispose of any left-overs in such a way that your dog will not find them.

EXERCISE
This is a subject about which many Newfoundland owners fail to agree. The amount of exercise a young dog should have is based on each breeder's own experience. Primarily, your breeder's advice should be heeded. When you ask for guidance, do not expect to be treated sympathetically by your puppy's breeder if you have broken every rule he or she has given you!

It should be obvious to everyone that a young puppy, like a human toddler, should not be expected to walk miles along roadways. However, this does not mean that the puppy should be confined to his garden for the first six months. Young animals have short bursts of activity followed by long periods of rest, and this pattern should be reflected in the type of exercise they take.

Our puppies are not restricted in any way and, if they feel the need to gallop about, they are allowed as much exercise as they want. A puppy who is allowed unlimited free running will learn to pace himself. A short gallop on grass may be followed by a lie-down for three seconds before he is away again, changing speeds and direction as he wishes, while the owner wanders in a slow circle. As soon as the owner calls and moves purposefully away, the puppy will catch up (especially if you are accompanied by an older dog) and can be put on a lead for a short 100-yard walk home. Compare this to a puppy being put on a lead and made to walk at the same pace over pavements and you will be able to understand why the former method is more suited to his physique.

It would be easy to state a set distance that puppies are capable of walking, but it is more sensible to treat each dog as an individual. If your puppy seems very tired or stiff after a walk, it is probably best to reduce the distance slightly (any persistent lameness should be treated by the vet and activity cut down to a minimum).

Much of your puppy's exercise will consist of games. This will stimulate his mind as well as his body. There is nothing so boring to an inquisitive puppy as plodding along on a lead with no opportunity to investigate scents. "Fetch" games are great fun and they teach the puppy some very basic obedience, although the direction and distance of the object thrown should be varied to prevent him becoming bored.

We have always made a habit of running a short distance away and hiding from our puppies, as it teaches them not to wander too far and to come when called. This method, however, only seems to work with a single puppy (or one accompanied by older dogs); two five-month-old littermates are just as likely to head for the horizon together and ignore any tactics you wish to employ!

Many breeders advocate exercising the puppy on relatively flat land, avoiding walking up or down steps. While running up and down stairs all day is obviously a harmful activity, your Newfoundland will need to be occasionally introduced to steps and other unusual walkways if he is to be a well-adjusted family member. It will be to the puppy's advantage, however, if you can avoid making him walk on slippery floor tiles or similar surfaces.

As for exercising on steep hills and slopes, it is unavoidable for us as we live in hilly Wales and would find it difficult to restrict ourselves to level land. To date, none of our puppies have shown any signs of unsoundness due to their exercise regime. *However*, exercise is a topic that must be ruled by common sense, so do not attempt to push the puppy too hard. One of the most appealing aspects of the Newfoundland temperament is the dogs' desire to please their owners, so it is not too difficult to make them walk further than they want to.

BASIC TRAINING
A well-mannered dog will be a happier member of your family 'pack' than one who has been unchecked and is unaware of his status within the home. A Newfoundland is too large to be allowed to barge through doorways before his owner, or to beg tidbits off the dinner table, so a few ground rules are essential. A dog who is *never* given tidbits from the table will not come to expect them. However, a few table left-overs added to his dinner will be equally pleasurable and you will never have the embarrassing task of removing your dog's drool-ridden face from the laps of dinner guests. Similarly, a dog who instantly leaps out of car doors or through doorways will soon learn that the door *always* shuts in his face when he attempts to pass through without being told.

A Newfie who constantly pulls on the lead is no pleasure to take for a walk and, as a consequence, is usually taken out less and less as the chore becomes increasingly unbearable. It will be natural for your dog to become excited at the prospect of a walk, but after the first few yards he should calm down. As you will always lose in a battle of strength with a Newfie it is more effective to use cunning methods of teaching. When our dogs pull, we stop walking. An intelligent dog will soon realise that pulling impedes rather than hastens progress. If the bad habit is too deeply ingrained, a head-collar can be used to control the pulling.

Basic training commands such as "Come", "Sit", "Down", and "Stay" cannot be started too early – not as formal 'lessons' but simply as part of the daily routine. In a similar vein you will also be teaching your Newfie not to climb on furniture or to bite you or your clothes. You will be showing plenty of love and affection, but he will also be aware that *you* are the boss! Dogs who obey a command simply because it is the most enjoyable option are far easier to train than those who respond out of force or fear. Constant rewarding (either with a tidbit or a cuddle) for good behaviour is far more satisfying for dog and owner than punishing for misdemeanours. Enrolling him in a 'Good Manners Obedience' class will be money well spent. If possible, try to avoid classes which are geared towards the Obedience competitor. These classes are usually dominated by Border Collies, and your Newfie's slower progress will be frustrating to all present. (Do not take this advice to mean that Newfoundlands are unsuitable for competition Obedience. We were 'owned' by one who could compete equally with Border Collies, and we have known of several since. Frankly, though, such Newfies are few and far between!)

Another important command to teach is "Give" when you want to take something from your Newfie's mouth. This can be a life-saver if he has picked up a cooked bone or something which may be poisonous. All Newfies should gladly give up their bone, bowl of food, or toy when told, and any growling or snapping is a sign of a questionable temperament. When teaching a puppy to "Give" it is important to always offer something else as a reward – another toy or a small piece of cheese or other tasty treat. Your Newfie will soon learn that "giving" has a pleasant result, and you will be confident that you have a dog who will not be possessive with food or toys.

AND FINALLY...
Your dog will be about five years old before you finally accomplish your ambition of owning a mature, relatively well-behaved and handsome Newfoundland. Even so, you will have probably encountered a stage where your dog has 'tried it on' in terms of defying your commands. Many dogs go through a phase when they try to promote themselves to a higher position within the family 'pack'. A Newfoundland usually does this without malice, and this must not be confused with the breed characteristic of 'smiling' when he shows his teeth and gums in a harmless, ingratiating manner.

Rearing a Newfie is a long process, and much of his character will be created by your actions. Nevertheless, he will still occasionally revert to his former 'Peter Pan' behaviour and you wonder if all your efforts to train him have been in vain. Rest assured that this inability to grow up is a typical Newfie trait, and each act of devilment will be outweighed by the devotion he shows to you.

Car stickers all over the world sum it up beautifully when they proclaim: *"If it ain't a Newfoundland, it's just a dog!"*

24

3 GROOMING

Any long-haired breed will need regular grooming to keep the dog's skin and coat healthy and clean. The Newfoundland is no exception, having a double coat consisting of a top layer of long coarse hair and a soft, dense, shorter undercoat which, being oily, repels the wet. It is also very effective at keeping out extremes of cold and heat.

When the original Standard of the Newfoundland was written, the coat was described as "a dull black". There is no doubt today that a clean (i.e. shampooed) Newfoundland will have a shiny coat. The older Newfoundland will sometimes show a duller coat, caused by less frequent moulting as the hair ages and is affected by environmental bleaching and drying. The top coat, with its long, harsh, shiny hair, tends to thin in old age while the dull, soft undercoat continues to grow, giving a softer, duller effect overall.

The puppy has several stages of coat growth up to approximately eighteen months of age when the new, complete adult coat will come through. Black puppies show a greyish or brownish tinge to their short, soft coats and, at about four months, a line of shiny, rather harsh guard hairs will start to erupt down the line of the spine and on to the tail. The short hair on the legs, feet and face also grows in at this time, giving some puppies quite a comical appearance. These changes continue throughout the first year. The primary, adult-type coat in the puppy will be slightly softer overall and shorter than the true adult coat with its very dense undercoat. Often the feathering is quite short, indeed almost non-existent, for the majority of the first year, then it gradually lengthens and thickens over the second, third, and subsequent years. The true coat grows in after the first complete moult in the second year. This can vary from quite straight or wavy to curly over the rump, back and ears. The texture can be fairly coarse or soft, and the length on the body can vary from 1 inch to 3 inches on the spine, getting longer as it grows down the sides, hips and chest. Depending on the type of coat, you may want to groom lightly every day, or more thoroughly once a week.

BRUSHING

Before you start to groom you must decide where the task is to be carried out. Some sort of grooming table is a must if you want to prevent backache, and it will help keep the dog still while you complete the job. Choose a time when your dog will be feeling relaxed – attempting to groom a dog who is excited, or eager to go for a walk, will be like

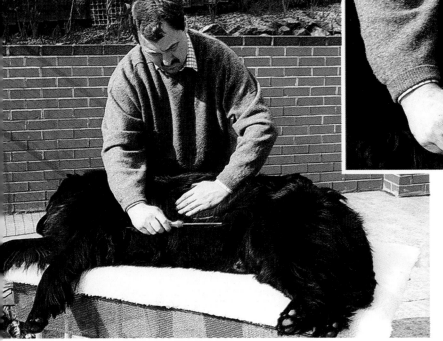

If you train your Newfoundland from an early age he will learn to accept the grooming procedure. The best method is to lift the hair upwards with one hand, and comb the hair below your hand down to the skin.

Photos: Keith Allison.

trying to groom an octopus! Once he knows what to expect, a Newfie may take up the chance to have a snooze while being brushed.

With so much variation in texture and length of hair, it is important to use the correct grooming techniques. Newfoundlands tend to lose a few hairs continually as new hair replaces the old, but, with heavy moults, the hair will tend to 'clump up' all over the dog. During the subsequent few days, or even one to two weeks, the undercoat and some topcoat will loosen and start to fall out. This is when mats can form – especially where the hair is longest.

A medium comb and slicker brush are necessary to remove this loose coat. Use the slicker brush to go over the entire dog, brushing the hair vigorously backwards. Then spray the coat with diluted 'leave-on' conditioner or plain water to prevent a static electricity build-up (also use if the coat is very dry). Next, using the comb, lift the hair upwards with one hand and comb the hair below your hand down to the skin. Work upwards in a line, and repeat in a line next to the previous one, eventually working from one end of the dog to the other. Get into a routine so as not to miss any bits. For example, I prefer to work from the front of the dog to the back. Lay the dog down to groom the belly and insides of the legs (under the armpit and between the back legs are particularly fertile areas for knots to flourish!). The leg feathering and the tail are done with the slicker brush working in layers against the lay of the coat. Be extra vigilant when grooming around the vulva, anus and testicles to avoid scratching the delicate skin of the genital area.

If the dog is severely matted, a special cutting comb with sharpened teeth can save cutting off great clumps of hair and can also be used to thin a very bushy coat. Bathing a matted dog will not make his coat harder to comb – on the contrary it removes the dirty grease and loosens shedding hairs. Squeezing neat hair conditioner into the mats and leaving for five minutes at the end of bathing will also help to loosen the felted hair when dry. Bathing at the 'clump up' stage will also hasten the release of the old coat and, once brushed out, the new coat will come in quicker and the skin will stay healthier. So do not be afraid to bath a neglected dog. It will make the job of grooming more comfortable for him and for you.

BATHING

Normally, bathing is only necessary two to four times a year for pets who are regularly groomed. However, if you are showing your dog, you may have to bath him almost weekly at the height of the season, and you will need to know how long his coat will keep that 'flyaway' look afterwards. Some return to normal within 24 hours, while others need a few days to 'settle'.

How soon to bath before a show also depends on your dog's lifestyle. If you live on a farm and your dog cannot be trusted not to roll in something disgusting for more than a few days, then the day before the show will probably be a must! With experience you will learn when your dog's coat looks at its best.

Bathing a Newfoundland is best done outside with a garden hose if you do not have a specially-made dog bath. Wet the dog all over as thoroughly as possible. Try not to get water or shampoo into the ears. Dilute a good all-purpose dog shampoo half and half with tepid water and soap the dog all over, working up a good lather. (A baby 'no-tears' shampoo is best on the face and around the eyes.) Hose the dog thoroughly until the water runs clear. Soap up again, this time using a special shampoo, such as one of the antiparasitic or fungicidal brands, and follow the instructions on the container for dilution and length of time to be left on the dog. The final rinse must be very thorough, paying special attention to areas where the coat is thickest and where there are many skin folds. A cream rinse can now be applied, diluted in a little warm water and rubbed well into the hair. Rinse thoroughly. Rub the dog down with dry towels, or blow-dry if you have a blower.

When the dog is thoroughly dry (possibly the next day), brush the hair backwards with the slicker; then, with the comb, groom in the direction of the lay of the coat until all the loose hair is removed. Stubborn mats must be worked out very carefully to avoid hurting the dog. Hold the mat firmly in one hand and comb from the outside end, working back towards the roots. If this is impossible because the mat is too dense or large, make cuts lengthwise in it with a cutting comb or plain scissors and groom as before. When cutting out stubborn mats, be very careful not to nick the dog's skin. It is best to cut the mats two-thirds off and tease the rest of the felted area out with the comb.

TRIMMING

The best time to trim the coat is when it is clean. A blower will remove all remaining loose hair and dandruff. These blowers or blasters send a high-speed stream of cool air to 'blast' the coat. It is the same principle as a hair dryer, but without the heat and far more powerful. The dog must be carefully introduced to the blower, as the air stream and noise of the motor can, at first, be very frightening. Blowers must also be used with care around the ears and eyes. They are, without doubt, one of the most useful tools invented for grooming since the comb. They

BATHING
Photos: Keith ALLISON.

It is a good idea to plug your Newfoundland's ears with cotton-wool before bathing.

Wet the dog's coat thoroughly. If you do not have a dog-bath, this can be done outside using a garden hose.

Dilute the shampoo and pour it over the dog's coat.

Work the shampoo into a good lather (left).

Rinse the coat, making sure you get rid of all the shampoo (right).

No dog can resist having a good shake after a bath (below).

Use a blower to dry the coat.

can also be used to blow clean a wet, dirty dog after walks or swimming, or used weekly to remove dirt and loose hair. They are best used before and after brushing, but be warned – use the blower *outdoors* or you will have hairy walls and ceilings!

In preparation for trimming, a blower is used on the lowest speed setting to spray a conditioner, or a light disinfectant, into the coat (dilute 1:20 in water). This is directed on to the skin, where the air blast parts the hair. When this is done all over the dog, it helps to keep the skin healthy. It will also lift and divide the hairs ready for trimming.

The amount of trimming necessary depends upon the type of coat your dog has, and whether you are showing, working or just keeping a house pet. Many Newfoundlands have quite short body coats with profuse feathering. These dogs are lovely to live with but not so glamorous for the show ring, hence the tendency to breed for heavier, longer coats which can be sculpted.

Most house pets who are not swimming regularly can be tidied around the ears, feet and hocks while allowing the rest of the coat to grow. But a dog with a long, heavy coat can be a nightmare if he lives in the house and sleeps in the bedroom! There is no reason why you cannot trim all the longest hairs down to a reasonable length with a pair of thinning scissors. The dog will look attractive and bring far less wet and dirt indoors.

Trim against the lay of the coat with thinning scissors, taking a little off at a time and following the contours of the body. Leave approximately 4 inches on the longest hairs at the very least. It is best to shorten half as much as you want all over, and re-assess before further cutting. Practice will improve the look. If you know a breeder or exhibitor, ask for a demonstration. To actually watch trimming being done is worth thousands of written words.

A Newfoundland should *never* be shorn

unless there is a medical reason. The coat insulates against heat and cold, and bare skin could be sunburned. I have never shorn even a badly matted dog. A sedative may be necessary if a dog is in a real mess and not used to being groomed. Most Newfoundlands are such loving characters that a little patience and care on your part will be enough to get the job done. A badly matted coat can be worked on over several days, an hour at a time, with gentle persuasion and, once again, much patience. However, if you have an old or sick dog who does not want to be groomed, some cutting of the hair in less accessible areas will be kinder than causing discomfort.

If your dog is doing water work, an excessively long coat will be a handicap as there will be more drag in the water. He will also bring far more water into the boat. Beware of over-bathing or removing excessive amounts of undercoat, as the grease and soft hair are necessary for insulation and buoyancy. The pet trim, as outlined above, is the ideal solution for a heavy-coated dog who is expected to work in water.

Trimming the hair around the ears is a sensible measure for every Newfoundland. Encouraging the circulation of air around the ears helps to prevent infection within the ear canal – a condition not helped by the heavy ear flap shutting out light and air. With thinning scissors, trim against the lay of the coat from the end of the ear flap up towards the root. Take a little off at a time until the hair is short and does not project past the edge of the ear. Leaving the hair slightly longer as you trim upwards will prevent a 'step' at the junction of the ear and skull. Trim carefully around the edge and under the ear – again, having a demonstration by an exhibitor is worthwhile.

The hocks and feet are trimmed for neatness and the hair can be cut down hard or shaped as you wish. Brush the hair upwards carefully from between the toes and

Use trimming scissors to tidy the ears.

Trim the hair, a little at a time, until it does not project past the edge of the ear.

The hair around the feet needs to be trimmed.

Lift the hair between the toes.

Cut upwards, using trimming scissors.

Trim around the foot, so you have a neat, round shape.

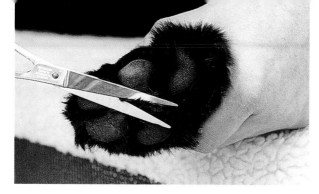

Trim the hair that grows between the pads.   *The finished result.*

trim off the tufts. Shape around the edge of
the foot and cut back the long hair under
the pads. The feathering is shortened as
required and the sides rounded to make a
tidy shape.

Finally the ears should be cleaned out
monthly, with cotton wool soaked in an
approved ear cleanser, to prevent ear
problems. The teeth can be scrubbed with a
brush and canine toothpaste, or a marrow-
bone or nylon chew can be given to help
polish and keep teeth tartar-free. Nails must
be regularly examined and cut with a special
curved clipper, back to just below the quick
if they get too long. Cut across the ends –
square to the nail – taking off tiny slivers at a
time. Black nails can be difficult to cut,
because the quick cannot be seen. They have
a greyish core, but cutting too far will reveal
the quick as a shiny black centre to the core.
It is best to have a coagulant to hand, such
as potassium permanganate crystals, in case
blood flows.

SHOW TRIMMING

When preparing the dog for a show, you
should always be assessing the body shape of
the Newfoundland. Trimming is done to
enhance and create a correct outline, but it
has to be remembered that a competent
judge will not be fooled by clever trimming.
A pair of scissors cannot perform miracles if
the dog is not correctly constructed.

It takes hours of hard work to prepare a
dog for the show ring and you will have
carried out all the basic grooming discussed
earlier – plus more! It is important, if you are

using any conditioners or sprays, that all
traces of the preparation are removed from
the coat. Under Kennel Club rules in
Britain, exhibitors are forbidden from using
any substance that alters the natural colour,
texture or body of the coat. In other
countries, coat preparations are not
permitted but, to date, there are no means of
testing coats for illegal substances. In the
US, however, a judge may 'excuse' an
exhibit who is showing obvious signs of
forbidden coat preparations.

The most effective tool for show trimming
is the pair of trimming scissors. These look
like an ordinary pair of scissors, but have a
normal blade on one side and dozens of
cutting teeth on the other.

Stand the groomed dog on a table and try
to picture where your dog needs to be
enhanced. Does the head hair grow into a
pointed tuft on top of the skull? If so, you
will need to cut the hairs down to similar
lengths to prevent the cranium looking
narrow.

If your dog has a profuse mane which
hangs in front of his chest, you may notice
that it makes him look 'front heavy'. Or, if
his body is slightly longer than you would
like, too much frontal mane will make him
look even longer. Cut away the excess by
trimming in the same direction as the hair to
leave a smooth, unbroken outline.

Similarly, excessive length of hair on the
sides and under the belly will make a dog
look too long in the body and too short in
the leg. The belly hair can be cut
horizontally, following the gentle curve of

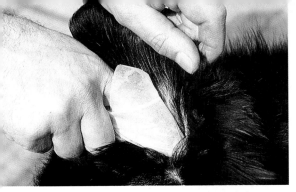

Clean the ears once a month, making sure you do not probe too deeply into the ear canal.

Tartar accumulates on the teeth.

This should be removed using a toothbrush and canine toothpaste.

BELOW: When trimming nails, cut across the ends – square to the nail.

the body; while lightly trimming the sides downwards, in the direction of the hair, will give a more natural finish.

Too much feathering on the front legs gives an illusion of not enough bone, as it is overshadowed by the hair. Tidy up the back edge of the leg by cutting away any uneven or wispy bits, then, cutting horizontally, merge the leg and feathering into one to create a rounded, chunky-looking limb. A dog who is 'out at elbow' will need more hair removed from this area than one who is correctly made. The bottom of the front leg (behind the pastern) will have to be done very carefully to avoid giving the dog weak-looking pasterns. Trimming in a broad curve from the back edge of the leg to *underneath* the foot usually has the desired effect, but this is something that has to be demonstrated rather than learned from a book.

The back legs are normally trimmed only below the hock, and this is just to take away any spiky or over-long hairs. This can be done by holding the hock hair in a 'scissor' fashion between the forefinger and middle finger of the left hand (your fingers will be pointing to the floor); then, with the right hand holding the scissors, cut the inch or so of hair, protruding beyond your fingers, in a downward manner. The bottom part is treated like the front leg, ending with a broad, blunt curve cut to underneath the foot (this will be easier to do if the back foot is positioned on tip-toe at the edge of the grooming table). If the dog has a great deal of hock hair, he may look as though his back legs are brushing together as he moves so you will also need to thin some of the hair between the bottom part of the back legs.

Contrary to popular belief, trimming can be very beneficial to an out-of-coat dog. Many owners are loath to take the scissors to their dog when he has lost so much coat through moulting! Watching from the ring-side though, there is nothing that gives away a dog's out-of-coat status more plainly than

It takes many hours to prepare a Newfoundland for the show ring. Am. Can. Ch. Jolly Roger's Tumblin' Dicce winning BIS at the Orangeville KC show.

Photo: Alex Smith.

seeing stringy, wispy strands of hair sprouting from various parts of his body. Barbaric though it may sound, cutting any hair that lets through daylight will smarten up a moulting dog, so do not be afraid to be a little 'scissor-happy'.

EQUIPMENT

The equipment mentioned in this chapter can be obtained from pet shops, grooming parlours, veterinary surgeries and from trade stands at dog shows. The initial expense is well worth the result. If possible, take an experienced Newfie owner with you to ensure that the right tools are purchased.

As a general guide, you will need the following.

• Slicker brush (flat or curved). These are also excellent for removing dog hair from your carpet!

• Medium comb.
• Wide-toothed comb.
• Bristle brush (for the show ring). Some people also like to have a 'pin brush' in their grooming bag. This is shaped like a bristle-brush but the 'bristles' are metallic blunt-end pins. Try to avoid the ones that have tiny 'bobbles' at the ends of the pins as they can rip out too much coat.
• Trimming scissors.
• Thinning scissors.
• Mat-cutting rake.
• A suitable box or bag for storage.

Grooming, if done with kindness and patience on a regular basis, will help to create a bond of trust and affection between you and your Newfoundland, and you will have a canine companion of which you can be proud.

4 THE NEWFOUNDLAND BREED STANDARDS

The official Standard of any breed gives breeders the 'blueprint' of the ideal dog to aim for. In this chapter we will look at three Standards for the Newfoundland breed: the UK Standard, which was acknowledged worldwide following its establishment in the 19th century; the AKC Standard, which *explains* rather than just itemizes the desired points; and the New FCI Standard, which was published in 1996. (Prior to this date, the FCI Standard was identical to the UK Standard.)

THE UK KENNEL CLUB STANDARD, MARCH 1994

This Standard was established by the Newfoundland Club in Britain in the 1880s, and has now been acknowledged by Newfoundland clubs throughout the world.

GENERAL APPEARANCE
Well balanced, impresses with strength and great activity. Massive bone throughout, but not giving heavy inactive

The Breed Standard gives a blueprint of the ideal dog. Ch. Ir. Ch. Sheridel Crawford – British breed recordholder and winner of several BIS awards.

Photo: David Dalton

appearance. Noble, majestic and powerful.

CHARACTERISTICS
Large draught and water dog, with natural life-saving instinct, and devoted companion.

TEMPERAMENT
Exceptionally gentle, docile nature.

HEAD AND SKULL
Head broad and massive, occipital bone well developed, no decided stop, muzzle short, clean cut and rather square, covered with short fine hair.

EYES
Small, dark brown, rather deeply set, not showing haw, set rather wide apart.

EARS
Small, set well back, square with skull, lying close to head, covered with short hair without fringe.

MOUTH
Soft and well covered by lips. Scissor bite preferred, i.e. upper teeth closely overlapping lower teeth and set square to the jaws, but pincer tolerated.

NECK
Strong, well set on to shoulders.

FOREQUARTERS
Legs perfectly straight, well muscled, elbows fitting close to sides, well let down.

BODY
Well ribbed, back broad with level topline, strong muscular loins. Chest deep, fairly broad.

HINDQUARTERS
Very well built and strong. Slackness of loins and cow-hocks most undesirable. Dewclaws should be removed.

FEET
Large, webbed and well shaped. Splayed or turned-out feet most undesirable.

TAIL
Moderate length, reaching a little below hock. Fair thickness, well covered with hair, but not forming a flag. When standing, hangs downwards with slight curve at end; when moving, carried slightly up, and when excited, straight out with only a slight curve at end. Tails with a kink or curled over back are most undesirable.

GAIT/MOVEMENT
Free, slightly rolling gait. When in motion slight toe-ing in at front acceptable.

COAT
Double, flat and dense, of coarse texture and oily nature, water-resistant. When brushed wrong way, it falls back into place naturally. Forelegs well feathered. Body well covered but chest hair not forming a frill. Hindlegs slightly feathered.

COLOUR
Only permitted colours are:
Black: dull jet black may be tinged with bronze. Splash of white on chest, toes and tip of tail acceptable.
Brown: can be chocolate or bronze. In all other respects follow black except for colour. Splash of white on chest, toes and tip of tail acceptable.
Landseer: white with black markings only. For preference, black head with narrow blaze, evenly marked saddle, black rump extending to tail. Beauty in markings to be taken greatly into consideration. Ticking undesirable.

SIZE

Average height at shoulder: dogs: 71 cms (28 ins); bitches: 66 cms (26 ins). Average weight: dogs: 64-69 kgs (140-150 lbs); bitches: 50-54.5 kgs (110-120 lbs). While size and weight are important, it is essential that symmetry is maintained.

FAULTS

Any departure from the foregoing points should be considered a fault and the seriousness with which the fault should be regarded should be in exact proportion to its degree.

NOTE: Male animals should have two apparently normal testicles fully descended into the scrotum.

AMERICAN KENNEL CLUB (AKC) STANDARD, MAY 1990

GENERAL APPEARANCE

The Newfoundland is a sweet-dispositioned dog that acts neither dull nor ill-tempered. He is a devoted companion. A multipurpose dog, at home on land and in water, the Newfoundland is capable of draft work and possesses natural life-saving abilities.

The Newfoundland is a large, heavily coated, well balanced dog that is deep bodied, heavily boned, muscular and strong. A good specimen of the breed has dignity and proud head carriage.

The following description is that of the ideal Newfoundland. Any deviation from this ideal is to be penalized to the extent of the deviation. Structural and movement faults common to all working breeds are as undesirable in the Newfoundland as in any other breed, even though they are not specifically mentioned herein.

SIZE, PROPORTION, SUBSTANCE

Average height for adult dogs is 28 inches, for adult bitches, 26 inches. Approximate weight of adult dogs ranges from 130 to 150 pounds, adult bitches from 100 to 120 pounds. The dog's appearance is more massive throughout than the bitch's. Large size is desirable, but never at the expense of balance, structure and correct gait. The Newfoundland is slightly longer than tall when measured from the point of shoulder to point of buttocks and from withers to ground. He is a dog of considerable substance which is determined by spring of rib, strong muscle, and heavy bone.

HEAD

The head is massive, with broad skull, slightly arched crown, and strongly developed occipital bone. Cheeks are well developed. Eyes are dark brown. (Browns and Grays may have lighter eyes and should be penalized only to the extent that color affects expression.) They are relatively small, deep-set, and spaced wide apart. Eyelids fit closely with no inversion. Ears are relatively small and triangular with rounded tips. They are set on the skull level with, or slightly above, the brow, and lie close to the head. When the ear is brought forward, it reaches to the inner corner of the eye on the same side. Expression is soft and reflects the characteristics of the breed: benevolence, intelligence, and dignity.

Forehead and face are smooth and free of wrinkles. Slope of the stop is moderate but, because of the well developed brow, it may appear abrupt in profile. The muzzle is clean cut, broad throughout its length, and deep. Depth and length are approximately equal, the length from tip of nose to stop being less than that from stop to occiput. The top of the muzzle is rounded, and the bridge, in profile, is straight or only slightly arched. Teeth meet in a scissors or level bite. Dropped lower incisors, in an otherwise normal bite, are not indicative of a skeletal malocclusion and should be considered only a minor deviation.

NECK, TOPLINE, BODY

The neck is strong and well set on the shoulders and is long enough for proud head carriage. The back is strong, broad, and muscular and is level from just behind the withers to the croup. The chest is full and deep with the brisket reaching at least down to the elbows. Ribs are well sprung, with the anterior third of the rib cage tapered to allow elbow clearance. The flank is deep. The croup is broad and slopes slightly.

TAIL

Tail set follows the natural line of the croup. The tail is broad at the base and strong. It has no kinks, and the distal bone reaches to the hock. When the dog is standing relaxed, its tail hangs straight or with a slight curve at the end. When the dog is in motion or excited, the tail is carried out, but it does not curl over the back.

FOREQUARTERS

Shoulders are muscular and well laid back. Elbows lie directly below the highest point of the withers. Forelegs are muscular, heavily boned, straight, and parallel to each other, and the elbows point directly to the rear. The distance from elbow to ground equals about half the dog's height. Pasterns are strong and slightly sloping. Feet are proportionate to the body in size, webbed, and cat foot in shape. Dewclaws may be removed.

HINDQUARTERS

The rear assembly is powerful, muscular, and heavily boned. Viewed from the rear,

the legs are straight and parallel. Viewed from the side, the thighs are broad and fairly long. Stifles and hocks are well bent and the line from hock to ground is perpendicular. Hocks are well let down. Hind feet are similar to the front feet. Dewclaws should be removed.

COAT

The adult Newfoundland has a flat, water-resistant, double coat that tends to fall back into place when rubbed against the nap. The outer coat is coarse, moderately long, and full, either straight or with a wave. The undercoat is soft and dense, although it is often less dense during the summer months or in warmer climates. Hair on the face and muzzle is short and fine. The backs of the legs are feathered all the way down. The tail is covered with long dense hair. Excess hair may be trimmed for neatness. Whiskers need not be trimmed.

COLOR

Color is secondary to type, structure and soundness. Recognized Newfoundland colors are black, brown, gray, and white and black.
SOLID COLORS – Blacks, Brown and Grays may appear as solid colors or solid colors with white at any, some, or all, of the following locations: chin, chest, toes, and tip of tail. Any amount of white found at these locations is typical and is not penalized. Also typical are a tinge of bronze on a black or gray coat and lighter furnishings on a brown or gray coat.
LANDSEER – white base coat with black markings. Typically, the head is solid black, or black with white on the muzzle, with or without a blaze. There is a separate black saddle and black on the rump extending onto a white tail.

Markings, on either solid colors or Landseers, might deviate considerably from those described and should be penalized only to the extent of the deviation. Clear white or white with minimal ticking is preferred.

Beauty of markings should be considered only when comparing dogs of otherwise comparable quality and never at the expense of type, structure and soundness.

Disqualifications: Any colors or combinations of colors not specifically described are disqualified.

GAIT

The Newfoundland in motion has good reach, strong drive, and gives the impression of effortless power. His gait is smooth and rhythmic, covering the maximum amount of ground with the minimum number of steps. Forelegs and hind legs travel straight forward. As the dog's speed increases, the legs tend toward single tracking. When moving, a slight roll of the skin is characteristic of the breed. Essential to good movement is the balance of correct front and rear assemblies.

TEMPERAMENT

Sweetness of temperament is the hallmark of the Newfoundland; this is the most important single characteristic of the breed.

FEDERATION CYNOLOGIQUE INTERNATIONAL (F.C.I.) STANDARD 1996

Utilization: sledge dog for heavy loads, water dog.

Classification FCI: Group 2 CPinscher and Schnauzer Type-Molossian and Swiss Mountain and Cattle Dogs

Section 2.2: molossian Type, Mountain Dogs without working trial.

Short Historical survey: the breed originated in the island of Newfoundland from dogs indigenous and the big black bear dog introduced by the Vikings after the year 1100. With the advent of European fishermen a variety of new breeds helped to shape and reinvigorate the breed, but the essential characteristics remained. When the colonization of the island began in 1610, the Newfoundland Dog was already largely in possession of his proper morphology and natural behaviour. These features allowed him to withstand the rigours of the extreme climate and sea's adversity while pulling heavy loads on land or serving as water and life-guard dog.

General appearance: the Newfoundland is massive, with powerful body, well muscled and well co-ordinated in his movements.

Important proportions: the length of the body from the withers to the root of the tail is equal to the distance from the withers to the ground. The body is compact. The body of the bitch may be slightly longer and is less massive than that of the dog. The distance from the withers to the underside of the chest is greater than the distance from the underside of the chest to the ground.

Behaviour and temperament: the Newfoundland expression reflects benevolence and softness. Dignified joyful and creative, he is known for his sterling gentleness and serenity.

Head: massive. The head of the bitch follows the same general conformation as the male's, but is less massive.

Cranial region:

Skull: broad, with slightly arched crown

and strongly developed occipital bone;

Stop: evident, but never abrupt;

Facial region:

Nose: large, well pigmented, nostrils well developed. Colour: Black on black and white and black dogs, brown on brown dogs;

Muzzle: definitely square, deep and moderately short, covered with short fine hair and free from wrinkles. The corners of the mouth are evident, but not excessively pronounced;

Cheeks: soft;

Bite: scissors or level bite;

Eyes: relatively small, deep set; they are wide apart and show no haw. Colour: Dark brown in black, and white and black, dogs, lighter shades permitted in brown dogs;

Ears: relatively small, triangular with rounded tips, well set back on the side of the head and close lying. When the ear of the adult dog is brought forward, it reaches to the inner corner of the eye on the same side.

Neck: strong, muscular, well set in the shoulders, long enough to permit dignified head carriage. The neck should not show excessive dewlap.

Body: bone structure is massive throughout. Viewed from the side, the body is deep and vigorous.

Top line: level and firm from the withers to the rump;

Back: broad;

Loin: strong and well muscled;

Rump: broad, sloping at an angle of about 30 degrees;

Chest: broad, full and deep, with good spread of ribs;

Abdomen and underline: almost level and never tucked up.

Forequarters: the forelegs are straight and parallel also when the dog is walking or slowly trotting:

Shoulders: very well muscled, well laid back at an angle approaching 45 degrees to the horizontal line;

Elbows: close to the chest;

Pasterns: slightly sloping;

Forefeet: large and proportionate to the body, well rounded and tight, with firm and compact toes. Webbing of toes is present. Nails black in black, and white and black, dogs, horn-coloured in brown dogs. In case of white toes, the nails should not be black.

Hindquarters: because driving power for pulling loads, swimming or covering ground efficiently is largely dependent upon the hindquarters, the rear structure of the Newfoundland is of prime importance. The pelvis has to be strong, broad and long;

Upper thighs: wide and muscular;

Stifle: well bent, but not so as to give a crouching appearance;

Lower thighs: strong and fairly long;

Hocks: relatively short, well let down and

well apart, parallel to each other; they turn neither in nor out;

Hindfeet: firm and tight. Nail colour as in forefeet. Dewclaws, if present, should have been removed.

Tail: the tail acts as a rudder when the Newfoundland is swimming; therefore it is strong and broad at the base. When the dog is standing, the tails hangs down with, possibly, a little curve at the tip; reaching to or slightly below the hocks. When the dog is in motion or excited, the tail is carried straight out with slight upward curve, but never curled over the back nor curved inward between the legs.

Gait/Movement: the Newfoundland moves with good reach of the forelegs and strong drive of the hindquarters, giving the impression of effortless power. A slight roll of the back is natural. As the speed increase, the dog tends to single track with the topline remaining level.

Coat:

Hair: the Newfoundland has a water resistant double coat. The outer coat is moderately long and straight with no curl. A slight wave is permissible. The undercoat is soft and dense, more dense in winter than in summer, but always found to some extent on the rump and chest. the hair on the head, muzzle and ears is short and fine. The front and rear legs are feathered. The tail is completely covered with long dense hair but does not form a flag;

Colour: black, white and black, and brown:

Black: the traditional colour is black. The colour has to be as even as possible, but a slight tinge of sunburn is permissible.

White markings on chest, toes and/or tip of tail are permissible;

White and black: this variety is of historical significance for the breed. The preferred pattern of markings is black head with, preferably, a white blaze extending onto the muzzle, black saddle with even markings and black rump and upper tail. The remaining parts are to be white and can show a minimum of ticking:

Brown: the brown colour goes from chocolate to bronze. White markings on chest, toes and/or tip of tail are permissible.

White and black dogs and brown dogs are to be shown in the same class as blacks.

Size and weight: the average height at the withers is:

for adult males 71 cm (28 inches);
for adult bitches 66 cm (26 inches);

The average weight is:
approximately 60 kg for males;
approximately 54 kg for bitches;

Large size is desirable, but is not to be favoured over symmetry, general soundness, power of structure and correct gait.

Faults: any departure from the foregoing points should be considered a fault and the seriousness with which the fault should be regarded should be in exact proportion to its degree:

- general appearance: Legginess, lack of substance;
- general bone structure: sluggish appearance, fine bone;
- character: aggressiveness, shyness;

- head: Narrow;
- muzzle: Snipey or long;
- flews: pronounced;
- eyes: Round, protruding, yellow eyes, showing pronounced haw;
- back: Roached, slack or swayed back;
- forequarters: Down in pastern, splayed toes, toeing in or out, lack of webbing between toes;
- hindquarters: Straight stifles, cowhocks, barrel legs, pigeon toes;
- tail: Short, long, kink tail, curled tip;
- gait/movement: Mincing, shuffling, crabbing, too close moving, weaving, crossing over in front, toeing out or distinctly toeing-in in front, hackney action, pacing;
- hair: Completely open coat;

Eliminating faults:

- bad temperament;
- overshot or undershot bite, wry mouth;
- short and flat coat;
- markings of any other colour than white on a black or brown dog;
- any other colour than black or white and black or brown;

Note: male animals should have two apparently normal testicles fully descended into the scrotum.

INTERPRETATION OF THE STANDARDS

Asking several people to explain and illustrate any breed standard will be like partaking in a game of Chinese Whispers. Everyone would have a slightly different idea of what the written word means. The following guide is a personal interpretation as we see it from a judge's and an exhibitor's viewpoint.

GENERAL APPEARANCE

"Well balanced" are the key words here. There should be no exaggerated features;
everything should fit together harmoniously, with no obvious feature standing out to the exclusion of all else.

"Strength and great activity..." The Newfoundland breed has a reputation for being a little 'dopey', but bear in mind that they should not be plodding or half-asleep when asked to move.

"Massive bone". It should be difficult for a man to close his hand around the foreleg of a mature, male Newfoundland. Bitches, being smaller, will naturally be a little finer-boned. A judge should always *feel* for bone, as profusely coated or out-of-coat dogs can give a deceptive appearance. A large dog should have correspondingly heavier bone than a medium-sized dog.

CHARACTERISTICS

Both the UK and US Standards mention "natural life-saving abilities" as a breed characteristic, while the New FCI Standard mentions "water and lifeguard dog", but these phrases have no value to a judge. Unless he is a clairvoyant, he will not be able to tell if a dog has natural life-saving instincts. Some judges, however, will be aware of the difference in muscle build-up of working and non-working dogs.

TEMPERAMENT

The word "gentle" is specified in both the UK and the New FCI Standards, and "sweetness of temperament" is how the AKC puts it. "Gentle" is a not a word that will be familiar to anyone who has been clawed by an attention-seeking Newfoundland! The only saving grace is that the dog is *trying* to be gentle and loving. A Newfoundland should love people, and any growling or nervous behaviour while being handled should be heavily penalised. Young males who display some macho behaviour towards each other can be temporarily forgiven, but a Newfie who has a total intolerance of other dogs is a poor example of temperament.

Typical head

HEAD AND SKULL

The head is the primary feature that owners recognize their dogs by; it is the part of the dog that you live and communicate with the most. Beware, though, this is not a 'head breed'. With some dogs, like Boxers, French Bulldogs and Shih Tzus, the Standard contains a long and precise description of the head. Judges and breeders forgive many faults if the head is right. A Newfoundland can have the loveliest of heads, but must also be sound in limb and temperament.

"Head broad and massive..." To achieve the desired balance, the head should not be so broad and massive that it looks wrong on the dog's body. Neither should it be so small that it sits like a pimple on his neck.

The occipital bone is singled out in the Standards. This feature is found as a bony bump at the back of the skull.The phrase "no decided stop" means that there should not be an impression of a 'doorstep' from the skull down on to the nasal bone. A gentle slope is ideal although, in profile, a sharper angle might be created by the slight jutting out of the eye socket bone.

The muzzle should display no excess lippiness and should have a general squarish appearance. A very strong head will be more disposed towards lippiness than a weak head, so both faults would have to be considered as to their severity.

The face should be "covered with short fine hair". The Newfoundland's face should not have a beard, moustache or eyebrows as seen in Briards or Irish Wolfhounds.

Incorrect: Overdone, excess stop, droopy eyes, loose flews, large ears.

Incorrect: Weak, pointed muzzle, large, round eyes, ear set too high.

*Incorrect: Ear
set too high.*

*Incorrect: Muzzle
too narrow, ear
set too high.*

EYES

The Standards give a straightforward description of the required eyes in a mature dog. A little haw (looseness of eye rims) may be forgiven in a young Newfie as it often tightens up with age. The eye shape is not mentioned in any of the Standards, but it is generally accepted that an almond shape adds to the dog's expression. Round eyes are very common and can sometimes give a hard, staring expression, which brings us to the question: "What is expression?"

Unfortunately, this is a vague term used by judges writing their critiques when they are unable to find any other virtues – "Good expression, nice colour!". We feel that a Newfie's expression can be summed up by what we call the "Aah factor". This means that any dog-lover looking into a Newfoundland's face should feel the need to give the dog a hug. Certainly, from a working point of view, it is likely that a person drowning in a lake would rather take his chances in the waves than be approached by something resembling a sabre-toothed tiger!

Conformation judges too, would probably prefer to see a friendly Newfie face coming towards them than a blank, wary expression. It may be their only guide to temperament while in the show ring.

EARS

The Standards call for "small" and "relatively small" ears. In fact, few small ears are seen nowadays, although any dog with exceptionally large ears is always noticed and commented upon. Ears that are proportionately the same size as a Retriever's or a Rottweiler's are most acceptable.

The UK and Australian Standards specify ears "without fringe". Actually, *every* Newfie would have a fringe like a Saluki if ears were not trimmed. Ears should look as if they do not need trimming, but not as if they have just been done. As this fault will be due to the owner's ignorance, then the dog should not be penalised if he is otherwise a nice specimen.

MOUTH

The New FCI Standard asks for a scissor or level bite, while the UK Standard states that, although a scissor bite is preferred, "pincer" is "tolerated". This is when the top and bottom teeth meet edge to edge. It is very

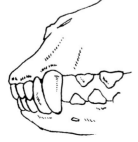

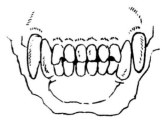

*Scissor bite
(preferred).*

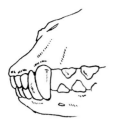

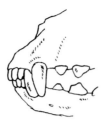

Level or pincer bite (acceptable).

Incorrect: Overshot.

Incorrect: Undershot.

common for Newfoundlands to have "dropped teeth", as mentioned in the AKC Standard, where the two central incisors on the bottom jaw protrude out of line with the rest of the dentition. Males of four years and over are particularly prone to this condition and it is considered acceptable within the breed. Unfortunately, accepting a deviation from the Standard then opens the floodgates to other inconsistencies, and it is possible to find champion Newfoundlands who are, frankly, undershot. A mouth fault, like any other, must be considered only in relation to the rest of the dog.

NECK

This is fairly easily understood and, as long as the dog appears to have a neck (in other words is not 'stuffy'), then this is one feature that will be difficult to fault.

FOREQUARTERS

The forequarters take most of the dog's bodyweight so it is important that the construction is as sound as stated in the Standards. In simple terms, a judge will be looking for the correct angulation; also while looking at a dog from the front he will be picturing two imaginary parallel lines running down through the Newfie's shoulders, elbows and feet. In order to emphasize the impression of strength, the front legs should not be set too close together and a good hand's-width will be needed between them at the chest.

BODY

The phrase "well ribbed" is simply another way of saying that the ribs should go far back along the body to give a shorter, stronger loin. "Chest deep, fairly broad" is a requirement of the Standards. A deep chest will reach as far as the dog's elbows, but do not expect young puppies to meet this criterion. There should be a medium "spring of rib" (how much the ribs curve out from the spine). A very barrel-chested dog (too much spring of rib) will always look unbalanced or even fat, while a slab-sided dog (not enough spring of rib) will be lacking in substance and strength.

A "level topline" will be easy to see, although a judge must make allowances for dogs being stood facing downhill. Some puppies and young dogs may be 'rump-high' or 'overbuilt' as part of their development, but will level out as they become older.

A 'roach-backed' dog may stand with a level topline, but the convex curve at the loin will soon show up in movement. Occasionally, a very silky coat can flick up over the loin during movement and this can, at first, look like a faulty topline if a closer examination is not made.

A curly or wavy coat can completely distort the topline, so it is most important that judging is not done by visual means alone. A curly coat is a far less serious fault than a constructionally defective topline.

HINDQUARTERS

If balance is to be maintained, it is important that the hindquarters are as strong and sound as the forequarters. A similar degree of angulation and strength of bone will ensure that wear and tear is equally

44

distributed throughout the body. From behind, the judge should again be looking for two imaginary parallel lines running from the hip bone, through the hock and down into the foot. As with the forequarters, the hind legs should not be too close together. From the side, angulation should be good enough but not exaggerated. Very straight hind angulation makes the movement look stilted, as there will be no perceptible 'bend' to the leg. Over-angulation can look very eye-catching as the dog thrashes his legs almost mechanically. However, this, is also a sign of impending weakness. (Think of the Leaning Tower of Pisa; just so much looks great, a little more and it will come crashing to the ground!)

FEET

Good feet will look like clenched fists and will have considerable depth if they are to carry a Newfie around effectively. Frank Cassidy (Littlecreek) once told us that in over thirty years he had *never* seen a

Newfoundland without webbed feet. This is hardly surprising as many other breeds also have webbed feet. All-rounder judges who are new to the breed often make a point of checking the presence of webbed feet. It is probably a futile exercise, but it is nice to know that they have read the Standard!

GAIT/MOVEMENT

As the word "slight" appears both in the UK and the New FCI Standards, and the AKC talks of "a slight roll of the skin" part, they represent an attempt to stamp out exaggeration.

The phrase "slightly rolling gait" means that loose skin around the rib-cage can be seen swinging clockwise and anti-clockwise as the dog moves. Dogs who are fat, barrel-chested or have a abundance of loose skin can look like living tombolas, and distract the judge's eye from the rest of the movement!

The New FCI Standard lists "distinctly toeing-in in front" as a fault, while the UK

LEFT: Correct: Good front, parallel limbs, with a straight line through the shoulder, elbow and pastern.

RIGHT: Correct: Converging on a single line during movement.

Incorrect: Wide at elbow, toeing in to compensate.

Incorrect: Narrow chest, tied at elbows, toeing out to compensate.

Standard contends that "slight toeing in at front" is acceptable. Many reasons, ranging from the bizarre to the ridiculous, have been given for the inclusion of this clause, and Newfie lovers everywhere have a different theory for and against it. Nonetheless, it is part of both Standards and is here to stay. Therefore judges need to accept that they should not fault it, while breeders need to realise that it is only "acceptable" and strive to produce stock that can also move without toe-ing in.

Good movement can mean many things to different judges, but anyone who is used to living with or judging horses, or is familiar with breeds like Siberian Huskies, will probably agree that an efficient gait comes from minimum effort and maximum progress. Apart from the aesthetic point of view, an effortless stride causes less wear and tear of joints over the years. Combine this with the correct angulation for longer strides and the parallel lines of the limbs as they swing back and forth, and it is easy to see why *good* movement is like running an economical car: you get more mileage and less expensive maintenance.

At slow speeds a Newfoundland steps out a relatively wide double track but at faster speeds he may converge into a single track, as mentioned in the AKC Standard and the New FCI Standard, and this should not be faulted or confused with moving "close behind" – a term which some use when they mean 'cow-hocks'. Other people use it when they see a narrowly-built dog whose hindquarters move "close" all the way down the back legs. Some judges forgive a poorly moving Newfoundland, as they believe that a giant breed cannot be expected to move actively and efficiently. Personally, we feel that if a heavily-built horse such as a Welsh Cob or heavy hunter can move well, even with a slight variation in construction, a Newfoundland can also move impressively.

Do not, however, confuse good movement with the high-stepping and kicking action of a Hackney horse; such deviation from the clean parallel lines expected from a Newfie would also result in unnecessary wearing out of joints, while the extra energy expended could be put to better use in assisting forward progress.

The hind movement of a dog going away from the judge can sometimes be disguised by a profuse coat. The motion of the hind leg will, nonetheless, always be given away by the position of the pad from behind.

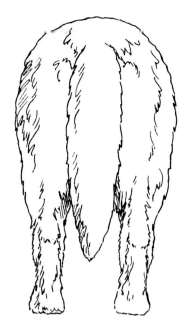

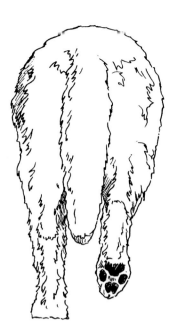

Converging on a single line during movement.

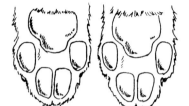

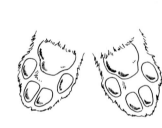

Incorrect: Cow hocks (can also occur while moving downhill).

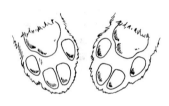

Incorrect: Barrel hocks.

Incorrect: "Throwing" one hock, or anticipating a left turn.

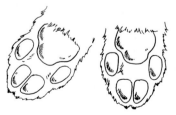

47

When the pad is not pointing at right angles to the ground the leg will not be moving forward in a straight line (unless the dog is turning to the right or left, when the relevant leg will also be tilted at an angle in anticipation of the turn).

TAIL

The tail is specifically described except for its set (which is generally accepted as being neither too high, nor too low). The AKC Standard includes a tail set which "follows the natural line of the croup".

A tail with "a kink" or one that is "curled over back" is undesirable. A kink in the tail will be easily felt and will resemble a knuckle or badly-set broken bone. A curled-over tail will also be plain to see – not only to the judge, but to the entire ring side. A very 'gay' tail is sometimes a temporary sign of male dominance, and it is possible to spot twelve to eighteen-month-old dogs who have just discovered what sex they are, by the way their tails are held aloft!

A kink in the tail is, according to the UK Standard, "most undesirable", but that is not to say that it is a fault worse than any other. A judge may have to decide between two dogs and should take into account whether a kinked tail is more serious than, for example, cow-hocks or a narrow skull.

COAT

The ideal coat will be flat, but it has to be remembered that a dog with a normally flat coat may, on the day of the show, have waves or curls due to having been blow-dried by an inexperienced owner. However, a judge has to assess each dog as he sees them, so, unless he is experienced enough to know when a coat has been dried wrongly, the fault has to be penalised accordingly.

"Coarse and oily" coats are called for. With modern trends of bathing the dog immediately before a show, it is unusual to find many coarse and oily coats. The show dog who also competes at water events may have a more oily coat and, if the water test has taken place a day or two before the show, may smell a little more 'doggy'. Assuming that the coat is not dirty (and this will show up on the judge's hands), the dog should not be faulted.

Occasionally, a dog is shown in a dirty or dusty condition. This is unpleasant and an insult to the judge but is not a reason for placing the dog far down the line or for not placing him at all, if he is correctly constructed and sound. A beautifully-presented and perfume-scented coat which only covers a slab-sided, fine-boned and long-muzzled creature will be lovely to touch, but will hardly do the breed any favours when the dog wins its title and is bred from. A dog with an unclean coat is the *owner's* fault, and it is he or she who should be taken to task when judging has been completed.

COLOUR

Although a dull black is called for, it is widely accepted that a shiny black bathed coat is equally suitable. A "splash of white" is open to misinterpretation and it seems that a white chest to any degree is accepted, while "toes and tip of tail" are more restricted. A brownish tinge throughout a black coat is perfectly correct although it is seen less often in latter-day Britain. Warmer countries, however, have more dogs with a sunburned tinge. The shade of brown preferred may be left to personal choice. Fewer people seem to favour the ginger colour seen in some Newfies, but it can be as attractive as a rich, dark chocolate shade. It is important to realise that brown, in genetic terms, is actually liver and therefore it is not possible for the dog to have dark brown eyes any more than it is possible for him to have a black nose. The eye colour of a brown dog will always be different to that of a black or landseer, and the specimen should not be faulted for having a light eye when it is simply and correctly matching the coat

COLOUR

1. Dutch and Int. Ch. Sita: The Standard calls for a dull black colour.

2. Aust. Ch. Mekong Rustic Warrior: A brown Newfoundland can be chocolate or bronze.

3. Am. Ch. Nomex De Nashau-Auke: In the US the grey colour is acceptable in the show ring.

4. A well-matched brace of Italian Champion Landseers: The colouring is white with black markings.

Landseer with good body markings.

A lightly marked dog gives the impression of a small head.

"One-sided" markings can make the topline look poor.

Heavy, "blanket" markings can create an illusion of too much body length.

colour. Browns who are moulting or immature may have lighter coloured shadings behind their ears, on their sides and on their 'trousers'. While an even shade is ideal, this, again, is a cosmetic, temporary fault and should be treated as such.

A landseer is a white dog with black markings, and not the other way around. Although the pattern of markings is described in some detail, it is quite rare to see a classically-marked landseer without any "ticking" (black spots on white areas).

Primarily, however, the dog should be judged as a Newfoundland first; the colour is a secondary consideration. A class of all landseers will obviously have their beauty of markings compared at some point, but when dogs of all three colours are in the ring the judge should be looking for good Newfoundlands and not coat colour. The black markings of a landseer can sometimes create an optical illusion, so it is important to correctly assess the construction of the dog.

"Grays" are allowed in the AKC Standard, and they should have an even colour all over. Like the browns, they are not able to have brown eyes or a black nose, but in all other respects should follow the Standard for blacks. Some lack of hair around the ears can be a colour-specific problem for grays, so it can be a challenge to breed a good gray.

SIZE

As the Newfoundland is a giant breed, it is understandable that the larger the dog, the more he will impress – as long as he still looks balanced and harmonious. An average height is given in all three Standards, which can be somewhat misleading.

As an all-rounder judge, the late Mr David Samuel, once said: "If there are six dogs in the ring and three are twenty-two inches high while the other three are thirty-four inches tall, then the average will be a correct twenty-eight inches." His observations are very true and, therefore, it may make more sense to assume that the Standards mean that a male Newfoundland should be *"around* twenty-eight inches" in height. Whatever his size, a Newfoundland's bulk should come from bone and muscle, never from fat.

FAULTS

This is the key to understanding the Breed Standards. No dog is perfect; they all have faults. The judge's task is to compare the severity of those faults as well as their importance in the overall quality of the dog.

COMPARISON OF STANDARDS

A diversity of opinion is a healthy state in all walks of life, and this is reflected in the slight variation of these Standards. Despite the few differences, the basic requirement is for a large breed of dog with life-saving tendencies, a gentle temperament and active movement. Breeding and showing Newfoundlands is a cosmopolitan activity these days, and the top-quality dogs are easily recognised by both national and international judges. The late Kitty Drury (Dryad Kennels, USA) could find a good Newfoundland in any country she visited or judged in!

The Newfoundland's colour is probably the most obvious point of difference. The AKC Standard allows grey dogs while, north of the border, the Canadian Standard (which was published in 1979 and falls somewhere between the UK and AKC formats) only accepts black or landseer. The rest of the world tends to agree that greys are not desirable, but that browns are perfectly acceptable!

Mouths have a slightly different emphasis in each Standard, with the AKC giving the fullest explanation. Most countries, however, make the same allowances for "dropped teeth" even though their Standards sound a little rigid.

The presence of webbed feet and a slightly toeing-in gait are omitted from the Australian and New Zealand Standards (who follow the UK Standard in all other respects). While webbed feet tend to be found universally in Newfoundlands, many Australian and New Zealand dogs have very good front movement.

5 THE SHOW RING

Many people showing their Newfoundlands are introduced to the show ring by a chance remark from someone who declares that the dog is of 'show quality'. Quite what this means (and how qualified the commentator is to make such a remark) depends on how seriously the owner intends to campaign his or her dog.

EXHIBITOR'S TEMPERAMENT

This is a very important factor in dog showing. As owners, we are all a little biased when it comes to assessing our own dogs. Like people, dogs can also have 'off days' and do not always look their best. However, the dog you viewed with great hopes when you left home in the morning will be the same one you bring home that night, regardless of how the judge rated him. The most important thing in a Newfoundland's life will be his owner's love, so do not be cold to him just because he played you up in the show ring or because the judge did not place him highly. There will be other days and other shows.

Similarly, you may encounter the occasional judge who places only the dogs of his or her friends, or one who is clearly incompetent and gives the awards to all the wrong exhibits. In these cases, you will want to call the judge some most unflattering names, and you may do so – providing it is done only *inside* your head! A Newfoundland is a loving and forgiving creature and does not deserve to be owned by someone who is forever complaining and insulting others.

If you enjoy showing your dog, gaining the occasional high award and having a pleasurable day in the company of other Newfie owners, then you have the correct temperament. If showing only brings out the worst in you, then it is time to look for another hobby.

PROBLEMS

What if your dog is out of coat? A Newfoundland's moult can vary in severity depending on many factors. A dog at fifteen months of age, having his first major moult, can look like a victim of starvation (until the body is felt), so it is hardly likely that he will win top honours. Unless you know that your opposition will also be minus their coats, you can save yourself a lot of time and effort by staying home.

Bitches who have had a litter in the previous twelve to twenty weeks will also be in a state of undress and not fit to be seen in public. Their tails, in particular, often resemble a length of tatty rope and this is an unmistakable sign of recent maternity duties. A normal moult, though, is not always extreme enough to keep the dog at home and, with experience, you will know when your dog is looking distinctly under par!

What if your bitch is in season? Entry fees are far from cheap, so it can be frustrating if your bitch comes in season before a show. As there are no rules forbidding a bitch in season to be shown, then the decision will have to be a personal one. However, showing a bitch on the thirteenth day of her season is a little irresponsible and owners of the male dogs present will curse your every step! The beginning or the end of the season should not cause too many problems if the owner diligently uses disinfectant wipes on the bitch's 'trousers'! Some bitches constantly smell 'interesting' to male dogs, and these, too, can benefit from similar treatment.

What if you know the judge? Most Newfoundland exhibitors know each other, so it is quite likely that you may have to enter your dog under a judge whom you see regularly. Unless it is your best friend's first judging appointment, then the most flattering action you can take is to enter your dog, as it shows that you have faith in the judge's integrity and competence.

AT THE SHOW

If you have entered a championship show, you will receive a 'pass' in the mail bearing your dog's name and exhibition number. There may be other information included, such as the number and location of your breed ring, the time that judging will commence or even details of possible traffic delays due to road maintenance near the show ground. Read the contents carefully, as they may be relevant to the time you set off from home.

Arrive at the show ground in plenty of time so that your dog will have an opportunity to empty his bladder and settle down on his bench in a relaxed mood. Offer him a drink of water, but do not leave the bowl on the bench with him in case he tips it – the water will not harm him, but a dripping wet Newfoundland will not look well-presented and the judge will hardly appreciate handling a soggy dog!

Shortly before your class is called, give your dog a final brushing and change his collar and lead for a thin, black show-lead (in the case of a black dog). If there are two sets of identical numbers on your bench, take one and wear it prominently on your arm or chest. If there is only one set, then it means you will be collecting your number in the ring so you will need to memorise it before the class is called.

While you are waiting outside the ring, look at the entrants in the previous class to see what they are being asked to do. Although you should have been to several training classes before attempting a championship show, some judges will have very specific directions for you, so it is a relief to know what to expect. Look also for any dips in the ground or a downhill slope. A Newfoundland rarely looks good facing downhill, so you may have to be a little selective over where you stand.

IN THE RING

At last your class is called and in you go! You will have 'butterflies' in your stomach but do not worry – so will everyone else, even the experienced handlers.

At some shows, exhibitors are expected to stand in numerical order and the ring steward will ensure that you are in the correct position. However, if you are not expected to line up in any particular order, you may tag along just about anywhere. It is very bad manners to barge to the front of the line-up or, indeed, in front of anyone who has already come to a halt with his or her dog.

Keep your Newfie on a short lead and be aware of any potential misbehaviour between him and his nearest neighbour. It is lovely to

WORLDWIDE WINNERS

The British show scene: Ch. Newfhouse Scandinavian Warrior for Merrybear, Top Working Dog in Britain 1996.
Photo: Russell Fine Art.

BIS winner Uk Ir. Ch. Leumasleiloc Penny Black – the first Northern Ireland bred dual Champion.
Photo: Carol Ann Johnson.

Am. Can. Ch. Seawards Blackbeard, the only Newfoundland to win Best In Show at Westminster. *Photo: Ashbey.*

South Africa: Sh. Ch. Carthew Born Free of Riverbears, CC recordholder for bitches in South Africa.

Swed BIS Ch. Qashiwas Big Bubble No Trouble. *Photo: Per Unden.*

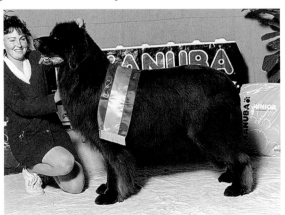

Australasia: NZ Grand Ch. Waterbear Winchester, a multi BIS winner.

see two dogs who have never met playing and having fun – but not in the show ring. The two will not only get themselves covered in dust, grass or slobber, but will also distract the other dogs in the ring. As the handler, your job will be to present your dog's best points to the judge, and you will not be able to do this if he is lying upside down with his paws in the air!

Once all the handlers have their dogs standing and the stewards have recorded the absentees, the judge will look briefly at all the dogs before sending everyone around the ring together. As many of the dogs will be of different heights and levels of fitness, you can expect some to move faster than others. If you are behind a fast-moving dog and your Newfie is finding it difficult to keep up, simply cut the corners as you go around the ring. Alternatively, if you find yourself behind a slow dog, then use the corners and the widest perimeter of the ring. *Never* be tempted to overtake the dog in front (unless the handler suddenly pulls up and tells you to pass), and do not go too close behind him. Even an easy-going Newfie can find this intimidating, and may try to defend himself against your dog.

When you have completed a circuit of the ring, the judge will examine or 'go over' each dog individually. You will have practised standing your dog at training classes, so, when your turn comes, you will know what to do. Walk your dog into a standing position while keeping the lead short and fairly tight behind the ears (do not become so nervous that you hold the lead too tightly). While keeping one hand on the neckband of the lead, use the other to place the dog's legs in the correct position (only if they are not already exactly as you want them). The front legs should be parallel to each other with the feet facing forward. If the legs are placed too far forward, your Newfie will look like a rocking-horse and will probably 'dip' in the middle. When you are moving the legs, hold them at the top, near

the elbows, rather than at the foot or pastern. Many Newfoundlands have ticklish feet, and you will find it much easier to grasp the top of the leg. You can position the hindquarters in much the same way, by holding the leg lightly near the hock. The hind legs should also be parallel to each other with the feet facing forward. If your dog is slightly 'rump-high', you may have to splay the hind legs a little in order to shorten the height of the rump. Placing the hind feet too far back or forward will spoil the natural outline of the dog, so it will take much practice to get it right. Juliet Leicester-Hope (Wanitopa) has a piece of ingenious advice for novice owners attempting to stand their dogs correctly. Stand opposite a plate glass window or large mirror where mistakes can easily be seen!

Once your dog is standing correctly, gently support his head so that it is held high and proud. The judge will then assess him by inspecting his teeth, eye colour, construction and coat. If the dog constantly fidgets or will not keep still, it may be that you are standing him in an unnatural pose and he is uncomfortable. Standing him should only enhance what is already there, so do not attempt to manipulate him into a shape that you think will please the judge; any competent judge will recognise poor construction as soon as he goes over the dog.

You will then be asked to move your dog. Some judges simply wave an arm vaguely in the direction they wish you to take, while others state clearly "Triangle, please", or "Up and down, twice". Whatever form the request takes, the judge will want to see your dog's movement from behind, from the front and in profile. You will know from training classes what speed suits your dog best, so you can set off confidently at that pace. Keep the lead fairly short so that your Newfie cannot sniff the ground as he moves, but do not string him up so much that he develops the stilted action favoured by terrier

fanciers. When you have moved your dog to the judge's satisfaction, you should return to the end of the row and wait until all the dogs have been examined by the judge. Newfoundlands have considerable patience, so do not take advantage of his good nature by making him stand during the time that other dogs are being assessed for the first time. Let him sit until the last dog in the ring is being looked at, then stand him up and brush him down before putting him into his final stance.

Whether or not you are placed in the class, you should pat your dog and quickly congratulate the winner. If you were lucky enough to win, you will need to stay in position for a minute while the judge writes a critique. This is *not* the time to tell the judge that "this is my first show, and I'm so glad he won because I bought him from the top breeders at Roverdog Kennels." In fact, unless you are asked a question, there is no need to converse with the judge at all, except maybe to say "Thank you" as you leave the ring. Some exhibitors, who should know better, never stop talking when they are near the judge. This is normally a vague conversation conducted with their dog, and goes along the lines of "What a good boy. Let's see if you can win the CC again today." As this is a complete waste of time (not to mention a breach of KC rules in some countries), you might as well start your showing career by omitting this particular tactic from your agenda!

PRESENTATION OF THE HANDLER

As you have spent hours preparing your dog for the show ring, it stands to reason that you will not want to look like a refugee from a war zone! A neatly turned out handler will complement the dog; it should make no difference to the judging, but it does look good to see a well-matched dog and handler who take pride in their appearance. Equally importantly – do not overdress. Long, fussy sleeves, or collar bows, are likely to end up in your Newfie's mouth as you bend over to place the legs, and anyone who has wrestled with a playful nine-month puppy who wants to eat her blouse will always thereafter be seen in a smart, but understated outfit! Ladies who display acres of cleavage and miles of leg impress no one unless they also happen to be starring in the latest Hollywood production.

Your attire at a show should be aimed at presenting your dog in the best possible light. Do not wear black when showing a black dog – the dog's neck and topline will be lost in the background colour. A bright or light colour, however, will emphasise his outline. A landseer looks particularly well against a vibrant mid-blue, but any colour not too dark or too light will be suitable. Browns stand out against a black background, but generally, this is one colour that is fairly easy to contrast with.

Make sure that you have appropriate footwear that will be suitable for running. High heels or slippery soles are obviously a hazard, but beware also of comfortable open-toed sandals. Should your Newfie stand on your foot (a habit of which they are very fond), then you will probably say something rather stronger than 'Ouch'!

AFTER THE SHOW

Following your first and second show (especially if you have won), it is very likely that you will have been bitten by the show bug. You will go home armed with schedules of forthcoming shows, you will study the judges to see which 'type' they favour, and you will practise your handling and presentation until they are perfect. Do not forget, though, that showing should take up only a small percentage of your dog's life and he is unlikely to be as enthusiastic about it as you. He will do his bit in the show ring just to please you, so try to return the favour by letting him live a 'normal' life the rest of the time. Walking in the woods, swimming and having a rough and tumble with another dog will be the pastimes he really enjoys, so let him have his fun without worrying that he will tear his coat out or injure his legs.

JUDGING
STARTING OFF

It is almost inevitable that exhibitors who, week after week, watch judges carrying out their duties eventually feel that they, too, could do a similar (or better!) job. The very ambitious (for want of another, less polite, term) feel competent to judge after six months or so as an exhibitor.

All prospective judges are asked: "Why do you want to judge Newfoundlands?" A variety of reasons may be given, but, in many cases, the true reason may be that the person concerned wants to feel more important in the world of dogs. Anyone who needs his or her ego massaged in such a way should look elsewhere. Judging dogs is simply a way of separating the good from the not-so-good, and the truly excellent from the ordinary. It is a way of assessing which dogs are good enough to be bred from and who will contribute the most to the breed in the future. Judging is not about self-importance or, worse still, revenge.

If a judge is incompetent or dishonest, it can have a disastrous effect on the breed in the long term. While breeders should not automatically use a dog at stud just because he is winning, they are certainly unlikely to use a dog who is consistently 'thrown out'. It also follows, therefore, that an exhibitor whose bitch is always being overlooked may decide not to breed from her – a wise decision if the judges were right, but the start of a decline for the breed if the judges were misguided or unscrupulous.

LEARNING THE BASICS

Judging looks easy; you go over each dog and pick the best four or five in descending order. We were once told an amusing story by a friend who had taken his dog into the town centre while his wife shopped. A man stepped out of a doorway and said: "What a lovely dog! May I stroke him?" On being given the go-ahead, the man carefully checked the bite, bone, front angulation and topline, exclaiming with delight the whole time. By then our friend was already picturing himself winning groups and BIS, and tentatively said: "You obviously do a bit of judging?", while trying to recollect who the man could be. "Oh no," said the would-be judge, "but I've watched Crufts on TV!" Although we laughed when we heard the tale, it does illustrate how anyone can go through the motions of judging dogs, but it is a pointless exercise if the hands are not able to tell the brain anything.

Judging, like most other skills, has to be learned and, these days, there are countless opportunities of doing so. Various breed clubs and canine societies often hold judging seminars and teach-ins. It is not essential to limit oneself to Newfoundland seminars, as basic construction can be learned equally well, if not better, by going over a variety of breeds. Points like correct dentition, sound movement and good angulation are similar in many breeds, so any opportunity to learn will not be wasted. Once the basic foundations are laid, read and re-read the Newfoundland Standard and go over as many Newfoundlands as you can. A word of warning though – keep your comments to yourself! When an owner has been accommodating enough to allow you to examine his dog, do not insult him by telling him (or others!) what faults you found, or you will find yourself with a marked shortage of dogs to practise on.

IN THE RING

When you have eventually been asked to judge Newfoundlands for the first time, it will probably be at an Open Show, and you can expect four or five breed classes to be provided. Shortly before the day of the show you will have been notified in writing of how many dogs are entered in each class. (Who they are will, of course, remain unknown to you until they enter the ring!) As judges are expected to assess between twenty and twenty-five dogs per hour, it will give you an indication of how long you should take to complete the breed. Open shows often average an entry of around twelve to sixteen dogs, so it is unlikely that you should take more than an hour to judge them.

Consider also how you will look in the ring. Smartness is essential, but an outfit that is either fussy or expensive will be more of a hindrance than a help. Scruffiness, too, is unnecessary these days, when everyone has access to an iron and a washing-machine. Choose an outfit that is comfortable, as you will be on your feet and moving around throughout the classes. It may be a good idea to restrict yourself to fabrics which do not produce static shock. Remembering that the first dog you go over is likely to be a puppy, you will not want to frighten him by 'crackling' as you make contact with him.

For a variety of reasons, you will

understandably be nervous before you begin judging; you may be worried about forgetting to check a particular conformation point or, more likely, you will baulk at the thought of upsetting exhibitors by not placing their dogs. We will always remember the advice of Frances Warren (Littlegrange) to new judges: "There will be no people in the ring. All you have to do is choose the best dog." If you offend an exhibitor by judging honestly, then it is unfortunate, but they have a choice whether or not to enter their dogs under you again.

It is likely that you will know the majority of dogs and exhibitors at the show, so it may be difficult to honestly assess a dog you saw winning his first CC the previous week. Dogs too, as we mentioned before, have their off-days. If a well-known winner is out of coat, lethargic and not moving well, do not be afraid to place ahead of him what is, in your opinion, an equally good dog with active movement. On the other hand, do not deliberately set out to find another dog just to prove that a winner can be beaten.

Try to ensure that each dog is given a fair chance to show his paces. If a dog gallops or plays up repeatedly, ask for him to be moved again until he gets it right. Many will settle down after their first few attempts, but, if not, then remember that the time you spend will be somewhat limited.

Some handlers are clever at disguising a dog's faults, so you will need to make a connection between what you *see* and what your *hands* tell you. Other handlers can be a little pushy – standing out from the line-up or obstructing someone else's dog. If you cannot see all the dogs properly, ask the errant handler to move. If you cannot get a good view of the dogs for any other reason

(bright sunlight for example), then move everyone around until you can.

When you have appraised all the dogs, you will be subconsciously placing them in order. Try not to fall into the trap of fault judging: "Can't place this one, he's got light eyes. Can't place that one, he's got a short tail", and so on. You could end up with a dog who has no great faults but no great virtues either!

When you have placed the dogs in your class you will need to write a critique on the winners. This need not be an essay, but should note the good and bad points. Just because a particular dog is your winner does not mean that he is the best Newfoundland since time began – simply the best one in that class on that day. He could be the best of a mediocre bunch or the best of a class of future champions, but you will need to elaborate on why you placed him ahead of the others.

It is doubtful whether the modern-day exhibitor really wants to know how awful his or her dog is, so do not be tempted into only listing shortcomings. A critique should be kind, but knowledgeable. An owner reading about the dog's faults will accept them far more readily if he or she can also read about his virtues.

The dread of every judge is the exhibitor (there is at least one in every breed) who confronts the judge when he has finished and demands to know why he did not like his/her dog. In extreme cases only, you can forget all you have learned about judging and offer the only feeble explanation available in these circumstances: "Madam (or Sir), I did not dislike your dog; I simply preferred the others!"

6 *WATER WORKING NEWFOUNDLANDS*

The Newfoundland is a working dog. His build, character, webbed feet and natural abilities make him uniquely suited for water work. A fit Newfoundland is a powerful swimmer, truly at home in the water, and to watch a dog work in rough conditions is an impressive sight.

Swimming and working with Newfoundlands is also tremendous fun and a great way to keep both people and dogs fit and healthy. The exhilaration of being towed in the water by one's own Newfoundland for the first time is one that should be experienced by all lovers of the breed.

TRAINING A YOUNG DOG

The younger the dog the better! If you are serious about wanting to train a dog to work at the highest level, then the younger he starts the more likely he is to achieve his full potential. All of our dogs are introduced to the water at around fourteen weeks of age, following the completion of their initial vaccination programme. I appreciate that not everyone will wish to put in the time and effort required to perform at the highest level, but, whatever your aspirations, swimming is a healthy and enjoyable exercise for a young Newfoundland. The basic rule is to keep it fun and not to expect too much too soon. Most Newfoundlands will be

around two years old before they are really capable of performing consistently at the higher levels.

FIRST STEPS

There are almost as many ideas on introducing young dogs to water work as there are trainers. However, the best advice is to know and understand the dog and to recognise what motivates him. Is it food, a toy, or is it simply your presence? Motivation is a key factor in all training. The best person to entice a young dog into the water for the first time is his owner – the person he knows best and trusts the most.

It is also important that you are patient, however long it takes. If one method fails, try something else. Use a favourite toy, or tasty morsel, walk up and down the bank and, gradually, both of you can enter the water.

One controversial method, used by some trainers but frowned upon by others, is simply to pick up the dog, wade out and place him in the water. This should *never* be the first step. A nervous dog could suffer a degree of trauma and consequent loss of confidence, which may take weeks or even months to undo. Nevertheless, it remains an option which, in appropriate circumstances, is adopted by many trainers.

The Newfoundland is uniquely suited to water work.

In practice, some dogs will paddle up and down in the water and retrieve or play, as long as their feet are on the bottom. They are clearly happy in water, but resist all attempts to induce that last step and start swimming. What do you do? You can carry on trying different forms of temptation, as patience usually brings its own reward, especially if the owner is in there with the dog. One method that often works is to include other dogs in the play session in the hope that, as the others swim off to retrieve a thrown float, the hesitant one will follow. With a young puppy, its mother or a litter mate is often a great incentive. An older male may well find any bitch an irresistible incentive, or even the scent (conveyed on a swab) of a bitch in season. However, with a dog you know well, who is clearly not nervous, there are times when a little bit of help is all that is required, either by applying a gentle tug on the harness or by lifting the dog into deeper water.

LEARNING TO SWIM

Newfoundlands are natural swimmers and have very powerful swimming actions. Nevertheless, some are better than others and indeed there is a small minority which have a very poor swimming action. The correct action – level in the water using all four legs to drive the dog through it – is essential to a good working dog. The dog's power in the water, the ability to swim long distances and pull heavy objects, derives from this action. You may have noted that most other breeds adopt a more upright position in the water and have a very energetic and less efficient style; they often use only the front legs in what is commonly referred to as the 'doggy paddle'.

Some Newfoundland puppies will take to swimming from the start and have few problems with its basics. Others will require a little assistance to perfect a good action. The most common fault is a failure to use all four legs and to adopt the level position. Such puppies will normally have a much more frantic and less efficient style.

How, then, do we overcome this problem in young or novice dogs? Again, you will not be surprised to learn that there are many ideas, but little evidence that any one is uniformly more effective. The alternatives include the following.

1. When the dog is in water that is sufficiently deep to ensure that he must swim, but shallow enough to enable the handler to stand, the dog's rear is manually lifted from behind so that it is level in the water. Most will then use all four legs to swim. The handler will hold the dog in that position so that he has to employ as much power as he is capable of to move forward. This is most effective if the owner, or someone else, calls the dog from the shore. As the dog adopts a correct swimming

position, he is allowed to make progress. The objective is to help the dog to realise that adopting the correct position gives him the power to progress. (N.B. Care needs to be taken to ensure that the handler is not harmed by the dog's rear paws, and that no stress is caused to the dog.)

2. A handler can walk beside the Newfoundland holding up the dog's rear as he swims through the water.

3. Some form of artificial float or inflatable can be attached, with the assistance being reduced as the dog increasingly adopts the right position in the water.

4. Ropes can be attached to the harness for the handler to hold and apply resistance, again forcing the dog to increase his power in order to make progress and hopefully adopt a more appropriate swimming style in order to do so. The ropes can be attached to a boat, but applying weight is more appropriate for older dogs and is not really suitable for young puppies.

With most dogs, the problem is temporary and they will eventually develop a reasonable swimming style. This is especially true for puppies. However, an older dog who has failed to develop an efficient swimming stroke can find this a difficult fault to overcome. At the core of all of the different methods is an attempt to instil into the dog a realisation that the correct action is the most efficient and involves least effort. In teaching swimming skills, it is much easier and more effective if the handler is able to stand as the dog swims. Alternatively, where that is not possible, support can be given to the handler by the use of a boat.

BASIC TRAINING EXERCISES
Keep training simple and make it fun! Previous training on land will have helped when a young dog takes to the water. We give our puppies ropes to play with as soon as they are able, at four to five weeks of age. A new puppy who has learned simple commands at home (such as "Sit", "Stay", "Take", "Hold" and "Fetch") will find initial water training much easier. A puppy who has played with his owner using a rope is more likely to hold a rope in water. A puppy who will fetch on land will often find little difficulty in performing a similar exercise in the water. It is also true that a dog who is familiar and confident with strangers will find training easier.

Always start by teaching the dog to swim safely at the side of the handler. Wade out with the puppy, but do not allow the puppy to climb on to a person even in play. If he attempts to do so, use gentle restraint and firm commands. It is tempting to see such climbing as a sign of affection and a lot of fun with a small, young pup. However, similar behaviour in an adult dog can be very dangerous and cause serious injury. At the very least, it is the cause of many torn wet suits, which are expensive to repair. A tear in a dry suit is potentially much more serious. Faults, like all forms of canine behaviour, are best overcome in a young dog.

At this stage, you should seek to use and develop the dog's natural instincts, e.g. his affection and desire to please you. Again, be patient. Use gentle persuasion, or try an incentive, but remember that it is all much easier and less stressful for the dog if you get in the water yourself. Others can help in sending and guiding, but there is no substitute for the owner being out in the water calling the dog to come. After these first steps, some trainers seek to use strangers from the early stages in order to alleviate difficulties at higher levels when a dog must swim to strangers.

TRAINING AN OLDER DOG
The principles used in training a puppy are equally valid in introducing older dogs to water, the major difference being the old

adage of 'teaching old dogs new tricks'. It is harder to overcome problems in an older dog, but most will learn to enjoy water training with time and patience. Many will take to it as if they have been swimming all of their lives. I can recall one retired show champion rising from a lively paddle to test passes at A and B within a few weeks of regular training.

THE RETRIEVE

As already discussed, exercises at home (disguised as playtime) will greatly assist in training a dog to retrieve an object in the water. However, it is no guarantee, since water is a different environment and some good retrievers will baulk at their first water retrieve. This is probably because of the fact that, as they open their mouths to take the object, they will also take in water, sometimes quite large amounts. For some dogs this will present an initial problem. I like to start with a piece of rope or a small float. However, when a dog is unfamiliar with these objects, it is usually best to start with something the dog enjoys playing with – normally a favourite toy. It must float, of course. I am no longer surprised by the variety of articles which are presented as favoured retrieve articles and, over the years, I have used most things that will float (and some that would not) in training dogs to retrieve. Again make training fun – get the dog excited and eager to complete the retrieve.

The object of a retrieve is for the dog to return to dry land, with the article, which he should present to the handler. A common fault in many dogs is that they drop the object before they leave the water, usually when their feet touch the bottom. This is less of a problem with dogs who have learned to retrieve and present the article in normal obedience classes. The problem can be overcome in a number of ways. It is essential to encourage the dog to hold the article until he is instructed to give it to the

handler, without making him feel that he has not performed the exercise correctly. When the dog has completed the retrieve, he merely needs to learn to finish the exercise in the correct manner. This is fairly easily achieved by one of two methods.

1. The handler walks backwards away from the water's edge as the dog approaches, encouraging him to fetch the object.

2. The handler walks into the water up to the point at which the dog is about to drop the object, and encourages him to continue to "Hold", until instructed to "Give".

The second common fault is a refusal to hand over the object when instructed to do so. I am not in favour of forcibly ducking a dog to encourage him to release an article and I believe that this is an obedience problem and is best tackled away from the water.

BUILDING ON BASICS

Water tests incorporate a building block approach that mirrors sensible methods of training. Whether for young musicians or Newfoundlands, all training has common rules and principles. You would not ask a person to conduct the band after one music lesson. Equally, there is no single, correct way to train a dog. One should use whatever works. I will use the exercise of jumping from a boat as an example. Some dogs will quite happily jump from a boat, while others require a great deal of encouragement and work to get them to do so.

JUMPING FROM A BOAT

A boat, afloat on water, is much less stable than dry land and many dogs will display some initial reluctance to jump out of one. So how do we train a reluctant dog to jump from a boat?

1. Start on dry land and train the dog to

Barney, the highest qualified water worker in Britain, leaping out of a boat.

enter and leave the boat on command.

2. Train the dog to jump on command. This was the method used successfully on one reluctant dog who was trained to exit a boat after many months of effort. Much of the training was carried out on land.

3. Hold the boat in shallow water and gradually increase the depth and distance from shore. Many dogs will happily jump in and out on land or in shallow water, but baulk when further from shore.

4. If the owner is in the water, most dogs will want to join him or her and will eventually get out of the boat.

5. Use a favourite toy or edible reward.

6. Use another dog. Place both dogs in the boat and throw out a favoured retrieve object. The sight of the second dog leaping out to steal a treasured toy is often sufficient

to encourage a reluctant dog.

7. Turn the boat upside down; some dogs are initially wary about climbing over the sides of a boat.

8. Use a boat with lower sides.

9. Take the boat and dog out into the lake and leave the owner on shore.

Again, be patient and persevere. If one method fails, try another. A good rule of thumb for all aspects of training is if you have tried one way five times without success, try something else. You can always come back to your original idea another time. Most importantly, keep the dog interested. Newfoundlands are not like certain breeds such as German Shepherds or Border Collies. They need persuasion and reward in training. They need to enjoy the exercise. It is also essential to retain their interest and attention, as this can soon

It is essential to keep the Newfoundland interested in his work.

wander, especially in young dogs. They also like variety, and quickly grow tired of repeating the same exercise. So, move on to something else frequently – there is always another day.

BOAT WORK
Let us look at the basic exercise of swimming out to a boat and see how this could develop.

1. The owner or helper stands in the water at a short distance and encourages the dog to swim out, using whatever method is felt to be best in each case. They can simply call by name, or wave a toy or a biscuit. If it works, the best incentive is a piece of rope. When the dog reaches the boat he is rewarded.

If the reward is the rope, then the dog can be encouraged to take the rope in his mouth for the return swim. If a different reward is used, then at some stage the dog will need to be trained to take and pull with a rope. This might be done by using lengths of ropes in controlled play and by using coils of rope as retrieve objects in water. All training is much simpler if a dog has been taught basic obedience. If he understands and obeys commands such as "Take' and "Hold", then teaching a dog to retrieve and work with a rope, or any other object, will obviously present fewer problems.

N.B. In asking dogs to retrieve lengths of rope, one must be aware of the dangers of snagging or the dog getting entangled in loose coils. Always pay attention and watch the dog. Intervene at the slightest suspicion of his being in any difficulty. In tests, all stewards are told to act on their own initiative to assist the dog whenever they suspect a problem, and not to wait for instruction.

2. The handler might stand beside a boat and give the dog a length of rope, which is attached to the boat, as a reward for the return swim.

3. The handler can sit in the boat and encourage the dog to swim out and be rewarded by being asked to take the rope. With a young or reluctant dog, a steward would push the boat from behind so that the dog does not experience the full weight. Gradually, the assistance given to the pull is reduced until the dog will tow the boat without assistance.

4. The distance is increased gradually over a period of time.

MOVING ON
TAKING A ROPE TO THE BOAT
When a dog is happy to perform the above exercise, then more complex exercises can be introduced. One element of water tests is for

the dog to take out a coil or rope to a boat and, on command, allow the steward to take it. He will then return to the shore pulling the boat with a second length of rope provided by the steward.

In training a dog to swim out and take a rope, a great deal of reliance can be put on a willing dog's natural instinct to retrieve and the enjoyment he derives from doing so. However, training your dog to take any object away from shore, to a person or boat, is very different and presents more difficult problems. In this exercise, the dog is being asked to work against his natural instinct to retrieve and return. He is being asked to leave his owner and take what is to the dog a very interesting object that would be great fun to play with out to a stranger. Even worse, he must give up that object on arrival then swim away and wait calmly nearby for the second rope.

At the higher levels of water tests, regular training and obedience is essential. A dog who will not respond willingly to commands such as "Take", "Hold", "Give" and "Wait" will present real problems to a trainer at this level.

'CHAINING'

One method of training for more complex tests is to break them down into their component parts, practising each part separately and then, when learned, linking them into the complete exercise. This is called 'chaining'. In the previous test, taking a rope to the boat, these elements might be:

1. "Take" and "Hold" the coil of rope, "Swim" to the boat and "Give" the coil on command to the steward.

2. On command, "Swim" calmly around the boat.

3. "Take" the second rope in the mouth and return to "Shore" using the rope to pull the boat.

Each element can be trained separately. The first part could be started by encouraging the dog to take a coil from one person to another over a short distance. This can be practised frequently on land or in the living room as a play exercise.

The second part is essentially about training the dog to swim close by or around the boat without climbing into it, or in any way endangering himself, the boat or its occupants.

The third part is the basic test of taking a rope and using it to pull a boat. The dog should already be familiar with this element

The dog's natural instinct to retrieve is harnessed as the tests become more complicated.

which should be the easiest part of the 'chain'.

TRAINING ON LAND

As I have already described, there is much that can be achieved on land, at home and in play. Some trainers simulate and practise even the more complex full exercises on land. However, it is doubtful that land work could ever adequately prepare a dog for completing a complex exercise in water. While great benefit can be obtained from dry practice, regular water training is essential to achieve success.

MOTIVATION AND REWARD

Most Newfoundlands love the water and derive a great deal of reward from being allowed to swim and play with their owners. However, when one is asking them to practise and perfect complex exercises, they need to be motivated and deserve to be rewarded for their efforts. For some, the only reward they ever require is a sign of your pleasure – an enthusiastic hug and pat after an exercise well done. One of my dogs is a case in point. As a young dog he loved to work, whether it was in water or on a long walk on the moors. His only motivation was being allowed to participate. He would always refuse food when out – 'at work' in

his view. Even in old age he remains a very good working dog capable of performing complex tasks, although he will now take a biscuit at the end! For other dogs, though, finding out what motivates them is your great aid to successful training.

SWIMMING TO A STRANGER

One method is to use obedience training and instruct the dog to swim to the person in the water. Alternatively, the dog can be instructed to swim to the stranger, who will call the dog by name or (more difficult) by a neutral term. The handler can swim with the dog to give encouragement and direction, gradually increasing the distance the dog swims alone. Helpers can stand in the water to ensure the dog continues on the line towards the person in the water.

How much simpler all of this becomes if the dog wants to go! Most Newfoundlands enjoy meeting new people and, for some, this is enough and the exercise never presents a real problem. However, a number of dogs are very reluctant to leave their owners, in which case the use of a reward as an incentive usually works.

1. The dog is shown the preferred reward by the stranger who then wades out into the water, stands a short distance away and

The dog must learn self-reliance in order to swim out to a stranger.

encourages the dog, using the reward.

2. The handler releases the dog and instructs him to swim to the person in the water. Some use the "Away" command.

3. The dog reaches the person in the water, is given the reward and instructed to return to shore.

4. The helper returns to shore with the dog holding a harness or the fur at the top of the tail, provided this does not cause alarm.

5. The distance is increased over time and the exercise repeated as required until the dog is quite happy to perform for the reward with this new person or, preferably, persons. The dog should think: "They are really quite nice, they give me a treat and all I have to do is pull them back. Easy peasy, what a great life!"

6. When the dog is performing to a satisfactory standard, the reward is withheld on one occasion, but given on the next. An element of uncertainty is thus introduced into the mind of the dog, who thinks "Will I or won't I get a treat? I have to go to that person if I am to find out."

7. Gradually, the number of times a dog is given a reward is reduced until he will perform the exercise without reward.

GOLDEN RULES
Always complete every successful exercise with an enthusiastic pat and say "Well done!". Let the dog know how pleased you are so that, when rewards are no longer the incentive, the pleasure remains.

Always finish with a success. If the dog is becoming bored by repetition or simply refuses to carry out a particular exercise, then ask him to do something he enjoys and reward compliance with a big "Well done!". Remember, Newfoundlands do get bored by

repetition and it is not unusual for performance to get worse with each repetition. Young dogs, in particular, tire easily, so be aware of their condition and feelings.

CONCLUSIONS
1. All dogs, like people, are unique. They have differing abilities; they work and learn at their own pace. The speed of learning and development will vary according to the ability of both the dog and trainer. Remember that the rate at which a dog develops is not directly related to ability. A slow learner might turn out to be a very good worker.

2. Always reward with enthusiastic praise. Your praise is probably the biggest factor in motivating your dog.

3. Keep it fun and, to retain interest, avoid too much repetition. There is strong evidence that too much replication can harm performance.

4. Regular training is essential for success and to maintain good performance.

NEWFOUNDLAND WATER TESTS
I do not intend to go into detail about every element of each test, as they are fully described in the regulations, which are available from the secretaries of your national breed clubs and are essential reading for anyone interested in taking water work with their Newfoundland to test level.

WATER TRAINING IN BRITAIN
There have, for many years, been a few individuals who have trained their dogs in water. The Ragley Trials have been held continuously since 1964, but there was little organised training in Britain before the 1980s. The Northern Newfoundland Club was the first breed club to take an interest, setting up a working committee in 1989 and

The first sea tests held in Britain were accomplished by Darkpeak Aryan Mist, who is also a successful show dog.

buying some equipment for use by a working group in Cheshire. It should be said that the vast majority of those involved in working Newfoundlands are committed to the non-competitive principle. I believe that this has been a major factor in retaining fun and camaraderie and avoiding the more unpleasant 'human' aspects that sometimes surface in the world of dog shows.

The first formal water test rules in the UK were compiled under the leadership of Paul and Christine Tedder, and the Northern Club held the first tests at Level A and B in 1990. From there things have progressed in leaps and bounds. Groups have been established in most areas of the country and the Newfoundland Club formed a working committee in 1990. Both clubs now hold three or more water tests each year. The water test regulations were revised by a joint working committee of both clubs in 1994 and the first tests under the revised regulations were held in 1995.

WATER TRAINING IN THE USA

Water work is immensely popular in the USA, with many informal and formal water events littering the calendar. As an added incentive, the successful water worker can earn the title WRD-NCA (Water Rescue Dog – Newfoundland Club of America) after his name. This should not be confused with the letters WRD and WRDX, which are the water work titles awarded to winners of the Junior and Senior Water Dog exercises held in Canada.

The US tests are also divided into Junior and Senior exercises, with points awarded for separate parts of the tests including Basic Control. The US tests appear to be popular, and the Newfoundland Club of Denmark is now basing its water training on the NCA exercises.

THE INTERNATIONAL SCENE

There is organised training in most countries where the breed is popular and many Newfoundland clubs have some form of trials or tests. International water trials are regularly held on the continent with handlers and dogs from many countries taking part. Rabies regulations prevent British dogs from participating, but many British trainers have travelled to watch or to take part using foreign dogs. The French, and in particular the Paris based TNS (Terre Neuve Sportif) group, are generally acknowledged as being leaders in the field. Their help and guidance has been invaluable over the past decade. The visits of French trainers to events in the UK remain popular dates in the working calendar.

SELECTING THE RIGHT PUPPY

How does one select the right puppy for

water work? As with training techniques, there are probably as many ideas as there are owners. But a few basic tips follow.

1. Look for a fit, healthy, confident and playful puppy.

2. Take note of the sire and dam; whenever possible, ask to see one or both of them in the water.

3. Are they fit and healthy?

4. Have they both got certified low hip scores?

5. Have they both been heart-tested and have their hearts been certified as murmur-free?

6. If the sire and dam are good water workers, then often this will be true of the puppies. There is some evidence that certain lines of Newfoundland have produced good water workers.

7. Go along to water tests or training groups where you will be able to see different dogs working and obtain advice from owners and trainers.

8. Do not listen only to the claims of the breeder, always obtain other opinions.

It is important that you *never* buy a puppy from a dealer or anyone other than someone who specialises in Newfoundlands. There is published evidence from animal welfare organisations that the healthiest dogs come from small breeders who breed few litters. Always ask to see certificates of heart testing and hip scoring.

One very experienced French trainer was heard to express alarm at the trend towards breeding larger dogs for the show ring, describing them as 'submarines' rather than potential swimmers. However, although

there is some evidence that very large dogs do not make good swimmers, in a lot of cases I suspect that many show dogs are simply unfit and a few weeks of training would produce a good working dog. It is certainly to be hoped that we will avoid the development of working and showing types, as has happened in some breeds. A properly constructed dog that excels in the show ring should also be capable, with training, of working at the highest level. If that were not the case then there would be a flaw in the Breed Standard, or the judging.

WHERE TO WORK

Most people will do the majority of their training in a particular location that is most convenient for them or their group. However, it is good to give your dog experience of different sites and types of water. A dog who only ever works in one place may have real difficulties in being tested at a different site, or in unfamiliar conditions. I have seen dogs perform well below their potential when asked to work in a new stretch of water.

RIVERS

Rivers must be suitable for training or testing. Avoid those with insufficient width and unsuitable currents. However, such rivers are often great places for exercise or to cool down on a hot summer's day. Beware of strong currents and underwater hazards.

LAKES

With a little effort it is possible to find somewhere suitable for water training. Get yourself a decent survey map and look for water. Try asking your local authorities, water companies, National Park authorities etc., all of whom can be valuable sources of information.

THE SEA OR OCEAN

The sea is the place to watch Newfoundlands perform as nature intended. Even the spirits of reluctant workers seem to be lifted by the presence of the sea. To watch a dog swim out through the breaking waves, resolutely pursuing an objective that is often out of sight, is to witness the Newfoundland at its most impressive. Many groups train regularly in the sea. Swimming and working in the sea presents different problems for dog and handlers, and good team work is even more essential. Changing tides makes sea testing more difficult, and demands a more flexible approach from judges, but it is certainly practicable and is great fun for handlers and dogs. However, the sea and coastline can be very dangerous places and must be respected.

Take note of advice from coast guards and never disregard weather warnings. Do not swim in areas declared unsafe. Beware of dangerous beaches, e.g. those with quicksand. Also beware of sewage outfalls and undercurrents. In Britain, most permanent hazards such as quicksand, military firing ranges etc. are shown on Ordnance Survey maps (the 1:25,000 series). Use your national equivalent, or the most detailed map you can find.

TRAINING GROUPS

It is always better to join a group, not to mention safer and more fun. In recent years, formal training groups have become much more common. If you want to swim with your dog, or just learn more about water work, contact your nearest group and go along to watch – they will be pleased to welcome you. If you want to find out about your nearest group, or are seeking advice on starting a new group, contact your national breed club which will have a working committee.

EQUIPMENT

At the start it is not necessary to spend a fortune and, if you join a group, its members will most likely already have or be raising money to obtain most of the things that you will require. I set up a new group with my wife and two other enthusiasts using a cheap inflatable boat, various bits of rope and other assorted floating objects. You will need a wet or dry suit, and some form of buoyancy aid. Boat sales and car boot sales are great places to pick up inexpensive equipment.

BOATS: The best training boats are 12-15 ft inflatables. A new boat can be an expensive item for one person to obtain, but adequate boats can be acquired second-hand fairly cheaply. Always use a boat with rounded edges.

OUTBOARD MOTORS: Again, check out the boat sales. Prop-guards are desirable, and automatic cut-outs are essential.

FLOATS: Make sure they do not contain wire or other metal fastenings. Modern ring floats are easily punctured by Newfoundlands, and are liable to fill with water.

RETRIEVES: Gundog training dummies are ideal. Plastic is best, as the older canvas-covered type can become waterlogged and sink.

ROPE: Make sure it floats.

WATER HARNESS: There are many types of harness, ranging from the simple tracking harness, used by many, to much more elaborate designs with handles and attached floats. I would recommend that a dog is always fitted with at least a basic harness when working in the water.

BUOYANCY AIDS AND LIFE JACKETS: Proper life-jackets are unsuitable for working with dogs, as they are too bulky and will seriously restrict movement. Buoyancy aids are, however, essential safety equipment and compulsory in many lakes.

WET SUITS AND DRY SUITS: Both types of suit are aids to buoyancy. Wet suits allow much more mobility and are easier for swimming. However, dry suits are warmer – especially important in winter. The main danger with dry suits is the risk of filling when punctured. Some trainers now use a closer-fitting type of dry suit.

HEALTH AND SAFETY ISSUES

The health and safety of both dog and handler should always be the primary concern. You should never train if you are feeling unwell. Similarly, it is essential to be aware of the condition of your dog and sensitive to any signs of ill health. For example, if the dog shows reluctance to get into the car, enter the water, or has had obvious tummy problems, then leave it for that day.

YOUNG DOGS: All water tests have age qualifications and these are good guides. There is much rot talked about what a young Newfoundland should not be asked to do, and some have been harmed through lack of exercise and over-feeding to produce too much weight on an immature and growing skeletal frame. Swimming is a great exercise for a juvenile dog. The body is exercised without putting strain on young bones and joints. However, you should never allow a dog under twelve months to jump in and out of boats, as this can harm the hips or shoulder and elbow joints. Also, remember that immature dogs tire more easily, especially in cold water. Young bodies are less able to regulate temperature, so watch youngsters carefully in all weathers and dry them thoroughly after a swim. In cold weather, let them rest somewhere warm and dry and keep an eye on them.

OLDER DOGS: Again, swimming is a great exercise for older dogs, with similar benefits for bones and joints. Even dogs with severe hip dysplasia have derived great benefit from swimming. However, too much exercise can put a strain on dogs who have chronic ill health such as heart problems, and veterinary advice should always be sought. Again, be sensitive to what your dog's mood and actions are telling you. My oldest dog still loves to swim and train, but he has poor hips. In his younger days he would happily leap out of a boat. He still loves a boat ride, but one day he resisted an instruction to jump out. This was his way of telling me his hips were causing him difficulty. I could persuade him to do it for me, but I care for him too much to do so.

PEOPLE: Use your common sense and be aware of your body! If you are unwell, stay out of the water. Remember that, when training with others, they are dependent on you, as are the dogs. If they get into difficulty they need you to help, which might be a problem if you are not up to it. Likewise, they are there to help you, but it is stupid to increase the risk by training when unfit or unwell.

Watch out for each other and, if someone seems in distress, suggest he or she leaves the water. People, like dogs, tire more easily in cold conditions so limit the time spent in chilly water, and do not stand around in a damp wet suit in inclement weather. Similarly, in hot temperatures it is essential to keep cool and take in fluids to avoid heat exhaustion and other more serious conditions. This is an especial problem for people in full, thick wet suits.

Swimming is a very effective way of getting and keeping fit; but like other forms of exercise, take it steady when you first start. Do not enter the water for the first time in ten years and try to cross the lake. Like starting to run, take it easy at first and build up gradually. If you are unfit or suffer from any form of ill health, seek medical advice.

SAFETY CHECKLIST
Always wear a wet suit or dry suit.
Always wear a buoyancy aid.

Do not train alone. There is always an increased risk to dog and handler in swimming alone. It is positively dangerous to swim alone with an inexperienced Newfoundland. Training should, ideally, be undertaken with a minimum of three people, a handler plus two assistants/stewards. Training a dog to swim to a person in the water requires: the handler, the person to whom the dog will swim, and the person/steward to assist.

In case of emergencies, make a note of the map co-ordinates of your venue, together with a mobile phone or the location of the nearest working payphone.

Always use safe equipment that will not harm dog or handlers, e.g. check for wire/staples and so on in buoys, floats etc.

Always check thoroughly the working area, especially the entry and exit. Remove all sharp objects or hidden hazards.

Always check for blue-green algae. *Never* enter the water if it is present.

Never ask a dog to perform a retrieve with sticks, or short-handled oars etc. A dog could be seriously injured if it stumbles with a stick held with one end in its mouth.

Always train a dog to hold larger oars in the middle.

Do not use the word "Help" as a call in training situations, unless you are in genuine difficulty.

Be aware of currents, undercurrents, tides etc.

Be sensitive to the needs and condition of dogs and other people, especially in cold weather.

Have a first-aid kit available.

Never run a boat motor close to dogs or people in the water. All engines should be fitted with an automatic cut-out. When training, always cut the motor as soon as an exercise begins.

Always keep details of local veterinary practices.

Above all, have fun and enjoy the unique bond between Newfoundland and owner.

Alan Farrar, and his wife Kirsteen, show and occasionally breed Newfoundlands under the Darkpeak affix. Alan regularly judges water events up to Level E, which is the highest test carried out in Britain. Both he and Kirsteen are also qualified Draught Test judges.

7 *DRAUGHT WORK*

Draught work should come naturally to your dog. Newfoundlands have been used for draught work as far back as records are held. These dogs were used, on the island which bears the same name, for many draught tasks, such as pulling felled timber from the forest (in teams of up to fourteen dogs), and carrying the mail and provisions to outlying settlements. They also hauled fishing nets.

In the UK, Newfoundlands are known to have been used to haul loads of fish and other merchandise such as milk, bread, vegetables and fruit from Southampton or other ports in the West Country (particularly Poole in Dorset and Bristol) to London. Dogs were banned from hauling loads in the London area in 1837, partly due to the fact that they were often loaded so heavily that once the trip to London was completed they collapsed. Other reasons were the noise that iron-rimmed wheels made on the cobbled streets, and the nuisance of dogs barking at each other when delivering milk or other such goods early in the morning. They were replaced by horses, which could pull heavier, more bulky loads and made less noise.

BASIC PRINCIPLES
Your Newfoundland will have an instinct for this type of 'work', and, usually, will not need to be taught to pull. When a puppy is first taken for a walk, he normally runs to the end of his leash and keeps on running. Unless he is taught not to pull, you could have an uncontrolled dog weighing 40kg by the time he is nine months old; you then have a problem. Any walk must start by your tying the leash tightly to the largest person available, in the vain hope of being able to control the dog!

Although this instinct to pull is utilised in draught work, it is just as important that the dog is under control, especially if he is giving rides to children. To be under control for safe draught work, the dog needs to have some training. Often, owners have simply put their dog in harness and the dog has happily pulled whatever the owners asked. Although this uses the dog's instinct to pull, the lack of training (control) means that there is a higher chance of something going wrong, resulting in damage to the dog, cart, passenger or handler.

Draught work is all about having fun with your dog. Once the dog is under basic control and the initial steps have been taught, opportunities are great. In winter, your dog can help to pull the sledge or toboggan back up the hill for the children (saving Dad's legs!). In summer, your dog can haul grass cuttings to the compost heap;

in autumn, he can haul leaves to the bonfire.

In the USA, Canada and New Zealand, people take their Newfies out fundraising for charity. For example, at Christmas-tree farms, they offer to haul the 'perfect' tree just picked out back to the family car, in exchange for a small donation to charity. Draught work gives the dog a greater sense of responsibility. Most owners notice obvious signs of a dog maturing when he first pulls children. The dog seems, while working, to abandon the usual devil-may-care attitude in favour of becoming a responsible (well, almost responsible, in some cases) dog with a 'proper' job to do. Your Newfoundland will do his utmost and generally take this job very seriously. Once unharnessed, however, he will be back to normal. The most enjoyment comes from simply being out with your dog doing fun things together and watching how he learns and enjoys himself.

TEAMWORK
Draught work is all about teamwork between dog and handler. Much of the pleasure comes from encountering a new situation or problem (a tree trunk across your path for example), and discovering how the pair of you can arrive at a solution. Most dogs work with their tails wagging and a smile. They love to be out with you, going to new places and 'helping' you. It is important to try to keep the dog feeling happy during training. 'Make-work' (in other words, asking the dog to do what to his mind is a pointless task) will soon bore your Newfoundland.

Draught tests have been set up for the breed in many countries, including the UK. These tests should not be considered the be-all and end-all of draught work. They merely give you and others a framework to gauge the progress of the dog and handler's ability to work together. It is unfortunate that, in the UK, handlers are not legally able to use dogs to haul carts, wagons or other draught apparatus on roads, footpaths or even bridleways. If an owner is sensible about the load the dog is expected to haul, then the police may turn a blind eye (especially if the event is for charity). There are, however, other organisations that may take legal action against the handler and/or owner of the dog even in such circumstances. If a handler has a problem with someone arguing that it is cruel to make a dog pull a loaded cart or wagon, drawing attention to the dog's demeanour (the dog pulling easily with tail held high and wagging strongly) is often enough to convert them to the idea that, as the dog enjoys draught work so much, it would actually be cruel to stop it.

BEFORE STARTING
Although the adult Newfoundland is a very strong dog, it takes time to build up the tendons, ligaments and muscles which support the bone structure. When you bring your Newfoundland puppy home (usually at seven weeks of age), he is already as big as some adult dogs, but his bones are still very soft. He will take a long time to mature physically. Your dog should be at least one year old before starting to pull anything. This gives plenty of time to build up the rapport and control necessary for draught work. For any breed of dog (be it pure-bred or cross-bred), training should start as soon as the puppy is brought home. This consists of the most basic leash training and very simple walking to heel and learning to sit. Take your puppy to a good obedience class, when he has had his inoculations (preferably a class where the trainers do not believe that a Newfoundland is just a large Border Collie). There they will teach you how to train your puppy, and the classes will help to socialise him towards other dogs and new situations. After a few weeks' attendance, your dog should be able to sit, stand, lie down on command, and he should walk calmly alongside you. All these skills are indispensable if you are to achieve the control required for carting.

The Newfoundland Breed Standard is designed to produce a sound specimen, well able to pull a cart. Unfortunately, there are a number of health conditions which occur within the breed and limit the ability of an individual Newfoundland to do draught work. Hip dysplasia (where there is an abnormality in the structure of the ball-and-socket hip joint) is probably the best known of these conditions. As the dog's musculature can often compensate for mild dysplasia, this should not bar a dog from draught work, although it is advisable to discuss this with your vet. In such circumstances, loads and distances should be carefully monitored. For dogs with severe dysplasia, draught work should not be attempted, as the work would put unfair strain upon the joints and, although your dog would try to oblige, he could suffer great damage.

Other such conditions include Osteochondritis Dissecans (OCD – also known as elbow dysplasia). In its mild forms, OCD would not exclude a dog from draught work, but veterinary advice should be obtained first. For more serious cases of these conditions draught work should be ruled out.

If a dog has had problems with stretched or ruptured cruciate ligaments (a knee joint injury) or luxating patella, then great care should be taken with draught work, only going ahead following veterinary approval. Sub-valvular Aortic Stenosis (SAS) is another condition which would limit draught work. If, at some point in the dog's life, he is shown to have a form of heart problem, again veterinary advice must be sought.

As stated above, draught work should not be started before the dog is at least one year old, or even older if a puppy is from some of the slower-maturing lines. The breeder should be able to give advice on whether or not the lines used are slow to mature physically. At this age (one year), only light work over short distances should be

attempted. In the US and Canada, it is advised that hauling loads, even small children, should not be attempted before the dog is two years old. In the UK, the Draught Regulations state that a dog must be at least fifteen months of age, prior to attempting the Level 1 (Preliminary); eighteen months before attempting Level 2 (Bronze); twenty-four months before attempting Level 3 (Silver); and thirty months old before attempting Level 4 (Gold). The regulations were formulated to help guide an inexperienced handler, so that a dog is not pushed through training at too fast a pace. For Levels 3 and 4, a Veterinary Certificate is required, dated within the last twelve months prior to the test. This states that the dog is fit to enter tests. The regulations also state that a dog over eight years of age cannot enter Level 4. This does not stop such dogs doing other draught work, but does indicate to handlers that, above such an age, they should watch the dog even more carefully for any signs of over-exertion.

Most dogs love to pull and, for draught work, it is necessary to control the dog's basic instinct. Sled dogs generally are given only commands for starting, stopping and turning left and right. On the command "Go", they are expected to immediately pull as hard as possible and keep going. Newfoundlands are not generally suited to the fast pace that is expected from Huskies, Malamutes, or other similar breeds. They were developed to provide good 'staying power' with a reasonable load. Although a trained team of Newfoundlands could enter one of the long-distance races, such as the Iditerod (1,100 miles from Anchorage to Nome in Alaska), they could not be expected to compete seriously with Huskies, Malamutes or other comparable breeds. Conversely, teams of Huskies or Malamutes could not have hauled the loads that Newfoundland teams pulled in the past, without having to significantly increase the size of the dog team required.

Newfoundlands need the same commands as Huskies and Malamutes, and more. Basic training for control teaches a dog to follow the commands of a handler. In Newfoundland draught work, the main commands also include those for waiting while the handler 'delivers' or 'receives' objects, and for waiting to cross a 'simulated' road.

As much of the draught work organised by Newfoundland clubs will be on forestry track or farmland, some may argue that exact control is not required. Yet many dogs take part in fêtes or demonstrations, or even give rides to children in the neighbourhood. If a dog is under only rudimentary control and is carrying children, then the lack of control is a recipe for potential disaster. Many times people will 'get away' with it, but if something goes wrong only once, that is one time too many! The more control over a dog the handler has, the better able he or she will be to cope with any sudden situation that may panic a less well-trained animal. Dogs have been seen to panic and run, pulling their draught apparatus and load with them. Often they end up overturned, with the dog struggling to get free from the shafts or harness. Calming a panicking dog is difficult, but is made easier if the dog trusts the handler. Such trust comes from training together.

FIRST STEPS

Once the dog is old enough to start draught work, the first step is to introduce him to the harness; these are usually made of either leather or nylon webbing and come in two general types, either Chest-Band or Siwash. Both will be discussed later.

With the harness in hand, walk up to the dog from the front. Allow the dog to sniff the harness before attempting to put it on him. Watch the dog's eyes – once he is relaxed, his attention will wander away from the harness. This might take only a second or it might take some minutes, but it is important to make sure that the dog is happy before proceeding. Praise the dog, and give him a tidbit. From in front of the dog (where the dog can see what is happening), slowly put the harness over his head. If the dog shows any sign of worry, take the harness off and talk gently to him. Once he is calm, try again. As the dog will be wearing the harness for all draught work, it is important that he looks forward to wearing it.

To get hesitant dogs used to wearing the harness, let them wear it while they are feeding. As most Newfoundlands enjoy eating, initially prepare the dog's meal in front of him. Then put the harness on and give the dog the food. After a couple of meals, lengthen the time the dog wears the harness before giving him the food. Then start putting the harness on just before taking the dog for a walk, but be careful not to let the dog become entangled.

The harness must fit correctly. It must not be too loose or too tight. If it does not fit properly, it may injure your dog. When trying on a harness, check that it is snug but not too tight. The handler should be able to slip two fingers between the parts of the harness and the dog where the harness fits most tightly during draught work, yet the harness should have enough freedom not to constrict the dog's movement. The fit should be such that it cannot ride up around the dog's neck and interfere with his breathing, nor should it drop to hamper the dog's legs.

TYPES OF HARNESS

As a dog grows, so the harness will either need to extend, or a new harness will be needed. Ideally, each individual dog should have its own fitted harness. In the UK, the most common routes to obtaining harnesses are either to approach a local saddler with a model to work from, or alternatively, make the harness at home. These home-made harnesses are more usually made of webbing with a synthetic material as padding. Some people prefer the look of a leather harness, but a properly-made harness may prove to be costly. A webbing harness can usually be bought for about half the price. Webbing and synthetic padding also has the advantage of being machine washable. Specialist suppliers exist in the USA, who will supply either a Chest-Band or a Siwash harness, but getting the fit right can mean returning it a number of times.

The Chest-Band type of harness has a thickly-padded strap that passes around in front of the chest and across each shoulder. A further padded strap loops up and over the dog's withers from either side of the chest band, adjacent to the shoulders, to take the weight of the shafts. On some designs there are two such straps. However, the handler must be careful that these bands do not transfer load to the dog's back. The chest-band is where the 'pull' is applied, and the strap that crosses the dog's withers supports the chest-band, holding it in position. This should be just above the point of the sternum (chest bone). If the chest-band is too high, it will interfere with the dog's breathing; if it is too low, it will obstruct the dog's leg movements. A further strap (or a continuation of the strap that passes over the withers) passes down around the dog's chest and has a buckle to allow it to be tightened to fit snugly. This type of harness looks similar to ones used for horses, although there are a few differences as a dog's bone structure is not the same. A dog's back is proportionately longer than a horse's, and the muscles supporting the dog's spine are weaker than those of a horse. The dog's harness must therefore be designed to avoid putting the weight of the shafts on to his back. All the shaft's weight must be transferred to the withers. This is more important for carts (two wheels) than for wagons (four wheels). The cart is supposed to be balanced by the load. However, during

loading or if the load moves, the shafts often take the weight. On a wagon, the shafts are usually hinged where they join the bed of the vehicle, so the only load that the straps over the withers have to take is the weight of the shafts themselves. The shafts are supported by loops of either leather or webbing called keeps, which are attached to the strap passing over the withers of the dog.

The Siwash harness has been developed from the types of harness used by sled dogs. There are a number of different styles, but essentially the harness is made from loops of leather or nylon webbing. These are connected in such a fashion that there is a well-padded loop through which the dog's head passes. This is joined to another well-padded strap that passes down the centre line of the dog's chest and up under the 'armpits'. This strap separates into two individual straps, one passing up each side of the dog's body. From the back of the loop through which the dog's head passes, straps descend to link up with those coming up from between the dog's legs. Depending on the style and purpose of the harness, various other straps pass around the dog's body, including one which passes around the loins and holds in place the 'D-rings' to which the traces are attached. For most practical purposes, such as use with carts and wagons, a strap is located over the dog's withers and passes around the dog's chest, just behind the front legs. The keeps are attached to this strap. Comments made regarding the Chest-Band type of harness (about the correct placement of this strap) apply equally to the Siwash if such a strap is fitted. On most harnesses of this type, this strap is removable as it is not required if the harness is to be used with apparatus without shafts (for instance, sleds or toboggans). Various other designs of Siwash harness are available, depending on the specific use required. As this type of harness does not interfere with the movement of the dog's shoulders, it is generally accepted as more efficient than a

Chest-Band harness. Traces are the means by which a cart or wagon is actually pulled. They are attached directly to both the harness and the cart, and generally comprise two straps of either leather or webbing, with connectors of differing kinds at either end. They often have buckles built in so they can be adjusted to suit many different dogs. When fitting traces for carts and wagons, it is important that the correct length is obtained. If they are too short, the dog will catch the cart or wagon with his feet as he moves forward. If they are too long, then often the shafts will not be positioned in the correct place. Also, if they are too long, the pull is transferred from the harness to the cart or wagon by the keeps that hold the shafts up. While initially this is not a problem as no weight is being carried, the pull is not being transferred efficiently from the dog to the cart or wagon via the harness. Once the cart or wagon is loaded, pulling by the keeps may lead to pressure being applied incorrectly.

HITCHING UP

There is no 'right way' to train a dog for anything. As long as the methods involved are not harsh and do not cause distress to the dog, then consideration should be given to using those methods. A happy, confident dog learns more quickly than a fearful, stressed dog. A self-assured and relaxed handler will give more confidence to the dog and so he will find it easier to learn. Many people have found that praising a dog for doing well, generally works better than shouting and other more physical methods. The techniques outlined in this chapter are distilled from many experiences training dogs not only for draught work but also for obedience, water work and training them to be good pets. The techniques should work for most dogs, but other approaches may be better for some, as not all training procedures work for all dogs. You should try to find the method that works best for both you and your dog. Listen to what others say when they watch you training your dog. Other people may be able to see the dog's reaction to an unconscious action on your part. Many people will tell you the 'best' method to train your dog. Listen to them, and evaluate what they say. Ask questions. If people cannot answer the question "Why?" when they have just told you that "the only way to train your dog is to...", this gives you a good idea as to the usefulness of the method. At all times, understand what you are asking your dog to do; try to anticipate what the dog's likely reaction will be. If there is a possibility of your dog becoming

A simple four-wheeled cart.

A two-wheeled cart can be equally effective, but care should be taken to correctly distribute the weight of the load.

In some types of terrain wheels can be a disadvantage.

worried, slow down, go back to something the dog can do, and build up his confidence. A dog cannot learn when he is stressed. Try to end a training session with something the dog enjoys and is able to do. If the dog has enjoyed the draught work training session, he will associate those memories with draught work. When you start the next session, the dog will probably be more willing to learn.

Once the dog is happy with the harness, then his introduction to draught apparatus can be started. Ideally, the dog will have been to many events, and seen and heard other dogs pulling draught apparatus. Watching other dogs do draught work often helps young dogs learn. It has been found that it is sometimes easier to start training with an object to drag, rather than one with shafts, as these may cause problems initially.

Such a 'drag' item must have sufficient weight to give the dog something to pull against and yet it must not bounce around. It should not be so heavy that the dog has to strain to pull it. Such items include a small log (5-10kg), a normal-sized car tyre, a short length of ladder, or even plastic milk containers filled with sand or water. The advantage of the latter is that they can start off only partially full, and then as the training progresses, the load can be increased gradually. With any 'drag'-type draught apparatus, it is usually necessary to use a 'spreader bar' to keep the traces apart, stopping them converging and catching the dog's legs. This 'spreader bar' also acts to even out the pull as one side of the dog moves forward.

When the dog is wearing his harness, have an assistant pull the 'apparatus' along in front of him. Let the dog follow behind and sniff it, listen to it and smell it. When the dog is happy (again watch the dog's eyes and body posture), talk gently and encouragingly and hitch the dog to the 'apparatus'. With some dogs, this stage takes only seconds; with others, it can take much longer.

STARTING TO PULL

Initially, just ask the dog to walk forward and pull for a short distance (say 2-3 metres) on a relatively flat surface such as grass or snow. On these types of terrain, the drag will be fairly quiet, whereas on concrete or tarmac it will make more noise. With most dogs this sound should not be a problem, but, with some, a noise that is always behind them can cause stress. When the dog is pulling happily while walking, try gentle running, but keep the dog from becoming tangled in the traces. Unhitch and play with the dog. Keep training times short and make them fun. Build up to pulling, say, 10 metres in a straight line, unhitch and play with the dog. Slowly start to introduce turns, and make them gradual. It is easier for the dog to turn using the handler as the pivot point, and this also allows the handler to stay in control. If you are standing on the right side of your dog, turn in a big circle to the right. Once the dog accepts this, swap sides and try a big circle to your left. The size of the turning circle can be slowly reduced, but keep a close watch that the dog does not become tangled with the traces.

Once the dog is happy turning in broad sweeps, walk him on to a different surface, again talking encouragingly. If the dog shows any signs of worry or stress, unhitch, move back on to the grass or snow and start again, but give the dog more time to become used to the drag. Once the dog is calm, unhitch and have someone pull the drag on to the concrete or tarmac in front of the dog, so that he can see it and hear the noise it makes. Walk the dog up to the drag as it is being pulled and then past it, so the

dog is now in front (yet not pulling the drag). Watch for signs of stress and, if there are none, calmly re-hitch the dog and start again. Keep the distance short. Some dogs work well for just praise, but most Newfoundlands like tidbits, so these can be used as a training aid. If the dog is stressed, it will not be able to eat. Once the dog is calm and happy, try turns again.

Take your time. Some dogs can do all of the above in one session; others can take much longer. Watch the dog; do not let him become stressed. Watch his eyes and tail posture. If the tail is up and wagging, the dog is enjoying the work; it is fun! If the tail is down and tucked between the legs, stop. Go back to a level where the dog was happy and build up more slowly.

BUILDING ON BASICS

When the dog can pull a drag in straight lines or curves, introduce him to a sledge or toboggan if the weather is suitable. In the same way as when the dog became acquainted with the log, tyre, ladder or plastic containers, introduce him to the toboggan or sledge. Let someone pull the apparatus in front of the dog on grass or snow. Let the dog catch up, sniff and pass the apparatus, before hitching him to it. Proceed as before, introducing the dog slowly, stage by stage, to new surfaces. Be warned, though, toboggans which are pulled over gravel tend to become damaged quickly.

Once the dog is completely happy with pulling a drag device on any type of ground, he is ready to be introduced to wheeled apparatus. The main difference between 'drag' and 'wheeled', is that the wheeled apparatus has shafts. Initially, dogs can see these as confining terrors. One way around this is to use equipment where one shaft can be removed.

Alternatively, an apparatus can easily be constructed from a plate of wood with a handle and two removable shafts. Introduce the dog to this; let the dog see and smell it. Then, firstly, only use a single shaft. With one person ready to walk alongside the dog guiding and holding him, and another behind supporting the wooden plate, insert the shaft into the keeps on the side of the harness between the dog and the helper. Traces are not needed yet. In this way the dog will not feel confined, as he can 'escape' to the free side. Start walking slowly forward. The person walking alongside the dog should talk encouragingly. The helper behind should make sure that only light pressure is applied by the shaft to the harness. The shaft should also be allowed to lightly tap against the dog's flanks. The person walking alongside the dog must keep him calm as this happens. Next, try slow gentle turns.

Once the dog accepts this, introduce the second shaft. Start again by walking in a straight line. Be very careful that the dog does not become stressed due to the proximity of the second shaft. Tidbits often help to direct the dog's attention away from the shafts. Slowly build up to turns, and allow the shafts to gently touch the dog's flanks. A slow slalom allows the shafts to touch the flanks in turn. Once the dog is used to this and is not perturbed by the shafts, then he is ready to be hitched to a cart or a wagon. If a training apparatus with removable shafts is not available, but one of the shafts can be removed from the wagon, then the introduction process is the same. Position the apparatus on grass or another 'quiet' surface. If the shafts are constructed in such a way that they cannot be separated, or the apparatus is a cart, then have the handler stand between the shafts in the position the dog will eventually occupy. Stand the dog with his harness level with the handler. Insert one of the shafts into the harness on the side of the dog between him and the handler, who should then take the weight of the shafts (so as not to off-balance the harness), and slowly walk forward while watching the dog.

If it is possible to have the shafts detached from the apparatus, it is best to do so. Once the dog is happy with the shaft between him and the handler, connect the apparatus. When the dog is unworried by this being in close proximity, the handler should allow some of the weight of the shafts to be felt through the harness. Add one trace so the dog feels the drag of the apparatus, then introduce slow, gentle turns and let the shafts lightly touch the dog's flanks as the turns progress.

If possible, use a light vehicle, but one that is heavy enough not to bounce around behind the dog when it crosses uneven ground. As before, let the dog see, sniff and hear the apparatus as it is pulled over the ground in front, then alongside and finally behind him. Once he accepts the sound of the apparatus being pulled along behind him, stand the dog and slowly bring it to him. Gently lower the shafts over the dog and put them into keeps. Attach the traces to the 'swingle-tree' (also known as a 'single-tree' or a 'whiffle-tree'), which is the hinged bar of wood attached to the centre of the cart or wagon. This converts the side-to-side movement of the dog, as he strides out, into a straight pull. If such a device is not part of the apparatus, as the dog stretches forward on one side, an uneven pull is applied to the cart or wagon. This is less comfortable for the dog, as it applies the pull unevenly and the passengers would experience an uneven, jerky ride.

Once the traces are attached, command the dog to go forward. Again, it is best to use two people; one to walk alongside the dog to encourage him and the other to look after the cart or wagon. If problems occur, the person walking alongside the dog should attempt to calm him, while the other person handles the cart or wagon and unhitches the dog. When he is happy moving forward, try some broad curves. Slowly increase the 'tightness' of the curves. Introduce some

The Sacco is ideal for the more experienced owner.

'stops' and 'waits', simulating waiting for traffic to pass before crossing a road. If there is an older, experienced dog available, some trainers have been known to hitch-up both and let the younger dog see and feel how the older dog works. This can be an advantage as the younger dog will often learn more quickly, or a disadvantage if the younger dog picks up bad habits from the older one. It has been said that a dog needs ten correct repetitions to learn how to do something properly, but only three wrong ones to learn to do it incorrectly!

By now the dog's obedience training will have included 'stays' and out-of-sight 'stays'. During draught work, it is sometimes necessary to check a route or move an object. In a real-life situation, for instance during a delivery, the handler may have to be out of sight for a short period. Consequently there is little point unhitching the dog. Some apparatus will not safely allow dogs to sit or lie while hitched; others will. If your apparatus is of the first type, you will need to teach your dog not to attempt to lie or sit while he is working. Dogs should not be allowed to eliminate while working. If a male dog attempts to do this with a loaded vehicle, he may overturn it. If there is going to be a lengthy halt, think about unhitching him.

Dogs must also be taught that, when working, they cannot go off to sniff that enticing scent, or to chase a cat that passes in front of them. To this end, during training,

artificial distractions should be introduced; these should include anything that the dog might conceivably meet. The more varied the experience of the dog and the greater his trust in the handler, the less likely he is to have problems with unexpected events during draught work. Such distractions could include children playing, cycling, running up to the dog, having a picnic, or noises such as chain-saws, cars, trains, music, radios, or the sight of balloons, loose dogs, and cats. Any chance to practise should be taken, as the more experience a dog has of different places, the more confidence he will have when meeting the unexpected.

There are many different types of draught apparatus, from simple box-carts (with two wheels, a box and shafts) to elaborate 'models' of horse-drawn carts or wagons. There are also different types of sledges or toboggans, from the plastic tray-like child's toy, to purpose-built, load-carrying ones used in areas of the world where there is snow for much of the year. Not seen very often in the UK are Travois, where a light load is supported between two poles. The fronts of the poles are hitched to the dog's harness and the rear ends are allowed to drag on the floor. These are useful for crossing rough ground as they allow a greater load to be pulled than could be carried, but they are not as efficient as wheeled equipment or sleds and toboggans where conditions allow such apparatus to be used.

Many of the wagons seen at UK draught

events are based on European 'goat-carts' (although they have four wheels). These have been modified for dog use or have been used as the basis for a design that has been improved upon. Many people have built their own version, utilising wood, metal and either bicycle or wheelchair wheels. Some Newfoundland owners are convinced that much of the fun comes from building and using your own apparatus, while others may opt for a more expensive, but 'once in a lifetime' piece of equipment. Designs for various items of equipment are available commercially, and some have been published via the Newfoundland Club of America's newsletter, *Newf Tide*. Alternatively, purpose-built apparatus is available both in the UK and by mail order from the US.

Many highly decorated carts or wagons are brought out for events such as The Newfoundland Club's Annual Fun Day at Ragley Hall in the UK. These frequently show much ingenuity on the part of the owners, and the dogs are often in fancy dress as well.

FIRST AID

There are many books written specifically on this subject, and it is recommended that anyone attempting draught work should have a basic awareness of First Aid. Some form of First Aid kit is strongly advisable when doing any draught work. It is unfortunate, but some people tend to leave broken glass around. Dogs' feet can easily be cut by such glass which often seems to be 'hiding' in long grass. Consequently, any handler should have the knowledge to deal with such injuries.

Another common problem for Newfoundlands is that of over-heating or even heat-stroke. These should be avoided by resting the dog as soon as he starts to pant heavily. If water is available, then offer the dog small quantities at frequent intervals. On hot days, if there is an opportunity, let the dog out of harness and send him for a

swim. The symptoms of heat-stroke include rapid panting, weakness, unsteadiness on the feet, tremors in the muscles, blue gums (cyanosis) due to lack of oxygen in the blood, and excessive salivation. If a dog is seen to be suffering from this, cool him immediately and seek veterinary attention as fast as possible. Try to avoid draught work during the heat of the day; training can be carried out early in the morning or late at night. If it gets dark, make sure that you have sufficient light to see and be seen.

Check with your vet as to what should be included in a First Aid Kit. The following items are recommended as a basic guide.

- An old sock or a purpose-made boot to protect dressings and keep everything as clean and dry as possible. To stop the sock wearing out, waterproof tape or similar can be stuck over it.
- 100mm square gauze pads to place over wounds.
- Cotton wool, useful for packing between pads to prevent chafing when the foot is bound up.
- Micropore tape to hold bandages in place.
- Crêpe bandages.
- Antiseptic powder, creams or solutions for cleaning and protecting wounds.
- Disposable razor for shaving hair to expose a wound.
- Tweezers for removing foreign objects.

DRAUGHT TESTS

In the UK, as I have mentioned, Newfoundlands can be measured against a standard of performance, which tests the step-by-step progression of the dog. It is hoped that the British KC will eventually accept the Diploma as the qualification required to become a Champion Draught Dog.

The Newfoundland Club of America, however, allows owners whose dogs have passed the US test to use the title draft Dog (DD) with the kennel name. Similarly, if the dog passes as part of a team, the title Team Draft Dog (TDD) can be used. In Canada there are Junior and Senior tests, while in New Zealand draught tests have recently been established in the North Island, though the NZ Kennel Club has not yet sanctioned the addition of the letters DD or DDX to the kennel name.

BACKPACKING

As the name implies, backpacks have been designed for dogs to enable them to carry loads in rough country. Owners and dogs can head off for either short day-trips or longer camping trips with the dog carrying a share of the necessary equipment. Backpacks are usually made of durable materials such as canvas or corduroy and are available from specialist suppliers in the US, or patterns are available for owners to make their own.

It is very important to keep the loads to a minimum during the early stages of training and to ensure that the backpack fits properly. This prevents chafing and distributes the load over the withers as much as possible. As mentioned before, it is important to avoid loading the dog's back.

There are various designs of backpack available, from day packs (usually made in one piece to carry the dog's bowl, water-carrier and first-aid kit) to expedition packs. These are usually made of a harness and panniers that are attached to the harness by clips and/or Velcro fasteners. This is to allow the load to be detached at intervals to give the dog a rest. It also allows removal at points on the trail where it is safer for the load to be carried by hand. The dog can then negotiate the obstacle without the extra width a full pack applies. It is important to load the pack evenly so that one side does not sag and unbalance the dog, thus causing discomfort which may quickly lead to sores due to chafing.

As with all draught work, the dog will require training to wear the pack and to carry any load. The steps for training are relatively simple. Introduce the dog to the idea of something resting on his back, by laying a folded towel over him while he is standing. When the dog ignores the towel, praise and reward him. Then get the dog to walk forwards, again rewarding him as he ignores the towel. Introduce the dog to the backpack or to the harness and pack, as you would for a carting harness. Once the dog has smelt it, put either the pack or only the harness on to his back. Ensure that the dog does not become stressed by this. If he shows signs of stress, go back to the towel and start again, but proceed more slowly. As with all training, dogs progress at different speeds, with some taking only minutes to accustom themselves to the backpack, while others need weeks of gentle training. With a two-piece pack, once the dog accepts the

Most dogs soon adapt to a correctly fitting backpack.

harness, put on the empty panniers.

When the dog accepts the pack, go for a walk. Slowly introduce a load. Old sweaters are good, as they supply bulk to fill out the panniers without too much weight. Then add something that rattles or rustles as the dog moves. This gets him used to the noise of packets of food or the first-aid kit moving as he crosses rough ground. As always, use slow progression with lots of praise and rewards to keep the dog motivated.

Gradually increase both the load and the distance the pack is carried. One word of warning, keep checking the dog's pads for signs of wear, especially during the early stages. Although the dog will initially barge into trees, bushes or whatever as he tries to get through gaps which he would normally (without the pack) easily negotiate, he will soon learn to allow for the extra width.

Most Newfoundlands enjoy going for walks (once they become used to them), as they offer the dog new sights and, more importantly, new smells. When the dog realises that backpacking offers even greater chances for exploring new places and scents, he will come to relish the sight of the pack coming off the shelf. Ch. and Canadian Ch. Sheridel Crakerjak could often be seen attending shows carrying his and his owner's belongings in a backpack. It only took a quick brushing to remove any 'strap marks' from his coat.

The load a dog can carry depends on the dog's age, fitness, weight and maturity, and on the weather conditions and the terrain to be crossed. A dog aged four or five, physically mature, fully-fit and conditioned to backpacking, should be able to carry up to 50 per cent of his body weight, but, at the start of the season, he should only be asked to carry about 10 per cent. If the dog has never done more than walk around the block or has just 'held down the carpet', then the maximum weight he should be expected to carry is about 10 per cent of his body weight. Load carrying should not be started until the dog is at least twelve months old, and then only up to a maximum of 10 per cent of body weight until he is at least two years old. Once again, be warned; certain individuals will view the carrying of any weight at all as 'cruelty'.

When out hiking, please be aware of your responsibility to others and keep your dog(s) under control at all times, including at night. Many people with different breeds get much enjoyment from hiking with their dogs; backpacking with your Newfoundland adds that extra bit of pleasure, and the dog generally seem to enjoy helping as well.

SKIJORING

This is a winter activity which dogs often love. When there is sufficient snow, the handler wears skis and is towed by one or more dogs. Most draught work harnesses are fairly easily adapted to allow the attachment of a tow line; however, a spreader bar may also be needed. The tow line is then attached to the handler, either with a body harness or with a wide belt. The point of attachment is usually a quick release buckle or knot. As before, slowly introduce the dog to the harness if this piece of equipment is not already familiar. Once the dog has accepted the harness, attach the line to the handler. It is advisable, initially, to do this in an open field.

Start the dog moving forward, with the handler giving the commands but with an assistant walking alongside the dog to reinforce the commands. The main commands are: "Move forward", "Turn left", "Turn right" and, most importantly, "Stop". Once the dog has learnt the commands and responds, off you go! Let the dog find his own pace, but help him where possible. For this 'sport', cross-country skis work best, but, alternatively, downhill ones can be used. Cross-country skis allow the handler to skate along behind the dog and so help him, especially when going up hills. When more than one dog is trained, they can be harnessed together to add to the thrill. As with all work on snow, be aware of the possibility of snow balls forming between the pads of the dog's feet and causing irritation; check his feet frequently throughout the excursion. As a preventative measure against snow balls, immerse the dog's pads in liquid paraffin and 'squeeze out' the excess.

SUMMARY

Draught work is about having fun with your dog. It is not about weight-pulling or speed competitions, but revolves around the teamwork between your Newfoundland and yourself. When training, progress slowly and in small stages, making sure the dog is not stressed. Control is necessary; not the control an Obedience champion needs, but plain control where the dog responds willingly to your commands that he has learned and understood. Without control, a dog and draught work is just an accident waiting to happen.

Gareth B. Williams has lived with dogs all his life and has been training Newfoundlands since 1987. He was involved in the production of the original Water and Draught Regulations and judges Water and Draught Tests at the highest level in Britain. He also has a profound interest in behavioural problems and obedience.

8 BREEDING A LITTER

In the world of dogs, there can be little as satisfying (or as traumatic) as breeding a litter of puppies. But if your view of breeding is watching over a heap of healthy, contented puppies before tearfully waving goodbye to them after eight weeks, then you are in for a great shock. The above scene is reminiscent of some of the old Hollywood blockbuster films where the credits roll as the handsome groom kisses his bride amid a shower of confetti. In real life, as anyone with a little common sense knows, it is often afterwards that the problems really start! Similarly with puppies, your greatest worries will be after they have gone to their new homes. So it is undoubtedly a good idea to honestly assess both your bitch and your own situation before you make the final decision to breed a litter, or to use your dog at stud.

IS YOUR BITCH A SUITABLE BROOD?
What makes a brood bitch? All too often people are heard to say: "She's not done much in the show ring. Never mind, I'll retire her. She'll make a good brood bitch." Sometimes, a bitch is unshowable due to some cosmetic injury. Apart from this, in our opinion, if she is not good enough to be shown, then she is not good enough to be bred from. The same applies if your

involvement is with working your Newfie bitch. Before you think of breeding from her, she should also have proven herself in terms of working qualifications.

If your bitch is just a loving pet and you think: 'It would be nice to have one of Bessie's puppies", then do yourself and the rescue organisations a favour, and forget it! Dogs' homes everywhere are full of unfortunate animals whose breeders fell under the same spell. If Bessie's temperament and character is second-to-none, then go back to her breeder for another puppy. The breeder is likely to know more about the pitfalls of breeding than you do and is probably better equipped to deal with a litter. If the thought of having to part with more money for a puppy is off-putting, then you are certainly not in a financial position to breed a litter, the economics of which can be terrifying.

So, having got that off our chests and assuming you still want to breed a litter, let us take a closer look at your bitch. She will certainly be at least two years old, probably older. She will either be a Champion or will have done a creditable amount of winning at championship shows. So far, so good.

She will have a good temperament. This is essential to any large breed of dog nowadays, but especially to a Newfie, who should be

Wooddales Louise of Wellfont: Dam of five UK, one Irish and one Canadian Champion.

basically 'a loving temperament wrapped up in a dog'. Is she the type of bitch who jumps at her own shadow or barks nervously for half an hour after hearing a car backfire? Of course, it is natural for even the most well-adjusted Newfie to jump or bark at some sudden, loud noises, but with some reassurance from her owner she should have forgotten all about it minutes later.

How does she react to strangers? Most Newfies love people more than their own kind, and a bitch who refuses the tastiest of tidbits from a stranger, when told to 'take' by her owner, is quite a rare sight!

Your intended brood bitch will be healthy. Not only in the most obvious aspects, but in terms of screening for hereditary defects. She will have an OFA number (See Chapter Nine: Health and Ailments) or a below-average hip score and will be certified free of heart murmurs. You will also be wise to check these details with regards to her sire, dam and litter mates. Remembering that puppy purchasers could well come back and sue the breeder at a later date, you really cannot be too careful where hereditary defects are concerned.

ARE YOU A SUITABLE BREEDER?

You are happy that your bitch passes the test. But, what about you, the owner? As stated before, you should have adequate funds set aside to spend on necessities like the stud fee, extra feeding for the bitch, possible veterinary fees, a heat lamp, whelping box and a mountain of puppy food. If you work full-time, are you able to take more than a month's leave, or can you afford to employ someone to be at home while you are out? Do you have a suitable quiet room where the bitch can whelp and spend the first ten days relatively undisturbed? Then, having crossed that hurdle, do you have a separate place where the puppies can grow, run around and see the comings and goings of the household?

Most importantly, do you have six or seven definite orders for puppies? In today's economic climate it makes sense to ensure good, permanent homes for puppies before the bitch is even mated. The first-time breeder will also have the added problem of not being known and therefore without the good reputation that many successful breeders have. Even if you have the facilities for running on four or five older puppies, it will be difficult to give them all the necessary attention and training that they need at this impressionable age.

THE STUD DOG

The words "stud dog" conjure up various meanings to different dog owners. Contrary to dictionary meaning, a stud dog is not just a dog that has been used at stud. With Newfoundlands, whose annual registrations are considerably fewer than some of the over-populated breeds, a stud dog needs to earn this label on the merit of his puppies rather than merely on his ability to produce offspring.

USING YOUR DOG AT STUD

Assuming that your dog meets the same health and quality criteria as discussed above for the brood bitch, how does your dog become a stud dog? Very often a dog's owner is approached by the dog's breeder, or another well-known (and hopefully well-respected) breeder, to discuss the possibility of using the dog at stud. Most owners are tremendously flattered at the thought of their dog becoming a father and common sense often flies out of the window. Certainly, the first time we were asked to use our first champion at stud we would probably have agreed if the bitch had had three legs and two heads! As it happened, the bitch's owner was a caring breeder who had done everything in her power to ensure a healthy litter. However, not everyone will be as lucky and it is worth taking a little time to consider whether you want to use your dog at stud.

If your dog is particularly eye-catching and of a good temperament, you will undoubtedly have had many stud enquiries. But if you have had only one enquiry (even if it is from the dog's breeder), it might be wise to evaluate the situation first. Once he is used at stud, your dog will probably never look at a bitch in the same light again. The once-docile animal who strolled casually by

at your side, will develop lightning reactions to the sight of a bitch in season. Unfortunately, it will not only be in-season bitches who will receive his unwanted inspection, as he will be keen to up-end the tails of *all* bitches he encounters – just in case!

If you own more than one male, using one, or both, at stud may upset the equilibrium between them and there may be fights (although it has to be said that this is not as likely between Newfies as in the case of more dominant breeds). Some males develop a self-imposed anorexia once they are aware of a nearby bitch in season. And 'nearby', to a Newfie male, may be quite some distance away by your standards, so you can expect this behaviour every time a bitch in the neighbourhood comes into season.

Scent marking can become very important to a male that has been used at stud, and you may have to suffer the inconvenience of 'mopping up' door frames, pairs of shoes or anything else which your dog believes to have been in contact with another canine scent!

Apart from the practical day-to-day changes, once your Newfie has added to the dog population, you will have a degree of responsibility for the resulting puppies. Any responsible breeder will take back one of their own breeding should the need arise; but if, for some genuine reason such as illness, they are unable to do so, then it is to *your* door that they will be coming next. Unscrupulous breeders and 'non-doggy' folk have always looked on a stud fee as 'easy money'. You provide a service, sign a form and promptly disappear from the equation. This could not be further from the truth!

As the stud dog owner you will be expected to pass on names of suitable, prospective owners, visit and vet homes in your area and go to see the puppies to honestly assess them. Also, should any hereditary health defect appear in your dog *after* he has produced puppies, then it will be your responsibility to make this fact known to bitch and puppy owners.

CHOOSING A STUD DOG

Now that you have decided to go ahead and mate your bitch, how do you decide which stud dog to use? It is very unlikely that the best dog for your bitch will live around the corner, and even less likely that he is also owned by you. Hypothetically, you have the finest dogs in your country to choose from so do not fall into the trap of using a dog because he is 'convenient'. It will take the same amount of effort and expense to rear a mediocre litter as a well-bred litter.

If you bought your bitch from a reputable breeder, your first step will be to ask his or her advice. The breeder will probably have more experience in knowing which lines tend to go well together. It is important to look at your bitch with a critical eye. Having found her faults (and there will always be some!), you will be able to eliminate those dogs who have the same faults. Your breeder will have probably advised you to 'line-breed' – that is, use a stud dog who is distantly related to your bitch, rather than 'out-cross' (two completely unrelated dogs) or 'in-breed' (father x daughter, sister x brother or a similarly closely related pair). So

you will be looking for a dog who has some common ancestry with your bitch. You will probably have two or three dogs in mind, well before any decisions are made. Use this time wisely by looking at the previous offspring they have sired. Just because a dog has won the most CCs during the past year it does not mean that he is necessarily the best dog for your bitch.

The best stud dogs are those who consistently stamp their type on their offspring, regardless of what bitch they are mated to. Having said that, if your bitch has a glaring fault or is generally lacking sparkle, do not expect the dog to work miracles. It is an ironic fact of life that when a poor specimen is seen, people are quick to say: "Did you know that dog is by Ch. Whatsisname?", forgetting to add that the dam was really nothing to write home about!

Look also at the dams of the offspring you are studying. If they vary greatly in type and quality, but the offspring are very similar in type, then your search will probably be over. Quite often, novice breeders with a bitch which is, say, too long in the leg will look for a stud dog who is too short in the leg, in order to compensate. If only breeding were so simple! If your bitch has one fault, do not be tempted to introduce yet another fault into the line, as your litter may well be split,

A stud dog should earn his title on the merit of his puppies. The German-bred Ch. Samson Von Soven of Swanpool sired nine Champions in the UK as well as Australian and NZ titleholders.

half having their dam's fault and the other half the sire's fault.

Only if you are lucky, in our hypothetical example, will you get any with the correct length of leg. Therefore, if your bitch has a very high tail-set, mate her to a dog who not only himself has a good, medium tail-set, but whose siblings and parents also have a correct medium set tail. You will still get some puppies with a high set tail, but at least you will not have introduced another fault into the line.

Having decided on a stud dog, contact his owner to ask if he or she will consider using the dog on your bitch. Do not ring up and say: "I've been thinking of using your dog on my bitch." It is good manners to ask first!

THE IN-SEASON BITCH

Prior to your bitch coming into season, you will have a fair indication of when she is 'due in'. Most bitches tend to fall into the five to eight-month cycle, and you will be able to plan ahead to a certain extent. As soon as she is in season, contact the stud dog's owners so that they can arrange to be at home at the right time. When she is first in season, you will see that her vulva is swollen and there will be a dark red, bloody discharge. If the bitch is very meticulous about cleaning herself, you may miss the bloody discharge for the first two days or so. A good tip is to quickly swab her with white tissue or cotton wool as soon as she stands up after sleeping and before she has a chance to clean herself.

If you also own a male dog it is quite feasible that he will show little or no interest in her at this stage. But, be warned, the *status quo* can change pretty quickly, so do not be tempted to leave them alone together. In fact, it is probably best to separate them totally from the beginning of her season.

From about ten days onwards you will see a slight change in the colour of the discharge. It will be either pink or straw-coloured and this indicates that the bitch is nearly ready for mating. The bitch's behaviour at this time may also change, with some howling to alert any nearby males, flirting with and mounting other bitches, or turning her tail to one side when her owner touches her back. Most people, keen not to 'miss' the bitch, shoot off to the stud dog as soon as they see her holding her tail to one side or 'standing' for another bitch to mount her. However, it is fairly common for a bitch to 'stand', for another bitch she knows, a few days before she is ready to be mated by a strange dog.

If you have agreed to use your dog at stud, you will receive a call from the bitch's owner informing you that she has come into season. If they are thoughtful people, the call will be to tell you that "She is on her second or third day today." If they are inconsiderate buffoons, it will be to say: "She'll be ready for mating the day after tomorrow," thus throwing your plans into disarray.

Although the bitch is traditionally brought to the dog's home, with the bitch's owners doing the bulk of the travelling, a mating can tie up a whole morning or afternoon of the stud dog owner's time. When the bitch's owners have travelled particularly far, you may feel obliged to put them up for the night (or even two!) so it is nice to know when to expect them well in advance. You should then warn them to keep the bitch away from any male dogs, and advise them not to use any scent-disguising sprays or preparations prior to mating.

These days there are on the market many scientific methods for ascertaining the bitch's optimum mating time, so it is possible to avoid much of the guesswork. Personally, we have found two reliable methods – a knowing stud dog, and the good old-fashioned swabbing by your vet.

Swabbing is such a simple exercise that we are surprised at how few breeders employ this method. The vet takes a simple swab from the bitch's vulva then transfers it on to a slide. It is quickly flushed with dye and then viewed under the microscope. Several swabs are taken from the bitch over the space of a few days. The changes in cell shapes are easy to detect and are a clear indication of the time of ovulation. Some stud dog owners insist on each bitch being swabbed to ensure that they are free of infection, so an additional check by the vet to determine the time of ovulation will be doubly convenient. A stud dog owner may ask to check the vet's report before going ahead.

THE MATING

If a dog has not been used at stud before, it is essential that someone experienced is in attendance at the mating. Ideally, his first mating will be to an experienced bitch, who will give him the necessary encouragement. However, this is obviously not always the case. With a maiden bitch it is even more important to have the presence of someone who knows what he or she is doing.

Before the dog and bitch are introduced, you will have decided on a suitable location for the 'nuptials' to take place. This should be a quiet room of reasonable size (so that the bitch does not feel intimidated), with non-slip flooring. Both dogs should wear strong collars and you will also need a muzzle (or length of bandage to use as such), a lubricant such as petroleum jelly, and some sort of ramp in case there is a great difference in height between dog and bitch.

When the two are introduced, do it in a fairly wide-open area. Keep the dog on a lead while the bitch is allowed to roam around him. With a little luck, it will not be long before she approaches the dog and attempts to flirt with him by pawing at his front and springing back down on to her elbows, or leaping away in order to entice him to play. By this stage, the person holding the dog will have a fair indication whether or not the dog is mentally mature enough to proceed. If the dog's handler has had to wrap the lead (and himself) around

the nearest fence post in order to remain in one place, then it is a good sign that the dog understands what is required of him. If, however, the dog treats the presence of the lead and strange people as the signal to go for a walk and ignores the bitch totally, you have a difficult task ahead of you!

Once the dog has experience of being in contact with in-season bitches, he will follow a set pattern each time. Some males pine continuously right through the bitch's season and will eagerly try to mate her at any opportunity. Others may be very attentive to the bitch up until the ninth day or so, and then pester her unendingly for the next five or six days.

The best stud dogs are those who show no obvious interest in the bitch until they know that she is 'ready'. Having owned such a dog, we are only too aware of how useful it is when an over-eager owner has brought a bitch too soon. Naturally, it can also be quite embarrassing if your 'pride and joy' turns his head away with obvious boredom when he is presented with a bitch who has made a six or seven-hour journey especially for him! But, rest assured, the very same dog will eat his way through locked doors to reach the bitch when he knows that the time is right.

The attitude of the bitch will also determine how easily things will proceed. Most pet bitches who have had no previous contact with a male dog will be the most difficult to mate. Having been brought up to behave as 'young ladies', with any sexual play being firmly discouraged, it is hardly surprising that they hold such strong views against being leapt upon by a strange dog. In some cases a bitch may play 'hard to get' only in the presence of her owners. Once they have been dispatched indoors out of sight, she may develop the morals of a harlot! Unfortunately, though, there are times when a bitch is obviously not going to be mated willingly. This is something the owners of a bitch must discuss. Do you want to go ahead with a forced mating, or are you prepared to forget the whole thing?

On many occasions, the bitch will simply have been brought too soon and another few days will see a dramatic change in her. Sometimes bitches constantly growl and grumble when the dog is nearby, while her rear end, with the tail held to one side, is giving a completely different message! However, in the event of a bitch being so terrified that she has to be held up, muzzled, and has her tail tucked between her legs, then it is probably time to call a halt.

Regardless of how keen the bitch is, it is still a good idea to muzzle her. Most people do this by wrapping a bandage around her muzzle a few times, tying it under her chin and then securing the loose ends around her skull, under the ears. Even the most eager of bitches can spin her head around to snap at (but rarely bite) the male, and a handler or helper getting in the way of that snap could be seriously hurt.

Once the scene is set you will need at least three people. One person (preferably the owner) to hold the bitch head-on with a hand on either side of her collar, one person ready to kneel at the bitch's side to either help support her or to help direct the male, and one more to hold the stud dog. You may be amazed at the amount of human involvement needed, and we have often heard the arguments: "How would they manage in the wild?" and "Street dogs are always mating bitches without any assistance."

Both statements have a grain of truth in them, but when you look at a magnificent, healthy Newfoundland with a beautifully cared-for coat, you begin to realise that these wonderful specimens cannot be produced by random matings in the wild; if your only intention is to produce dogs of the quality of those strays seen on the street, then you have made a big mistake in purchasing this book.

Once all three people are in their allotted place, the dog's handler should bring him forward behind the bitch's tail; alternatively,

the handler may be dragged up behind the bitch's rear end, depending on whether the dog is of the "Oh, all right, if I really must", or the 'You hold 'em and I'll mate 'em' type.

If the dog mounts the bitch from the rear, the handler can let go of his collar, but if he naively tries to work his way around to her head, he can be gently pulled back to the correct end. Once he has mounted her, the person holding the bitch's head will have to prepare for a token protest, and the person kneeling at her side must be ready to intervene if the rear end collapses.

If the bitch becomes seriously uncomfortable, or the dog appears to be going off course, the handler can pull him away by his collar in order to start again. Do not attempt to pull him backwards as he will have discovered supernatural strength, and you both may end up with slipped discs! If the dog has to be taken away, stand at the side of the pair and pull him off sideways.

At this point, if the dog is a novice, the bitch's vulva can be lubricated with petroleum jelly. Doing it earlier can confuse a young dog by disguising the scent. With an experienced dog, it can be applied immediately. (You can do this wearing disposable gloves if you are squeamish.)

When the dog mounts again, the person kneeling will slide an arm and hand (palm upwards) lengthways under the bitch's belly until the fingertips reach her vulva. If a slight pressure is applied the vulva will be made to tilt upwards and open slightly. This will make it easier for the dog's penis to enter. If the dog is still not quite on course, a subtle manoeuvring of the bitch's pelvis should ensure a result. It is understandable that the first mating may be a little uncomfortable for the bitch, and she may begin to struggle at this critical time, so all concerned should be forewarned.

After thirty seconds or so, the glands at the base of the dog's penis swell and a 'tie' occurs when the bitch 'grips' the glands internally. If penetration is not entirely successful and the dog's glands become enlarged *outside* the vulva, it is important to hold the pair together for as long as possible (ideally about five minutes), so that the sperm still has the best chance of reaching the egg. At about this time, regardless of whether or not a tie has taken place, the dog becomes very relaxed and rests all his weight on the bitch's back. Some bitches find this very objectionable and can become quite agitated. Whenever we are present at a mating, we prefer to put both of the dog's front legs on the floor (next to the bitch's front quarters) as soon as he starts to relax. This has to be done by a fairly strong person as his front legs will be firmly clasping the bitch around her ribcage. Once back on the ground, the two will probably stand quietly until the tie is over.

Some dogs instinctively want to 'turn' by lifting a back leg over the bitch's croup until they are standing tail to tail. If he does want to turn, you can gently help him, but if he shows no inclination to do so, do not be concerned – it is not essential and will make no difference as to whether or not fertilisation takes place. Personally, we have found that not turning can be an advantage to an older stud dog and lessens the risk of a leg injury. However, we have also found that younger dogs are more prone to constantly washing the bitch's face and ears if they have *not* turned and this can be irritating to some bitches, making them snap or fidget.

The tie itself may last for only five minutes or, in rare cases, two hours or more. About twenty to thirty minutes is usual, and we know of nothing that can be done to hasten the process. So, if you have chosen to go ahead outdoors, and a thunderstorm breaks out – then, quite simply, you will get wet!

When the tie is over (and this happens instantly), both dogs will immediately clean themselves and it is a good opportunity for the owners to check for any sign of injury or bleeding. The dog should be walked quietly away before he starts to show a renewed interest in the bitch. It is quite commonplace for the dog's penis not to return immediately to its sheath and, although it is an alarming sight for the novice owner, it gradually returns to normal without the need for any cold-sponging.

The bitch should also be taken to a place where she can continue to clean herself and be offered a drink of water. The dyed-in-the-wool dog men of the past used to believe in up-ending the bitch's hindquarters for a few seconds and preventing her from urinating for at least half an hour after mating. This was to ensure that she conceived. Although the practice has since been proved to have no scientific basis, it can do no harm, so if it makes either the dog's or the bitch's owner feel happier, then go ahead!

Occasionally, the dog becomes so eager that he spends himself before a mating is accomplished. In these cases, both animals can be separated for half an hour before another (usually more controlled) attempt can be made.

SIGNS OF PREGNANCY

After the mating, many over-anxious owners can convince themselves, and their bitch, that she is in whelp. All too often we have been called to see a bitch who is allegedly nine weeks in-whelp, only to discover a smug-faced, overweight Newfie who is no more pregnant than is the man on the moon!

There are many indications as to a positive result. Old-fashioned breeders used to take notice of how soon after mating a bitch's season finished. The sooner the season ended, the more likelihood of the bitch being in whelp, was the theory. It is not a practice we have ever adhered to, as we have had bitches ready for mating at such varying times in their season that we feel the results would be inaccurate. But for someone else, it might work.

Three weeks after mating, some claim that there is a change in a pregnant bitch's teats.

They appear to be a darker colour and more prominent. At around twenty-four to twenty-eight days after mating, your vet will be able to externally palpate the bitch and will feel small 'golf balls' (or large 'marbles') if there are puppies present. This method of checking the bitch has often been patiently explained to us by our vet, but, to date, we are still unable to feel anything in our bitches! Personally, we believe that using a good vet is the safest way of palpating a bitch just in case we should do any unintentional damage to the unborn puppies.

For those owners who like to know what is happening well in advance, there is ultra-sound scanning. Not all veterinary surgeries have a scanner, but most farming practices will have one as it is a very useful tool for detecting pregnancy in sheep. We have never used a scanner, but have heard enough about them to realise that the equipment is only as clever as the operator; mistakes can easily be made. We were once told by the well-known all-rounder judge, Ann Arch, about the owner of a recently scanned bitch who proudly announced that her bitch was carrying two puppies. A later scan revealed the 'puppies' to be the bitch's two kidneys!

Scanning bitches is very much a case of 'counting chickens', and seven puppies seen on the scanner does not automatically mean seven live puppies at birth. Some may be absorbed by the bitch, some may be born dead and others may have severe congenital defects. It may all sound very depressing, but unfortunately there are no written guarantees when one is dealing with living creatures. If you feel that you want to scan your bitch, and it makes you feel better, then by all means do so. Our own feelings are that, if she is in whelp, great! It will soon show. If not, better luck next time, but life has to go on as normal for the bitch.

A slight increase in food at five-and-a-half to six weeks after mating might be a good idea and, if you feed a complete food, it is probably just as well to change to a different grade. We have found that dismissing a bitch as not in-whelp at six weeks and entering her for a championship show seems to be a sure-fire way of having a litter. No sooner does the show society cash your cheque, than the bitch becomes pregnant overnight!

CARE OF THE IN-WHELP BITCH
Once you are certain that your bitch is in whelp, you may notice a change in her eating habits. This ranges from "I'm eating for twelve, so I'd better have another helping", to "I feel a bit delicate today, but you could tempt me with some pilchards and scrambled eggs."

We have found that the easiest and most nutritious method of feeding an in-whelp bitch is to use a graded complete food. A gradual increase in food from 10 per cent up to 50 per cent during the final three weeks of gestation is adequate. Most complete foods have a printed feeding guide, so do not be tempted to exceed this guide by vast amounts. A greedy bitch will only end up overweight and unfit and, maybe, will cause herself a difficult birth.

A 'picky' bitch is much more difficult to feed, and especially so when the owner is convinced that she is going to starve herself. Try, as far as possible, to give her the usual meal but add a little of something tasty to tempt her. Bitches carrying large litters, or who carry their puppies very high in the abdomen, often have insufficient room for the stomach to expand. Understandably, this constant 'full' feeling contributes to their lack of appetite. Therefore, it makes sense to feed the bitch 'little and often', rather than two normal meals daily. Even the pickiest of bitches will not starve herself. They are very cunning, and know that they will be offered a variety of tempting fare. Such bitches can also be very trying. For two days a bitch may eat prime steak, then, on the third day, sniff it and turn her head away looking decidedly green! However, there is a marked difference between being 'picky' and being unwell. If a bitch is refusing water, is lethargic, has no interest in anything, or has a discharge, then there is only one place to be – the vet's surgery.

Most of the time, however, try to keep her to her usual routine; she is not an invalid. She will need her walks to keep herself fit and well-muscled. Your bitch will tell you how far she wants to walk, and whether or not she wants to fetch a ball or stick. It is probably not a good idea to be climbing mountains or going on fifteen-mile hikes once you are certain she in-whelp!

Keep her to her usual grooming regime – although she may not be able to leap on and off the grooming table, so this may have to be done on the floor. Many owners notice a thicker coat on an in-whelp bitch, so regular grooming will be even more important. It is not advisable to use insecticidal sprays or preparations on an in-whelp bitch, so grooming will be your only method of keeping her coat in good order.

Naturally, your bitch will have had her booster injections some months before she is mated, so you will have no reason to add any extra toxins to her system. Some vets recommend a daily worming for the final ten to fourteen days gestation, to ensure that the mother and puppies will be worm-free. It is a method that we follow and, although we find a slight reduction in birth weight, we generally do not have an obvious worm burden when the bitch and puppies are older. Your vet will have very definite thoughts on the subject and, as he will be your bitch's best friend during this time, it would be wise to heed what he says.

PREPARING FOR WHELPING

You will have set aside a quiet room as your 'maternity ward' and, from about ten days to a week before the big event, it is best to take the bitch in there for short periods every day. If she is also allowed to sleep in there alone she will come to regard it as her private quarters. There should be some sort of whelping box provided. This can be easily made by the handyman of the family using plywood, conti-board or something equally suitable bought at any hardware store. But, for those whose practical skills are non-existent, ready-made whelping boxes can be purchased. These are naturally more expensive, are usually made of more durable, hygienic material, and can be used for years.

If you are making your own whelping box, ensure that its sides are long enough for a bitch to lie stretched out in any direction. Three sides should be rigid and at least knee-high, while the fourth should be able to be folded down (or removed) to half the height of the others. This is to allow the bitch to leave the whelping box without scraping her udder on the edge, while the remaining half-height can still contain the puppies and protect them from draught. It can also be quite useful to put in a puppy rail to enable the puppies to lie safely around the edge of the box without being squashed and killed by the dam. The box should be fairly close to an electrical plug-point, and should also be situated under a beam or hook so that a heat lamp may be used.

The final few weeks of pregnancy should be used to beg old newspapers from friends, relatives and neighbours. (Incidentally, we prefer to have newspapers from people who are not dog owners, for fear of introducing germs.) When you have got stacks of newspapers and think you may have gone a bit over the top, that is a good indication that you will need about half as many again! Equally important are the fleecy synthetic pet blankets – a good supply of these is essential.

You will also need a thermometer, some puppy feeding bottles, a tin of puppy replacement milk, artificial colostrum, a bottle of liquid calcium and some baby bottle sterilizing fluid. And these are items you may not even use!

The week before, trim or shave the hair off

the bitch's udder and, if necessary, around her vulva and breeching. Wash the teats with a good antiseptic soap and dry thoroughly. This reduces the chance of parasitic eggs being swallowed by the puppies.

THE PUPPIES' ARRIVAL

This, according to the textbooks, should be sixty-three days after mating. Unfortunately, bitches do not read textbooks, so you can expect puppies any time from six days before to a few days after her due date. During the last week, the bitch's temperature should be taken daily. The normal temperature is 101.5 degrees Fahrenheit, but drops to under 99 degrees F during the twenty-four hours prior to whelping. Although there are exceptions, this is a fairly reliable guide as to when to expect the litter, so you can safely line the whelping box with newspapers at this stage. From our own experience, we find that the temperature drops enticingly near to 99 degrees F in the run-up to whelping, and then shoots back up towards normal just as we are rolling up our sleeves in readiness. There will usually be at least one false alarm, when the bitch's behaviour changes and she becomes restless. This passes in an hour or so, and is quite mild compared to the symptoms displayed when whelping has really started, but many people breeding their first litter are understandably concerned when the false alarm stage occurs.

When whelping starts in earnest the bitch will pant heavily, scratch up her bed, get up and lie down numerous times and cannot be pacified by anything. It is natural for her to constantly ask to 'go out' and, up to a point, she should be allowed to, while the owner follows at a discreet distance. Do not be tempted to leave the bitch out in the garden on her own as she will probably revert to natural canine behaviour, such as digging large holes to whelp in. Subsequently persuading her to use your whelping area instead of hers will be a difficult task. Also there is the added worry of a bitch digging

underneath a wooden shed or tree root and giving birth to puppies that no-one can reach.

Bitches who are house-clean are obviously going to feel a little uneasy initially about what they probably regard as 'fouling' indoors. Once the first puppy is born, however, they are much happier about the whole thing.

In due course you will see your bitch straining. How much heavy weather she makes of it depends on the bitch herself. Some just stop panting for a few seconds, grit their teeth, and out comes the puppy immediately. Others indulge in several long, grunting strains, so that the helper almost suffers a hernia just watching. As long as the bitch is not straining often, or for over forty minutes or so without results, then it will be 'normal' for her. Some bitches strain lying down or half sitting, while others stand up to push, so do not feel you have to make the bitch lie down if she is happier standing. It is as well to remember that the bitch's instincts tell her that the whelping process is one she would prefer to do in a dark, quiet and private corner. An owner flapping and fussing will be of no benefit to her.

As the puppy is being born, you will see a dark fluid-filled sac appearing through the vulva. A second later and the same sac containing the puppy should be expelled completely. At this stage, the puppy's survival will depend on it being able to breathe air for itself. Its link to its mother's oxygen supply will have been severed during the birth, and therefore it will be up to you, the midwife, to ensure the sac is broken and the puppy's head freed. On occasions, the puppy may be three-quarters of the way out of the vulva but is trapped there by the rest of the sac and the umbilical cord which has not yet been pushed through. In these cases, we always break the sac to free the puppy's head. Once it is able to breathe, it does not matter that everything else takes a minute or two to be passed. The owner can help by gently pulling the sac end of the cord – not the puppy – away from the vulva. This should be done in a gentle, downward curve, as you would with a puppy that was stuck at the shoulders.

Occasionally, maiden bitches will immediately attend to their new puppy, tearing the sac, vigorously washing the puppy and eating the afterbirth. But, more often than not, they will gaze at it in horror with an "I don't remember eating *that*!" expression, so it is important that there is someone capable at hand to prevent the puppy drowning. This bewilderment is probably a major cause of first-born puppies not surviving, although it is also quite common for puppies to be born without their placental sac.

If the bitch is not taking any notice of her baby, do not force her, but carry on drying the puppy. Its squeaking will eventually trigger a reaction in the mother and, when that happens, stand back and give them time to bond. When the bitch is happily washing the puppy and chewing at the umbilical cord to shorten it, you can then make her lie down and put the puppy on a teat to suckle. Newborn puppies can seem incredibly stupid at first, and turn their heads away from the teat you offer them. They will, however, choose their own teat and, once latched on, will be difficult to dislodge.

You will notice that up until now we have not mentioned weighing the puppy. This is deliberate. Anyone responsible for the family laundry will know the great difference in weight between wet and dry fabrics. Weighing a wet puppy can give an inaccurate result and, if you wish to weigh puppies daily at this stage, you will suffer unnecessary stress the following day if they appear to have lost weight.

We have the heat lamp switched on during the whelping and the puppies are soon warm and dry. Once another delivery is imminent, we place the previous arrivals in a smaller box inside the whelping box. In between

puppies, the bitch may take a drink of water, or even a little milk, to keep her energy up. We do not recommend feeding solids to a whelping bitch in case she should have to be operated on for the rest of the litter. (Although one bitch we whelped for friends happily ate chocolate wafers and tea in between each puppy and the next and suffered no ill effects!).

When the litter is complete (or when we believe it to be complete – anything from two to twelve hours!) we weigh and sex the puppies. In the absence of identifiable markings we use a dab of nail varnish on different parts of the puppies' bodies (taking care that it has dried before the puppy goes back to mum). This can then be renewed as necessary.

If there are more puppies than teats, and the bitch has a plentiful supply of milk, it will be vital to rotate the puppies to ensure that all are fed. Rarely, the bitch does not produce any milk and, although the vet may be able to administer a hormone to help things along, in the meantime you will have to give them the artificial colostrum and start hand-feeding. Bottle-feeding puppies is a daunting, never-ending task and doubly upsetting when one of them dies.

There have been books written on the subject of hand-rearing puppies so we will not dwell on what is obviously an extensive topic, but the most helpful hint we have found is to take care that the bottle teat does not have too large a hole. Too much flow of milk can easily end up in the puppies' lungs, drowning them, or causing coughing, distress and even fatal infections.

The whelping process is a messy business, and you will have used a large quantity of newspapers for 'mopping up'. Once whelping is complete, some new layers of paper can be put down and partly covered with fleecy synthetic blankets. Ensure that the bitch is lying comfortably on her side and that the puppies are lined up on her teats. At this stage, they will spend hours simply latched on to their teat waking every so often to take another feed. It is best to leave mother and babies in this position for as long as possible, but also wise not to leave the whelping room. Newfie mothers can be remarkably clumsy, and have to be constantly watched for the first week (and sometimes even longer.)

Some bitches incessantly wash their puppies and investigate every squeak, while others are more relaxed, giving a 'once over' at less regular intervals. Watching a bitch washing her puppy while it hangs on to the teat can be frightening, as she usually shoves its rear end into the air while its neck takes on a strange angle in an effort to hang on to the teat. However, no action is needed, save for the owner having a calming cup of tea, or a large scotch or two!

During the washing the bitch's tongue stimulates the puppy's bladder and bowel. This is another frightening occurrence, as the first bowel movement looks like a length of intestine that has been expelled. This is normal and nothing to worry about.

It is a good idea to have a vet check out the bitch soon after whelping (depending on the time of day), and this will also be the time to have any sick or defective puppies culled. Puppies with cleft palates or who are deformed in some other way are more kindly euthanised at this stage, rather than suffering and dying a week or so later.

Some breeders also cull mismarked puppies, or two or three others if it is a very large litter. This is not a practice that we would ever be comfortable about carrying out. However, everyone has a right to their own belief and that is probably enough said on the subject.

Your task for the next two weeks will be to ensure that the bitch is cared for and the puppies kept warm and adequately fed. Quiet puppies are contented, well-fed puppies. If they are huddled together and crying, lower the height of the heat lamp, but if they are spread out apart from each other then raise it slightly. If everything goes well, your role will be a very passive one – changing bedding, feeding the bitch and checking the puppies for any warning signs of ill health. In short, as little interference as possible is best. Some bitches spend the whole of the first two weeks lying on their sides and having to be literally forced outside to go to the toilet. These are usually the careful mothers who are more watchful as to whether or not they are lying on a puppy. Other bitches, after four or five days, prefer to be out of the whelping box, but they go back in every time the puppies cry or need cleaning. These are the ones who test your nerves, as they stomp about the whelping box and suddenly collapse with a sigh, regardless of babies yelling and struggling beneath them.

REARING THE PUPPIES
Shortly after the puppies' eyes are open (at ten to fourteen days) they will start to show an interest in food. Certainly, by three weeks of age, they should have been offered their first 'solid' feed. As we feed our adult dogs on a complete diet, we also believe in giving our puppies a complete, puppy-graded food. There are several on the market and they have the advantage of being soakable with warm water to form a 'gruel'. The first time you attempt to feed the puppies you will need only to prepare a saucerful of 'gruel' for a litter of eight or so puppies. Very little is ingested at this stage, and you will find that most of it goes over yourself and the puppies (with mum sitting hopefully nearby, waiting for a chance to come in and 'clean up'!).

To start, hold a puppy in your lap and dip your finger into the food before offering it to the puppy. At first, it will attempt to suckle the food off your finger. The next step will be to put the puppy on the floor with the saucer while you put your finger into the food, tilting the fingertip up slightly. The puppy will still attempt to suckle the food

By the time they are ready to go to their new homes, the puppies will be fully weaned and eating from their own bowls. *Photo: Keith Allison.*

and your finger, but will also be taking in small amounts of food. By the time you have repeated this exercise with all the puppies, you will be very messy indeed and the puppies will look like toddlers who have been allowed to eat a choc-ice unsupervised! We find it useful to have a bowl of warm water and a cloth nearby to wipe the puppies after they have finished. Give the puppies a solid feed *before* they are allowed a feed from the bitch.

We start the puppies with one feed on the first day, two on the second and so on until we are giving them four or five feeds per day. By then, they will be eating with some relish although they will still need a wash after every meal. It is important to keep the feed fairly sloppy and lump-free until they have grown an efficient set of teeth and are able to swallow properly. Most puppy food manufacturers have a general, printed guideline as to how their feed should be given, and these can be safely followed. If you give each puppy a dish to itself you will be more informed about how much each one is eating.

WORMING
We treat our puppies for roundworm at two weeks of age, and continue every two weeks until they are aged eight weeks. After that, any puppies we keep are wormed monthly until they reach six months, and every three to four months afterwards.

ASSESSING THE LITTER
By the time your puppies are three weeks old, your approved, prospective puppy owners will be clamouring at your door wanting to see them and wanting to be the first to choose their puppy. It will be good for the puppies to be handled by as many different people as possible, but personally we have doubts about choosing a puppy so young. We often hear of people who proudly announce that they picked their puppy at two days old and it went on to be a Champion. That is probably a case of good luck rather than sixth sense or any particular skill on the part of the owner.

Having said that, the breeder, being with the litter constantly since it was born, will probably have a slightly more educated view of the puppies than anyone else. There will usually be one that catches the eye and every time you pick it up thinking "That looks like a nice puppy", it will be the same one.

Do not be misled by the size of the puppies. It is easy to fall for the biggest in the litter. Because its growth rate is slightly advanced, its head will look bigger, broader and deeper. Its bone and feet will look more impressive, but it will be simply a stage ahead in development at that moment. If you are

By the time the pups are over eight weeks old the breeder will be able to assess their quality.

not convinced, just think back to your schooldays when there was a 'giant' who towered over everyone else in the class and then remember the lightweight, skinniest kid in your year. Chances are that if you met them now, the positions would be reversed or about even. This theory rings even truer with sibling puppies. Judge each one on its proportions to its *own* body and, unless you have an abnormally small puppy, forget about its size compared to others in the litter.

If you bred your litter specifically to keep a bitch puppy, but you are not over-keen on the only bitch in the litter, think hard about whether you really want to keep a male instead. Do not be tempted to keep just anything if it is not right for you.

Ask the stud dog's owner to take a look at the litter. He or she will undoubtedly have seen many of their dog's puppies, and can give you some valuable input about the puppies' good and bad points.

Once the puppies have turned six weeks old, you (and the prospective owners) will be able to make a choice. Stand each puppy on a grooming table and go over it point by

point. Then put the puppy on the floor while someone drags a toy along the floor in front of it. Watch how it moves both before and after picking the toy up. There is an increasing interest in Puppy Aptitude Tests, in which each puppy's reaction to a set of controlled circumstances is noted and graded by an independent person. These tests, done usually at seven weeks, establish such factors as touch and sound sensitivity, stability, restraint and touch sensitivity, social attraction and social dominance. The tests are more popular in the US, but some British breeders are finding it a valuable exercise in matching puppies with owners.

At six weeks we have all our puppies checked by our vet. This is a general health check, but they are also given their first inoculation against Parvovirus and their hearts are listened to for any obvious murmurs. The male puppies are looked at, to ensure that both testicles are present, and coats are examined for any sign of parasites. Many vets are happy, for a small fee, to provide a certificate following their examination of the puppies. This might be an idea worth considering, but it has to be understood that this is no guarantee against heart murmurs, parasites, etc. occurring at a later stage.

REGISTERING THE LITTER
In between the Herculean task of cleaning up after the puppies, feeding them and washing them, you will have to complete the paperwork required by your national kennel club. A five-generation pedigree may have to be filled in for each puppy, along with a diet sheet and general directions for the new owners to follow. The most important part of the paperwork will be each puppy's registration form. Make sure you send off the forms early enough to have the certificates back in time to hand over to each new owner at collecting time.

Most national clubs allow breeders almost unlimited freedom when it comes to naming puppies, and the result is a wide selection of weird, wonderful and sometimes embarrassingly unsuitable choices. Remember that your puppy will carry its name for the duration of its life, and a whimsical choice made now may come back to haunt you for years. If you intend to breed more than once you will appreciate the need for some sort of system. Graham Birch (Wellfont) once told us: "Keep your names simple and catchy. If the puppy becomes a top winner, everyone will be able to remember it."

Long and intricately-spelt names create misunderstandings and inaccurate pedigrees. We followed Graham's advice and named each litter in alphabetical sequence. This works for us, but other people prefer a theme for each litter. Such an approach can be equally effective, and tells you immediately who the sire and dam were. Particularly effective Newfoundland themes were Mrs Wilson's Ashness Italian wines litter and, in the early 1980s, Mrs Colgan's Karazan Gold litter.

INSURANCE

Insurance is a must when selling a puppy. So many things can go wrong and, for the sake of a small premium, at least potential financial heartache can be catered for. There is a variety of insurance companies who will issue you with a free book of cover notes. It cannot be simpler. The breeder pays the first month's premium on the day the puppy leaves home, and the company then contacts the new owner with the opportunity to continue the cover for twelve months.

In Britain, the KC also runs a free insurance scheme provided the new owner transfers the puppy into his name within ten days of purchase. It matters not which company or method you use as long as the puppy is covered.In countries such as the USA and Australia, insurance is a slightly different matter. A few commercial companies supply vet care insurance and it is

Even after the puppies leave home, the breeder has a responsibility for the puppies for the rest of their lives.

also possible to insure your dog along with your home contents. Although vet care insurance is somewhat limiting, especially for owners of large numbers of dogs, it is worth considering for the average pet owner. Breeders should ensure that puppy owners are aware of this option as many vets are notoriously forgetful of the fact!

LEAVING HOME

This is quite a sad day for many breeders. Life has revolved around these little lives for the past eight weeks, so it is understandable to feel a little protective when it is time for them to go. Remember, though, that as their

The brown, black, and Landseer colours are acceptable in most parts of the world.

breeder you will be responsible for all of them until the day they die. On the practical side, you will need to make the transition from 'litter member' to 'family member' as smooth as possible for the puppy. A supply of its usual food and water, a familiar bowl and perhaps a piece of pet blanket will all help the puppy to feel 'at home' in its new abode. Meanwhile, along with the rest of the paperwork, an indication of feeding times, familiar words to use and other everyday habits will establish a set routine which can then be changed gradually as required by the new owners.

Once all the puppies (except yours) are gone, sell your TV set and buy a new microwave. If all your approved owners take to heart the instruction to keep in touch, for the next ten or twelve years you will never again finish a hot meal or watch a programme in peace due to the constant ringing of the telephone.

A BRIEF LOOK AT COLOUR INHERITANCE

Genetics is a complex subject which has been written about by those with greater knowledge than ourselves. However, breeders and exhibitors of Newfoundlands need to have a basic understanding of how the colours are inherited.

Black is the dominant colour of Newfoundlands. In other words, a Newfoundland can *always* produce black offspring, regardless of its own colour (providing it has been mated to a dog of a different colour, if it is not black itself). A genetically solid black dog does not carry any other colour gene so cannot produce browns or landseers. He will look exactly the same as a black dog carrying brown or landseer genes so there is no way of telling by just looking at a Newfoundland.

In very simple terms, if a solid black Newfoundland is represented by the symbol BB and a brown by bb, then the following table shows the colours inherited when the two are mated:

Litter X

	b	b
B	Bb	Bb
B	Bb	Bb

Litter Y

	b	b
B	Bb	Bb
B	Bb	Bb

104

This shows that all the resulting puppies will be black, but will *all* be carrying the brown gene and will therefore be capable of producing brown puppies themselves, if mated to a suitable dog. If one of the members of litter X is mated to any one of litter Y, the following will occur:

Litter Z

	B	b
B	BB	Bb
b	Bb	bb

Some puppies will be born solid black (black coats BB), most will be black carrying brown (black coats Bb), and some will be brown coated (bb).

When a solid black (BB) is mated to a black carrying brown (Bb), the results will be as follows:

	B	b
B	BB	Bb
B	BB	Bb

All the puppies will have black coats, but approximately half the litter will be genetically solid black (BB), while the others will carry brown (Bb). Brown, being a recessive gene, cannot be produced unless it is present in both parents genetically.

The tables work in exactly the same way to show how the landseer colour is inherited. Again, solid black is represented by BB, while landseer is shown as ll:

	l	l
B	Bl	Bl
B	Bl	Bl

This litter is again all black in colour, but *all* the puppies carry the landseer gene and will be able to produce landseer when bred to the right mate. When two black-carrying landseer dogs (Bl) are mated, the resulting litter will fall into the same pattern as the black carrying brown dogs:

	B	l
B	BB	Bl
l	Bl	ll

A quarter of the puppies will be genetically solid black (and black coated BB). A further half will also be black coated, but carrying the landseer gene (Bl). Another quarter will be black and white piebald coated (ll) – landseer.

If two browns or two landseers are mated together, they can only produce that same colour but, from here on, the whole process becomes very complicated. If a brown is mated to a landseer, every one of the puppies will have black coats, but could be carrying any permutation of the other colours!

As well as the straightforward coat colours there are other shades, points or markings which have a similar genetic pattern.

Breeders should also bear in mind that the reference to 'half the litter' or 'quarter of the litter' and so on is only an average when applied to the results of a hundred litters or more. It is not an exact specification, as one misguided breeder some years ago seemed to think. Having mated his black-carrying landseer bitch (Bl) to a black-carrying landseer dog (Bl), he then arranged to have the bitch scanned. On seeing eight puppies on the scanner screen he was well pleased. "That means I'll have two landseers," was his response. He was adamant in his argument, up until the day the bitch whelped four blacks and four landseers!

9 HEALTH AND AILMENTS

It is said that a little knowledge is a dangerous thing and, for Newfoundland owners, this certainly rings true in relation to veterinary matters. Concerned Newfie owners often diagnose a multitude of rare diseases in their dogs – a condition not helped by their clever dogs' ability to use the situation to their best advantage!

However, although a great number of Newfoundlands live their lives with hardly a visit to the vet, it does no harm to recognise certain symptoms, or to be aware of hereditary conditions if your intention is to breed from the dog.

COMMON SENSE
Many of your dog's illnesses will be short-lived and will, hopefully, not require the services of a vet, so it is important that you are able to assess when veterinary attention really is needed and when a little common sense will do instead.

When your Newfie has vomited or had diarrhoea on a single occasion, but no raised temperature or obvious pain or distress is present, then a diet of boiled water for twenty-four hours, followed by feeding little and often for a further day, will probably be all that is needed. Try to think back to what he has eaten prior to the incident (and this includes anything disgusting which he may

have gulped down during a walk), but it is unlikely that you will need to consider changing his brand of food.

Lameness, too, can be a 'here today, gone tomorrow' type of condition. Lameness is the gait developed by the dog to put less weight on the painful limb, so stopping his exercise can only be beneficial to a minor injury. Incidentally, it is surprising how few people can identify *which* limb is the painful one – the foot which is slammed down quickly on the floor, thus showing up the condition and taking the bulk of the weight, is *not* the one which will be affected. We have also heard people say "He's lame, but he's not in pain"; one of the silliest arguments ever. If a dog becomes lame, he is doing so *because* he is in pain which the lameness helps to alleviate. So, unless a dog is lame out of habit following a long-term injury or operation (and even this could be due to some arthritis), when a dog is lame, it is due to pain.

Giving medication sometimes causes problems for owners (although many Newfies happily swallow tablets thinking they are being given a treat!). We have never attempted to struggle; instead we place the tablets in a spoonful of butter or dairy spread. This works so well that whenever the fridge door is opened and the butter is taken out we can guarantee a row of Newfies sitting smartly to attention hoping for a treat!

BREED DISEASES AND CONDITIONS

EAR CONDITIONS

The heavy, dropped ear of the Newfoundland, surrounded by thick hair (often made wet by swimming) makes it a natural site for problems to occur. Prevention is often more effective than treatment of an ear condition, so it is as well to get into the habit of routinely cleaning your dog's ears. You can purchase a cleanser from your vet – this will be suitable for the delicate lining of the ear, so do not be tempted to use anything else. The cleanser will be easy to use. Gently squirt the liquid into the deep part of the ear; it will help if your dog is lying on his side. Then massage the underpart of the ear for a few moments – you will probably hear a 'squishing' sound as you do so. When you have finished, the dog will shake his head to rid his ears of liquid and other debris that may have been in them. You can then wipe the ear flap and hair with cotton wool to prevent the mixture of cleanser and wax from making the ear region look greasy. Some Newfies object quite dramatically to having their ears cleaned and may bury their head in a corner or under their front paws. If you are certain that you are not being too rough, then it is probably because the liquid is cold, so stand the container in a bowl of lukewarm water before you begin.

INFECTIONS: If you suspect that your dog has an ear infection, you will need to take him to your vet who will probably prescribe drops, tablets and precise directions as to how and when they should be used. If an infection is present your dog will probably scratch his ears, shake his head or even hold his head to one side. The skin inside the ear may be inflamed and red, while the waxy discharge will probably be dark brown or black. There will also be a strong odour coming from the ear.

EAR MITES: The symptoms of ear mites are similar to those of infection, although there may not be odour or inflammation. If your dog is shaking his head and scratching (*and* you have a cat) then it almost certainly due to ear mites. Another visit to the vet will soon clear up the problem – but remember to treat the cat as well!

AURAL HAEMATOMA: A haematoma is a blood blister. Haematomas commonly occur in the ear flap and are easily recognised, as the ear looks as though it has been inflated with a pump and feels yielding and balloon-like. The condition can occur after an injury or fight, but most often develops after the dog has had extreme bouts of head shaking because of ear mites. The constant shaking ruptures a blood vessel in the ear flap, and the blood collects in a blister as it has nowhere else to go. Your vet will probably drain the blister by inserting a needle. If the draining has not been entirely successful, the dog may be left with a slight 'cauliflower ear'. Some vets prefer to solve the problem by simple surgery, when a small opening is made in the blister and buttons are stitched around it; this exerts pressure to assist draining and stops the blister re-forming.

EPILEPSY

This is a disorder in which fits occur, either as a result of damage to the brain or for no apparent reason. There are many Newfoundlands recorded as having epilepsy, but not so many as to make it a breed-specific problem. The condition normally occurs in the young dog (under four or five years), so fairly effective steps can be taken to prevent the affected animal being bred from.

The size of the Newfoundland makes 'fitting' a particularly distressing episode for the owner, as he or she may not be able to move out of the way. It is best not to touch or move the dog during a fit, but calmly wait until he has come round. Epilepsy *must* be treated by your vet and his directions followed precisely.

EYE CONDITIONS

ENTROPION: This is an irritating condition where the eyelid (usually the lower) rolls inward causing the eyelashes to rub against the cornea. The symptom is a constantly weeping eye which can, in some cases, be seen in young puppies. Surgical correction may be needed if the condition is severe. There are three kinds of entropion – congenital (being born with the condition), spastic (which is secondary to another painful eye condition making the dog squeeze his eyes shut), and trauma-induced (following an injury or surgery to the eye area).

Treatment of the primary condition is the best course of action for spastic entropion, while surgery might be the answer for the other two. Breeders in the USA and Canada are particularly vigilant in checking for a variety of eye diseases, and many will not breed from stock without a CERF (Canine Eye Registry Foundation) grading.

ECTROPION: This is best described to the lay person as the opposite of entropion. The lower eyelid is too large and long, and so does not fit snugly around the eyeball. The vulnerable conjunctiva or 'haw' is displayed and is often red, due to constant contact with atmospheric dust, grass seeds and other foreign objects. If the conjunctivitis is severe and recurring, surgery may be an option. Bear in mind, though, that a dog who has had surgery in order to live a normal life is not the ideal breeding prospect. (In the UK any surgical correction is reported ultimately to the Kennel Club, and the dog may not be allowed to be shown or bred from.)

HEART DISEASES

We make no apologies for devoting so much space to this subject as it is a matter of great concern to us. The heart is such an important organ that we feel breeders should go to great lengths to learn about it, and so try to avoid producing puppies with life-threatening conditions.

DILATED CARDIO-MYOPATHY (DCM): This is a disease of the heart muscle in which the organ becomes very dilated (enlarged) and produces a feeble beat. The blood circulation then becomes poor, resulting in an intolerance of exercise in the affected dog. Some are even known to faint. Irregular heart rhythms (arrhythmia) may be detected, and the progression of the disease may lead to heart failure, when pressures build up in the heart causing fluid to accumulate in the body. The fluid can sometimes invade the air-filled spaces of the lungs (pulmonary oedema) and the dog will be noticed to cough or show signs of breathlessness. Fluid can also collect in the abdomen, giving the dog a pot-bellied appearance. DCM is fatal, but can sometimes be controlled by various methods until either sudden death or euthanasia follows uncontrollable heart failure. The symptoms may not be apparent until the disease has been present for some time, so it is important to have the dog's heart checked regularly in an effort to recognise the signs at the earliest opportunity. A diagnosis of DCM, however, is unlikely to be made in its early stage by a simple examination by your vet, who is neither a cardiologist nor a magician and should not be expected to detect abnormalities which are often only obvious after specialised tests have been carried out.

A suspicion of DCM on the part of your vet will often mean that the dog is already in the early stages of heart failure, so a series of methods may be used to assist diagnosis. This will probably mean an electrocardiography (ECG) to show if there are abnormal heart rhythms, an X-ray to ascertain whether the heart is enlarged or fluid is present in the lung, and a Doppler echocardiogram (heart scan) which is an ultrasound scan of the heart. The scan is able to show the blood flow through the heart and valves and is the most sensitive method of diagnosing DCM. A further advantage is that ultrasound scanning is a non-invasive technique which results in many dogs falling asleep during the test!

Although DCM can be treated to an extent by drugs and careful management, it is ultimately a killer. The disease has a strong tendency to run in certain family lines, so omitting some dogs from the breeding programme (even if they are champions) has to be a sensible move for breeders.

SUB-VALVULAR AORTIC STENOSIS (SAS): This is an abnormality of the heart in which fibrous tissue develops in or near to the aortic valve, thus narrowing it. The narrowing (stenosis) causes the blood to be forced through the valve faster, resulting in a turbulence (murmur) which can be heard by auscultation (examination by stethoscope). The louder the sound (murmur) the greater the degree of the disease. The most severely affected dogs may collapse or die during exercise. The worse cases usually die at a young age, but for those moderately affected there does not seem to be a general worsening of the problem after they have reached full maturity.

A recent investigation of the problem by Newfoundland clubs in the UK rated the number of affected dogs as being as high as 20 per cent (although not all kennels had their dogs tested) and, with expert veterinary opinion proving the disease to be inherited, there is no denying that it is a condition which must be carefully monitored.

Puppies should be checked by a vet before leaving the breeder, but remember that your vet is not a cardiologist and may only detect the louder murmurs. Similarly with adult

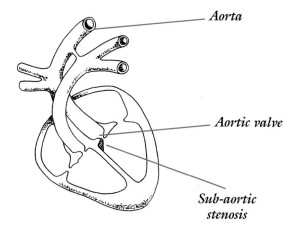

Heart disease (sub-aortic stenosis).
The stenosis can be seen as an obstructing lesion of fibrous connective tissue.

dogs, it is unfair to expect your vet to distinguish lower-scale murmurs. Some puppies develop suspicious 'swirling' sounds in their chests which then disappear by the time they are three or four months old. These should not be confused with stenosis murmurs, but, if there is any doubt, it is best to be referred to a cardiologist.

Checking dogs for evidence of SAS is done by cardiologists when the animal is twelve months or older. It is a simple test which involves listening to the heart with a stethoscope and grading any murmur heard. A 'murmur-free' dog will be given a certificate marked 0/6 and stating that no murmur could be heard.

Others may receive gradings of 1/6, 2/6 and so on up to 6/6 (a severe murmur). While gradings of 1/6, 2/6 and 3/6 are unlikely to affect the dog's lifestyle, it is unwise to breed from them bearing in mind the hereditary factor. However, gradings of 2/6 and upwards may be offered the opportunity of being referred for further testing on a Doppler scanner. This measures the flow of blood through the valves; the accepted upper limit of normal blood velocity through the aortic valve is 1.5 metre/second. For example, a dog having a reading of 1.65 m/s would have mild aortic stenosis, while 2.5 m/s and 6.5 m/s would be progressively worse (with the latter being extremely life-threatening).

Responsible breeders usually have their dogs checked by a cardiologist with the stethoscope on more than one occasion, in order to rule out the possibility of a 'lucky shot'. Unfortunately, as with all matters genetic, there will always be an exception to the rule and even the most careful of breeders can occasionally produce an affected puppy. Nevertheless, rigorous testing and judicious breeding can be the only way forward from this disease.

OTHER HEART CONDITIONS: Some other conditions recorded in Newfoundlands are Pulmonic Stenosis (narrowing of the Pulmonic valve), Patent Ductus Arteriusus (PDA – in which a blood vessel to by-pass the non-breathing lungs while the puppy is still in the uterus does not shut off after the puppy is born), and Tricuspid Valvular Dysplasia (similar to 'blue babies' in humans). These conditions do not occur with great frequency, but are serious and should be managed under the directions of a cardiologist. Veterinary treatment is now considered to be very advanced and much can be done to enrich the quality of life of a well-loved pet, although breeding from an affected dog would be extremely unwise.

HEATSTROKE
The Newfoundland's thick coat (plus, all too often, an ample covering of fat) can pre-dispose the breed to heatstroke following exercise during the hottest part of the day. Even in the UK, owners avoid walking their dogs during the afternoon in the summer. In countries such as Italy, breeders prefer not to have bitches in whelp during the month of August, as the heat and extra stress can

prove too uncomfortable for Newfie dams.

Heatstroke, at its most extreme, causes difficulty with breathing (panting sounds, rasping and laboured), and the dog may collapse. Hosing down the dog or immersing him in a child's paddling pool may provide a little relief before the vet arrives (ice-cold water should not be used as the dog could go into shock).

Prevention is the best course of action; as well as a careful exercise regime in summer, owners must ensure that their dogs have adequate shade on sunny days. It goes without saying that *no* dog should be left in a vehicle on even a moderately warm day.

INTESTINAL DISORDERS
BLOAT (GASTRIC DILATION VOLVULUS)
This is the one true emergency that all Newfie owners dread. Any time wasted could mean the difference between life and death for your dog.

Bloat symptoms are easy to recognise: the stomach becomes hard and bloated; the dog looks uncomfortable or even in distress; he may try to vomit but will be unable to do so. He must be treated by a vet immediately as he will rapidly go into shock. The vet will probably sedate the dog and orally insert a tube into his stomach to release the gas. If, however, the stomach has already twisted (this is caused by the pendulum-like movement of the stomach as the dog walks), then a major operation will be necessary. Because the condition is likely to recur, the vet will not only untwist the stomach during the operation, but will perform a 'belt and loop' procedure. This is where part of the stomach is surgically secured to the abdomen wall (depending on the vet's preference, the stomach may be secured to a rib instead or a tube may be placed in the aperture of the stomach). Sadly, there are times when the twist has cut off the blood supply to several organs and the operation will not be successful in saving the patient's life.

Following such an operation, post-surgical care is vital, with food and water being withheld for twenty-four hours. Fluids and then bland, sloppy foods can be built up gradually until normal intake is reached about ten days later. The dog may need to be kept on several small meals a day for the rest of his life. Some people also use a high feeding stand for the dog's bowl.

Despite considerable research, there does not seem to be a course of action which will absolutely prevent the condition from occurring. General opinion dictates the following.
1. Feed two or three meals a day.
2. Feed soaked rather than dry foods.
3. Avoid high-cereal content foods.
4. Do not allow strenuous exercise immediately before or after feeding.

It is unfortunate that, despite the best of management, some Newfies will still suffer from bloat, so any feelings of guilt on the owner's part will be misplaced.

DIARRHOEA OR VOMITING
Given the Newfoundland's propensity for eating anything – however disgusting – it is not surprising that they get the odd attack of sickness or diarrhoea. Unless the dog seems listless or in pain, or if he is a young puppy, or has blood in the faeces, no action should be necessary except for withholding food for twenty-four hours (and in some cases giving the dog kaolin and morphine).

FLATULENCE
This is definitely a 'big dog' problem, but, although embarrassing when the boss comes to dinner, be grateful that intestinal gas is able to escape and is not trapped in the stomach! Charcoal tablets can be quite helpful, as can a change in diet sometimes.

EXTERNAL PARASITES
Fleas, lice and ticks are the commonest problems. Fleas are extremely resilient against our attempts to eradicate them, and it is unlikely that you will ever be totally 'flea-free'. There are many preparations available for treating the dog and his surroundings, carpets and furnishings. People still feel, however, that to admit to having fleas on their dog is a slight on their personal hygiene and they may not take immediate action. Fleas and ticks can be picked up on walks, from other dogs or livestock, or you may have a colony hatching out in that warm spot under the radiator! Use anti-parasitic preparations routinely – it is the best way to control the problem. A flea-bite can sometimes cause an allergic reaction in the dog and these patches, when constantly gnawed at, become sore, sticky areas which have to be clipped back and bathed in salt and water.

Mothballs crushed up in the vacuum cleaner bag can be an effective deterrent against fleas in household furnishings and there are many more herbal or natural solutions.

Ticks can be found where deer, sheep or cattle live, and can latch on to your dog with annoying regularity. They can also cause Lyme Disease, a long-standing and debilitating illness. Once ticks have been in place for a day or so, they are easy to spot by their light-coloured bloated bodies. Removing the insect by pulling it out is not a good idea, as the mouth part is sometimes left behind and can set up an infection. Again, insecticidal sprays are effective, but the simplest method of removing a tick is to smear its body in petroleum jelly; unable to breathe it soon falls out or can be removed. Alternatively, apply a pad of cotton wool soaked in alcohol to the tick for a few minutes.

INTERNAL PARASITES
INTESTINAL WORMS
Roundworms and tapeworms are usually present in dogs unless they are routinely treated. Contrary to popular belief, the dog does not *have* to be thin, pot-bellied and

displaying a poor coat to have worms. To date, no-one has begun a campaign to save the roundworm or tapeworm from extinction and they are not an endangered species, so you can be quite ruthless when it comes to treating them!

We treat our puppies for roundworms every fortnight from two weeks of age until twelve weeks old. Further treatment is monthly until six months of age. From then on, they are treated every three or four months along with the adult dogs and the preparation used is also effective against tapeworm. We try to rotate the brand of the wormer every two or three treatments in case effectiveness becomes reduced. Tablets can easily be given as stated at the beginning of this chapter; liquid wormers are most easily dispensed in a syringe. Hold your Newfie's head up slightly, and gently trickle the contents of the syringe into the pocket of the dog's cheek. He will then swallow the liquid, albeit with great drama! If your Newfie really hates the taste of liquid wormer then put the bottle in the fridge for an hour until it is cool and has less flavour.

Dogs in warmer countries can also suffer from an infestation of heartworm. This can cause coughing and loss of energy but can be prevented and controlled by following your veterinary surgeon's advice.

REPRODUCTIVE SYSTEM
SEASONS
Some bitches come in season at fairly regular six-monthly intervals, others may go as long as ten or eleven months without showing any signs. If you intend to breed from your bitch, it will be useful to keep a record of previous seasons and behaviour throughout. If, however, a previously regular 'six monthly' bitch goes an extra two months, you have no cause to worry (unless the bitch appears seriously ill), but you will need to make some changes to your breeding plans! Similarly, some bitches are late coming into season for the first time (we know of a few

who were nearly two years old at their first season) and this, too, is no cause for concern. In fact, if you own a male dog, you can look upon this relaxing 'heat-free' time as a blessing!

PHANTOM PREGNANCY
Many unspayed bitches (and a few spayed ones!) have at least one phantom pregnancy during their lives. This may be fairly mild or it can be a full-scale affair, when the bitch refuses to leave her 'puppies' to go for walks and fills up with milk. In most cases, keeping the bitch's routine fairly busy with lots of short, interesting walks will soon bring her round. Giving her toys as 'babies' and pandering to her whims will only make her more confused and is, in our opinion, rather cruel. It may be kinder to spay a bitch who has regular 'phantoms'. A bitch who behaves in this way has no guarantee about her maternal instincts when she has real live puppies. Our Ch. Merrybear Jennah of Sheridel suffered from phantom pregnancies – her final theatrical effort being at a show where we had camped overnight. She flatly refused to come out of the van where she had had her 'litter'. However, when we eventually had puppies from her, she decided that the real thing was a dreadful experience; she was subsequently spayed and lived happily ever after!

PYOMETRA
This is another emergency, and the bitch will probably need an operation to remove her womb and ovaries (spaying). The bitch will be obviously ill, will show a marked increase in water intake, and vomiting is often seen. There may be a reddish or pus-coloured discharge from the vulva. In the absence of a discharge, the bitch will be even more unwell, as the toxins are retained inside her. In a few, less severe cases oral and injectable treatment may be sufficient, but, unless there are plans to breed from her, it is probably kinder to let her be spayed. The condition

usually occurs about five to ten weeks after a season.

WHELPING DISORDERS
ECLAMPSIA (MILK FEVER)

This condition occurs when the bitch develops a calcium deficiency either shortly after whelping or when the puppies are too suddenly weaned away from her. A bitch may develop eclampsia even if she is having calcium additives in her diet, so it can, sometimes, be unavoidable. Making sure that the puppies are suckling 'little and often' may help. (Dairy cows also have the condition when too much milk is taken from them at a single milking, whereas it is seen less often in beef cattle who have a calf constantly 'at foot'.)

At its most extreme, symptoms are panting, shivering and loss of consciousness, leading to death. An intravenous injection of calcium, however, has almost instantaneous results. In milder cases, the bitch may just be restless, panting and over-washing her puppies. Your vet may give oral treatment in these instances.

MASTITIS

The bitch's udders will be hot, red, swollen and painful, while the milk will be an unnatural yellowish colour with small 'flakes' in it. The puppies will become restless and cry constantly as the milk will be distasteful to them. Your vet will prescribe a suitable course of treatment.

METRITIS (WOMB INFLAMMATION/INFECTION)

We have come across this condition only once (it usually occurs within a few days of whelping), and have no desire to see it again. The bitch appears very unwell, has an orange-coloured discharge and does not have any interest in her puppies or her food. Immediate veterinary attention is needed, along with plenty of TLC (tender loving care) afterwards.

PARTURITION (GIVING BIRTH)

A first-time litter (for either bitch or owner) can give cause for some concern. It is difficult to assess what is 'right'. Ideally, you should be accompanied by an experienced breeder when your bitch has puppies, but this is not always practical. If in doubt, call your vet.

UTERINE INERTIA

As 'inertia' means 'inactivity', the condition is somewhat self-explanatory. Sometimes, if the bitch is only carrying one or two puppies, the womb is not sufficiently full to send the necessary messages to the brain and no contractions occur. The inertia can also be due to lack of muscle tone, fatigue or even an abnormally large litter resulting in the uterus being unable to contract. The least severe cases can be treated by your vet with the use of a hormone injection, but occasionally the puppies will need to be delivered by caesarean section.

Look out for the bitch's temperature dropping to under 99 degrees Fahrenheit for twenty-four hours, then rising again without any signs of whelping. Also, be aware that if the bitch goes into the first stage of whelping (panting, digging etc.) but has never had a temperature below 99.5 degrees F, then it may also be an inertia.

INABILITY TO PASS A PUPPY

Occasional straining (two or three times every fifteen minutes) for over one hour indicates some difficulty, and may need action if it persists for another half hour. If the bitch strains violently almost every minute and does not produce a puppy within thirty or forty minutes, she will become distressed, exhausted and will need veterinary attention.

INFERTILITY

Infertility often turns out to be poor timing on the part of the dog or bitch's owner. In the rare case of a 'low fertility' dog or bitch, it may be worth remembering that going to extremes to produce a litter may be counter-productive as the resulting puppies may also be affected. Male dogs may suffer a temporary 'summer sterility' due to overheating, so it is especially important to ensure that they are as cool as possible during long car journeys.

Both male and female dogs may be affected by treatment with corticosteroids, so do not be surprised if there are no results from a mating if one or the other has been similarly treated. In the event of your Newfie being genuinely sterile, it is unfortunate if you had planned a breeding programme, but you will still be living with the same wonderful character as before.

MONORCHIDISM (retained testicle),
CRYPTORCHIDISM (both testes retained)
These conditions represent not only an inconvenience to the serious exhibitor, but also worrying conditions with regard to the dog's health. If one or both testicles have not descended by the time the dog is a year old, then castration should soon be considered, as the retained gland will have a 50 per cent chance of becoming cancerous when over six years old. Monorchids are usually fertile, so it is important that castration is carried out to prevent the condition being passed on. Cryptorchids are almost always sterile.

SKELETAL DISEASES
HIP DYSPLASIA
This hereditary condition is often seen in Newfoundlands to the extent that they are the fourth worst-affected breed in the UK.

As our vet often points out, it is a disease of the *hip socket*, but the head of the femur also becomes altered, taking on a squarish or flattened shape. In severely affected dogs, an operation to cut the pectineus muscle may give relief, but some animals may even have to be euthanised. Some badly affected dogs may live as normal a life as those only mildly afflicted, but it is usually unwise to breed from them. The complicated genetic factors mean that progress to lower incidence of the disease is slow, and breeders can expect the odd poorly-hipped puppy even in good hip-producing bloodlines.

The British Veterinary Association/KC Hip Dysplasia Scheme (BVA/KC/HD) assesses the degree of hip dysplasia present by using a scoring system. The minimum (i.e. best) score for each hip is 0 and the maximum (worst) is 53, giving a total range of 0-106. The average score for Newfoundlands in the UK is 31. This could be made up for example, of left hip, 14, plus right hip, 17. The owner of a hip-scored dog, may say: "My dog's got a hip score of 12" or "My dog's hips are 7-5", so it is important, if you are thinking of using the dog at stud, to find out what his *total* score is (12 in this case). It is useful to know the average hip-score of progeny produced by a dog you wish to use at stud. It is also unreasonable to expect low-scoring offspring from a stud dog with a score of 8, if his mother scored 68 and all his litter mates scored over 50!

Hip scoring (an X-ray procedure) is done under anaesthetic or deep sedation by your veterinary surgeon when the dog is at least one year old. The dog has to be placed on his back with the pelvis positioned centrally and hind legs extended. If there are no problems with positioning, the procedure should take no longer than ten or fifteen minutes. The X-ray plates are then sent to a recognised panel which assesses the hip-scores of all the relevant breeds in the country. The results are usually returned within a few weeks. It will have been necessary for you to bring your dog's registration certificate and pedigree to show your vet prior to the X-ray being taken. The details are checked and entered on the X-ray plate.

It will be tempting to ask your vet what sort of score to expect, but it is hardly fair to

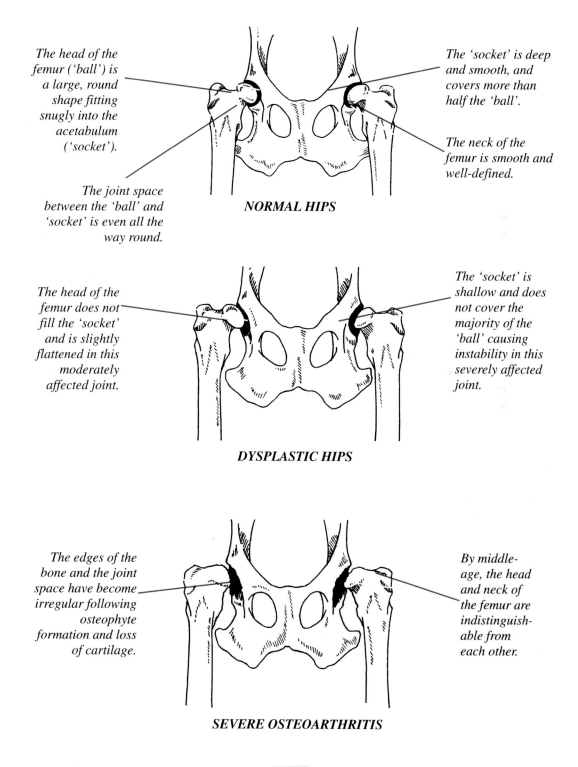

The head of the femur ('ball') is a large, round shape fitting snugly into the acetabulum ('socket').

The 'socket' is deep and smooth, and covers more than half the 'ball'.

The neck of the femur is smooth and well-defined.

The joint space between the 'ball' and 'socket' is even all the way round.

NORMAL HIPS

The head of the femur does not fill the 'socket' and is slightly flattened in this moderately affected joint.

The 'socket' is shallow and does not cover the majority of the 'ball' causing instability in this severely affected joint.

DYSPLASTIC HIPS

The edges of the bone and the joint space have become irregular following osteophyte formation and loss of cartilage.

By middle-age, the head and neck of the femur are indistinguish-able from each other.

SEVERE OSTEOARTHRITIS

demand an answer when he will not have the measuring apparatus or expertise needed to give an accurate prediction. He will, however, be able to tell you whether the hips were generally good or rather poor, so, until the results return, you must be content with that. The BVA system is also used in Australia and New Zealand.

In the USA and Canada a different system based on the OFA (Orthopedic Foundation for Animals) procedure is used. An OFA number is assigned to dogs whose hips are considered to be within the normal range for the breed. There are seven recognised grades of hip status: Excellent, Good, Fair, Borderline, Mild, Moderate and Severe (based on the percentage of the femoral head within the hip socket). Only the first three are eligible for an OFA number. Dogs are graded at two years old or over. In parts of Europe and Scandinavia the gradings are again different and unique to each country's system.

ELBOW DYSPLASIA
Elbow dysplasia, like that of the hip joint, is when the joint does not fit together properly or well enough to function normally. The ill-fitting joint then puts pressure on areas that take the majority of the weight. Over time, uneven pressure can cause a number of problems within the joint. These conditions are:
• Fragmented Coronoid Process (FCP).
• Osteochondritis Dissecans (OCD) – the most common occurrence in Newfoundlands.
• Ununited Anconeal Process (UAP).
• Arthrosis.

These can occur singly or in conjunction with each other. Symptoms show up as lameness (usually in the young dog), although a degree of dysplasia can be present without any clinical signs.

The number of Newfoundlands X-rayed globally shows a significant percentage of affected dogs, and high heritability seems likely. The Elbow Scoring Programme is a

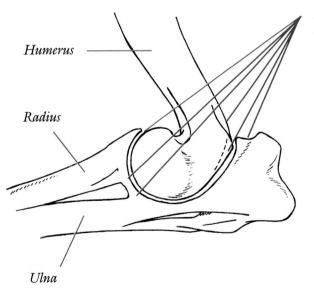

Areas where arthrosis may show up on X-ray

Humerus

Radius

ELBOW DYSPLASIA

Ulna

116

useful tool for breeders wishing to monitor the situation. Elbows are X-rayed singly while the dog is anaesthetised or under sedation; this can be done at the same time as hips are scored. Elbow screening, too, requires the dog to be over twelve months old. The same pedigree details are given and a similar procedure is followed when the X-ray plates are sent away to be assessed.

The results will be one of the following for each elbow.
Clear (no arthrosis visible).
Grade I (minimal arthrosis).
Grade II (moderate arthrosis).
Grade III (severe arthrosis).

Owners of Newfoundlands which have been operated on for OCD report that the post-operative period is particularly painful and distressing, thus emphasising the importance of breeding with stock that is less likely to produce the defect.

CRUCIATE LIGAMENT RUPTURE

The two cruciate ligaments (the cranial and the caudal) are present in the stifle joint (knee), and it is the former which is most liable to injury in the Newfoundland. Sufferers occur at both ends of the scale – the middle-aged, overweight and rather inactive dog or the very athletic and energetic specimen. Owners commonly report a sudden cry from the dog before it resorts to holding the injured leg off the ground. By the following day, although still lame, the dog may, lightly, put some weight on the tip-toe of his hind foot. Surgery will usually be necessary to correct the problem, following which a strictly controlled rest and exercise regime must be observed.

SKIN PROBLEMS
ALLERGIES

Any suspected allergy needs to be treated by a vet and may, depending on the allergen(s), need a series of tests to determine the cause. Skin allergies do not suddenly get better overnight, so it is important to be patient

and to feed only what you are advised by your vet. Flea allergies, as mentioned earlier, can be controlled by careful management.

Allergies giving skin irritation may fall into the following categories.
• Contact, e.g. blankets, cleaning agents.
• Food, e.g. beef.
• Inhaled, e.g. dust mites.

ECZEMA ('HOT SPOTS')

These are the most common complaints reported by Newfie owners. In rare cases, they are due to food allergies or some minor trauma, but most of the time the blame lies with the ever-present flea!

Food allergies can be controlled by restricted diet and regular monitoring of the situation. 'Hot spots' due to stress need a little more hard work, as the dog's routine may need to be changed so that he does not become stressed.

FEET CHEWING

This is an annoying habit to watch, but remember that your dog is not doing it for fun – he is reacting to an itch in his feet. Shouting at him will not solve the problem, as he will simply continue to chew when you are not around and, possibly, cause himself even more damage. This is also a condition which needs to be investigated for a possible allergy or grass mites. It can also be caused by bacterial and fungal infections, parasites, or physical and chemical irritants.

Some Newfie owners are completely satisfied with the results of using a haemorrhoid cream on the feet (although how this 'cure' came about is a question we are far too polite to ask!).

DEMODECTIC MANGE

A serious condition caused by a mite living in the dog's hair follicles. The mite may be present but causing no harm to the dog. However, it may become diseased and destroy the hair. It can also burrow through the skin, causing infections. This condition will respond to veterinary treatment but is notoriously difficult to cure. It is believed to be an hereditary condition, and an affected animal should not be bred from.

SARCOPTIC MANGE
Another burrowing mite causing irritation, spots and patches of hairlessness. Eventually the patches can become infected with secondary bacteria causing eczema. Unless the correct treatment is followed, you could find yourself sharing your dog's problem, as this condition can be transmitted to man in the form of scabies. Treatment must be continued over several weeks.

WARTS, LUMPS AND GROWTHS
The older Newfie, like most dogs, is prone to the occasional lump or cyst. Most of the time they are quite innocuous, but you will need this confirmed by your vet. If a lump is harmless, the best course of action is to leave it there, but to keep a regular check on its progress.

TEETH
Your Newfie's teeth should be large, strong, white and set into healthy pink gums. In order that they remain in that condition you will need to give large marrowbones and nylon chews, or your dog will need to have his teeth brushed (start when he is young and he will soon get used to it). Orangey-brown teeth covered in tartar are not only unsightly, but the gums soon become inflamed too. While a healthy mouth is necessary to all dogs, it is doubly important to a bitch who will be used for breeding, as infections can be passed on through the puppies' navels when they are being washed.

As Newfies often like to carry objects in their mouths, the teeth soon become worn down and the centre core revealed. The teeth will probably be checked annually by your vet when the dog has his booster vaccinations, but if, in the meantime, your Newfie's teeth show a pink-coloured core

and some inflammation of the gums, it may mean that the nerve is exposed and prompt action is needed. Broken or split teeth should be also checked by your vet.

THYROID DISORDERS
This deficiency of the thyroid hormone is seen only occasionally in Newfoundlands in the UK; but in the US and Canada a perceived breed disposition has resulted, very sensibly, in the routine screening of breeding stock.

Symptoms do not usually present prior to the dog reaching four years of age. These symptoms are so many and varied that it would be of little value to list them all. However, changes in coat, skin, appetite and general behaviour may be noticed. The *only* diagnosis and treatment should be via your veterinary surgeon, as it is usually a long-term disorder and should not be treated as a result of the owner's suspicion alone.

VACCINATIONS
Puppies now begin their inoculations at an early age, and owners are usually eager to complete the first course so that training and socialization can begin. However, by the dog's second year, owners are notoriously lax about administering boosters! Speak to an older or retired breeder about the heartbreak caused before modern vaccination programmes were discovered, and stay up-to-date with your dog's boosters.

Vaccination covers diseases such as:
- Distemper – a fatal virus which attacks the nervous system causing fits and coughing, to name only two of its distressing symptoms.
- Hepatitis – jaundice accompanied by diarrhoea, vomiting and abdominal pain, leading to death in extreme cases. There may also be damage to the cornea, and the eye colour becomes a shade of blue.
- Leptospirosis (liver form) – another type of jaundice which can be passed on to humans. It is potentially fatal if not treated.
- Leptospirosis (kidney form) – the cause of

a potentially fatal kidney disease.
• Parvovirus – a virus causing extreme vomiting and diarrhoea (often blood-stained). This is a killer of young dogs up to about fourteen months old and can wipe out whole litters.
• Kennel Cough – a very distressing and contagious condition for young puppies and older stock. Dogs of all ages can be affected, displaying a distinctive, hacking, 'something stuck in the throat'-type cough and, in some cases, nasal discharge.

WHEN VETERINARY ADVICE IS NEEDED
This chapter is intended as a guide to the Newfoundland owner to help understand what to expect when confronted with certain conditions. It is not meant as a substitute for your vet's diagnosis, which comes from five years' training and in-practice experience.

Unless you are certain that your Newfie has an ailment which can be treated by first-aid and common sense, then he must be examined by the only person qualified to do so.

If your vet diagnoses an hereditary condition in your dog (which ruins your breeding plans), do not search in disgust for another vet. Hereditary conditions *do* exist and, therefore, your vet must not be blamed for finding them. However, your dog will still be the same character that endeared you to the breed, so cherish him while you have him. And, while on that sombre note, do not forget that there may come a time when you have to make a difficult decision about the quality of your pet's life. Even seriously-ill Newfoundlands seem to make a great effort to greet their owners or do something 'special' to convince everyone that all is well. Living with a sick Newfie, it is easy to imagine that his condition is improving slightly, so heed the advice of your vet and your friends, remembering that, sometimes, saying goodbye is the kindest thing you can do.

10 NEWFOUNDLANDS IN BRITAIN

We may be a little biased, but it is widely believed that making up a champion in Britain is more difficult to achieve than in almost any other country in the world. Whether this is true or whether it is a theory which stems from wishful thinking is difficult to prove either way, but the gaining of a title for a British show dog is no mean feat.

A steadily increasing registration figure of around 800 Newfoundland puppies a year (where all puppies are registered at birth or, rarely, not at all) puts the breed in the mid-range of popularity and one does not have to travel far to see a Newfoundland. Unfortunately, such large figures for our small island often means that dogs are re-homed with worrying regularity.

Present-day urban trends dictate that many successful breeders own only a few dogs and produce puppies rarely. With space and facilities at such a premium, each litter is very carefully thought out, as breeders realise that they may not get another chance for up to four years or so. Those breeders may not have the impressive tally of champions produced at the more populated kennels but, in terms of percentage, their contribution to the breed is often greater than that of much larger establishments. The fact that Newfoundlands are not, by nature,

ideally suited to kennel life also means that the part-time breeder is more prevalent in our breed.

The following kennels are just some of the proven producers of quality dogs in Britain today and up until recent years.

ASHNESS (Christine Wilson)
The Ashness affix has developed a reputation for selective but quality breeding. Following the acquisition of a much-loved pet in 1983, two bitches from the Stormsail and Wellfont Kennels joined the Wilson family. Wellfont Rosanna of Ashness was, in time, mated to Ch. Wellfont Macillon to produce a single bitch puppy who became Ch. Ashness Naomi.

The next litter out of Stormsail Mountain Ash of Ashness (2 CCs), by Italian import Asterion Canis Venatici, went to the other extreme, as thirteen puppies were produced! Their performance in the show ring was consistent with three becoming champions (including CCs won at Crufts and a BIS at a Group Championship Show). A further three won CCs (one at a Club Championship Show) and each of the others, lightly shown, won their Stud Book numbers.

A visit to Canada in 1990 resulted in the importation of a landseer male, Topmast's

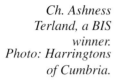

Ch. Ashness Terland, a BIS winner. Photo: Harringtons of Cumbria.

Jimmy Canuk for Jean at Ashness, and he has been used selectively at stud as well as winning a CC and two Reserves.

A particular landmark for the kennel was when the littermates Ch. Ashness Lugano of Stormsail and Ashness Aleatico of Bessibear won BIS and RBIS at the Newfoundland Club Championship Show. Owned by the same person, this was a first-time occurrence since the show's inception in 1976.

As well as being show winners and house pets (never more than six), many Ashness dogs also hold draught test qualifications, while Ch. Ashness Terlano has also acquitted himself well at water tests. A further landseer import from the Topmast Kennel has provided some useful bloodlines and will, hopefully, continue to be successful for the Ashness line.

ATTIMORE (Esther Denham)
Esther's first Newfoundland, a black bitch, was purchased from Juliet Leicester-Hope's Wanitopa Kennel in 1965. Wanitopa Mermaid not only fulfilled her role as the family's pet but was a very able worker, winning the Water Trials 1965, much to her owner's amazement as she had never been trained for water work!

When bred to Lord Hercules of Fairwater she produced the first homebred champion bitch, Ch. Attimore Aquarius, the male Ch. Laphroaig Attimore Aries and Attimore Libra, a CC winner. Also in this litter was Ragtime Attimore Sirius who won 3 CCs but not his title, as two of the Certificates were awarded at different times by the same judge. (This is a situation which happens occasionally when a last-minute change of

121

Ch. Laphroaig Attimore Aries.

judge occurs or if the show in question is especially prestigious – such as Crufts or a Club Show.)

A repeat mating yielded Ch. Attimore Minches who also found favour with such respected breed judges as Mr Handley, Mrs Roberts and Mr Blyth. Aquarius was eventually mated to the Dutch import Avalons Ikaros of Littlegrange (owned by Frances Warren) to produce Ch. Attimore Royal Sovereign who won the CC and BIS at the Newfoundland Club Show in 1976 – the first year the show was given championship status. Sovereign was also an influential stud dog producing champions for the Stormsail and Shermead Kennels.

Another success story was Ch. Attimore Cutter (owned by Mr and Miss Ward) who won BIS at the National Working Breeds Championship Show at a time when Newfoundlands were rarely considered for such high honours.

There have been landseers and even browns at Attimore, although their breeder says that producing this colour came as quite a shock as there were also two greys in the same litter! However, one of the browns, Ketch, became a CC winner.

Being an experienced veterinary surgeon, Esther is watchful of the health of the breed and proud to have the second lowest HD average (7.33) in the UK. The working instincts of Attimore dogs have remained constant, with a total of ten winning the

Water Trials. The latest successful water worker, Attimore Mary Rose, has achieved a pass at Level D – a qualification which stood her in good stead when she was recently swept off a beach by a giant wave. Fortunately, she was able to save herself and is still enthusiastic in the water.

CEILIDH (John and Jenny Davie)
The Ceilidh Kennels were established in 1979 with the purchase of a black bitch puppy from the Wellfont Kennels. The puppy became Ch. Wellfont Angie and was one of the famous Wellfont 'A' litter which contained Admiral, the one-time breed record holder. Angie was mated to the Danish import, Ch. Ursulas White Sails (landseer) and a landseer bitch, Wellfont Eriskay, was kept. Eriskay's pet name was 'Ceilidh' as her character matched the fun-filled musical evenings much loved by the Scots, and this also became the kennel name of the Davies. Eriskay, a very large bitch, gained her title and was Top Bitch in 1987. When mated to Dk. Import Ch. Ursulas Admiral Ascot she produced only one puppy – Ceilidh Solitaire – who lived up to her early promise by winning the CC at only eight months old! A somewhat reluctant brood, Solitaire eventually whelped two black males to Ch. Wellfont Macillon. These

Ceilidh Uisge Beatha.   *Photo: Yvonne Kent.*

122

Culnor Lord of the Ring with his brown son Culnor Snuff-Snuff.

were Ceilidh Carrick of Seaking (a RCC winner) and Ceilidh Cruit Mo Cridh, winner of a CC, Open Show Groups and Top Puppy in 1990.

Meanwhile, in 1988, John and Jenny bought in a bitch puppy by Ch. Wellfont Macillon and Ursulas Renata of Wellfont. The puppy was to be Ch. Krystalcove Karagh for Ceilidh, a great character in the show ring and with excellent movement which she passed on to her eventual progeny.

Karagh's first litter to Cruit Mo Cridh produced, as well as a consistent Championship Show winner, two super working dogs in Ceilidh Islay Mist and Ceilidh McTavish, the latter being one of the first dogs to reach Level Four (top level) at Draught Tests. The second litter, to Ch. Topsy's Offenbach, clicked extremely well with a champion, two CC winners and a group placing so far.

Ceilidh dogs are all hip-scored, elbow-scored and heart-tested, while John and Jenny continue to aim for the sound temperament of their previous generations.

CULNOR (Lucy Stevenson)
When Lucy was eleven she encountered her first Newfoundland and unsuccessfully tried to persuade her father to allow one to join the family. She had to wait many years until 1982 when she purchased her first Newfie, Coalfern Windy Ridge at Culnor 'Bear' (Ch. Stormsail Matterhorn x Esmeduna's Thorsanne), having first researched the results of the show ring.

Lucy was very lucky with Bear. Not only did she win Best Puppy at her first show and, later a RCC, but she also had excellent hips. Lucy also gave a home to her two sisters and these were the basis for the Culnor line.

She enjoyed showing, but was more concerned that the puppies produced went to loving pet homes where they could enjoy life by doing a little carting or swimming. She has always tried to aim for a large dog that looks like a Newfoundland, but even more importantly, one that has an excellent temperament and as few health problems as possible. She believes that Culnor was one of the first kennels to publish all its hip scores.

Lucy refuses to inflict on her dogs hours or days of rigorous show training, which is considered essential by the more dedicated exhibitors. In spite of this, her dogs have managed a fairly creditable performance over the years with title holders Ch. Culnor Fuzzy Sea-Wuzzy (BIS at the Newfoundland Club Centenary Show 1986), Ch. Culnor Monsoon Disaster, Can. Ch. Culnor Falls Down Laughing and Irish Ch. Culnor Starshine Dugald on Startrek, as well as many other CC and RCC winners.

Her recent import of the young Canadian dog, Greer's Canadian Trader at Culnor (one RCC), appears to have been successful, as his offspring so far look very promising.

Lucy has had mainly blacks, but also breeds and shows browns, the most well-known being the CC winner Culnor Snuff Snuff. She has also recently resumed an interest in landseers, who she feels are on the decline generally. She does not formally work her dogs, but living near the sea provides an ideal opportunity to have fun with them and to retain their swimming instincts.

Ch. Hambledown Hornblower with his canine family.

Photo: Pearce.

HAMBLEDOWN (George and Freda Pratt)
During the war, when Freda was five years old, a large, black dog followed her home from school one day and, on being allowed to stay the night, rewarded the family by producing twelve puppies before morning. The family did not have the facilities to care for the dogs and they had to go, much to Freda's despair. She consoled herself with the ambition that she would eventually own a great black dog.

The dream did not become reality until 1971 when she and her husband George bought a male Newfoundland, Clywoods the Bomber. The following year, a bitch arrived on breeding terms and Lady Delia of Esmeduna was mated to Bomber. From the litter the couple kept Hambledown Boatman (2 CCs) and his sister Hambledown Pitch and Pigtail, a RCC winner. Together they travelled enthusiastically to every show possible, as well as to the Water Trials, where not only did the dogs demonstrate a flair for working, but George earned his own reputation for building the decorated carts which the dogs pulled.

In between visiting local schools to promote responsible dog ownership, George and Freda bred CC-winning dogs like Seafarer (for the Merrybear Kennels) and Flagship (Swanpool Newfoundlands). Many other CC and RCC winners followed, including the Ch. Hambledown Shantyman and the top winning Ch. Hambledown Hornblower.

The Hambledown dogs were no strangers to charity work as they often donned their harnesses and collecting tins to raise money for the Royal National Institute for the Blind and the Royal National Lifeboat Institute. (This work prompted an invitation to appear in the first Personality Parade at Crufts and also at the second, a year later.)

Over the years, George and Freda have attended numerous lectures and seminars in an attempt to learn more about dogs in general and Newfoundlands in particular. Freda is now a championship show judge, while both are active participants and organisers of the Welsh Newfoundland Activity Group which regularly meets for owners to swim their dogs and share experiences.

Hambledown dogs have been exported to the USA, France, Italy, Spain and South Africa, and the present aim is to continue to produce family companions with an excellent temperament.

HIGHFOO (Warwick and Peggy Winston)
You may be forgiven for identifying the Highfoo name with the Toy group, as quality Pekinese are also bred under this affix. However, Warwick's affinity with the Newfoundland breed means that there is usually at least one Newfie in the family.

The Winstons' association of almost thirty years with the Newfoundland has, by choice, been limited in terms of breeding, but nevertheless the percentage of quality, typey dogs has been high.

Their earlier dogs were based on the well-

Ch. Honeybears Moondust – the first bitch to win RBIS at an all breeds Championship show in Britain.

Photo: Carol Ann Johnson.

known Harlingen, Harratons and Esmeduna lines, with landseers featuring prominently from this background. The first champion to bear the Winstons' affix was the landseer bitch Ch. Highfoo Harratons Ocean Queen (Suleskerry Sailmaker of Fairwater x Whitehouse Sea Diver). She also passed on her good qualities when mated to Ch. Sigroc King Neptune, resulting in the black dog Ch. Highfoo Big Baloo.

Meanwhile, another landseer bitch, Harlingen Puffin of Highfoo (who went on to be the base of the early Karazan litters), had also produced a litter to Neptune and a black bitch was exported to South Africa. She became SA Ch. Highfoo Sea Urchin and was extremely useful to the breed there, at a time when Newfoundlands were thin on the ground.

The landseer bitch Highfoo Karazan Veuve Cliquot became a RCC winner and was eventually mated to the Dk. import Ch. Ursulas White Sails to produce an all-landseer Highfoo litter.

Today, the resident champion in the Winston household is Ch. Karazan Sugar In My Tea of Highfoo (Ch. Karazan Rockafella x Ch. Shermead Coco Chanelle), a black bitch who was successfully campaigned to an early title despite competition from top winning littermates. When mated to Ch. Karazan Chocolate Buttons, the first Highfoo brown was produced.

Warwick's involvement with the Kennel Club and the Northern Newfoundland Club leaves little time for breeding or showing these days, but the Highfoo name has earned its reputation and association with quality and good temperament.

HONEYBEARS (Carol Stuckey)

Carol and Peter bought their first Newfoundland, a landseer dog called Monterosa Sir Julian, in 1978. Although purchased as a pet, he was mainly from Fairwater, Attimore and Harratons lines which also went back to good dogs from the well-known (and by then historic) Sparry, Suleskerry and Harlingen Kennels. A show was attempted and at only his second outing he won both his classes and the RCC! Needless to say, from then on Carol was bitten by the show bug.

Of the two bitches to follow, one was never shown or bred from due to severe hip dysplasia, while the other became the Stuckeys' first champion, namely Ch. Mapleopals Honeybear. Born in 1981, by Ch. Ursulas White Sails out of Ch. Mapleopals Sleepy Time Girl, Honeybear tragically died, shortly after gaining her title and before producing any progeny. In recognition of her 'special' status, the kennel was named after her.

The next bitch to come to Honeybears with the hope of becoming the foundation of the kennel was unfortunately diagnosed with Sub-Valvular Aortic Stenosis (SAS), and was not expected to live more than twelve months or so (although she actually lived to be seven years of age). By then, Carol was almost ready to give up showing Newfoundlands when she heard that Phyllis Colgan had a litter of puppies from Ch. Samson von Söven of Swanpool ex Karazan Goldbreeze. A bitch puppy was purchased and, as if to make up for all the previous heartache, Sophia was a flyer. Winning her first CC at fourteen months of age, she went on to become Ch. Karazan Sophia of Honeybears by the time she was seventeen months. Her twentieth and final CC was as a veteran at Crufts 1994, collecting on the way the title of Top Newfoundland in 1988 and Top Newfoundland Bitch in 1990. Sophia also proved herself as a brood bitch, producing several offspring who won major awards, the best-known being Ch. Honeybears Moondust who, on two occasions, won RBIS at Championship shows and is the only bitch to have reached this level at All Breed Championship events.

Carol has since introduced Pouch Cove bloodlines and is co-owner of the Ch. Karazan Love's a Risky Business, as well as breeder/owner of the young CC winner Honeybears Dream Boat. Honeybears is known mainly for blacks, but a young brown bitch has recently been retained. Carol and Peter's dogs number around twelve and include retired pets. All have access to the house with the older dogs enjoying permanent residency.

KARAZAN (Phyllis Colgan)
The Karazan name is surely known by Newfoundland breeders all over the world, not only for its top winning dogs but also for its owner's skilful handling and presentation.

Ch. Karazan Chocolate Buttons.

Photo: E. Gascoigne.

The numerous Karazan champions seen today come in all three colours, but Phyllis was first smitten by the eye-catching landseers. The two original bitches were this colour and the early Karazan breeding programme aimed for typey landseers, rather than simply well-marked dogs. Indeed, by following this trend, their first two champions were landseer, Ch. Shermead Fragrant Cloud of Karazan and her son, the homebred Ch. Karazan Bollinger (by Ch. Ursulas White Sails). Fragrant Cloud was also mated to Ch. and Irish Ch. Wellfont Admiral, with the resulting puppies taking the show ring by storm! Ch. Karazan Golddust of Wellfont won her first CC at only eight months of age, and went on to be the bitch record holder with 22 CCs, group placings and a BIS. Her brother, Ch. Karazan Goldigger, did not exactly hide his light under a bushel and notched up an impressive list of CCs himself.

A trip to Denmark saw the importation of the brown bitch puppy, La Bellas Abba of Karazan, along with a black male, Klondyke of Karazan – the first of several influential imports for the kennel and for other Newfoundland breeders. Klondyke produced a CC winner, but Abba, when mated to Admiral, became the dam of the first brown Karazan titleholder, Ch. Karazan Sweet Charity (as well as of other notable winners including NZ Ch. Karazan Hot Chocolate), and produced a CC or RCC winner in every litter. Another well-known Abba daughter was the Top Newfoundland 1991, Ch. Karazan Blackberry Blossom.

A Bollinger daughter mated to the German import, Ch. Samson von Söven of Swanpool, resulted in a good litter containing the excellent stud dog Ch. Karazan Rockafella (sire of Blossom and many other champions). Karazan Gold Breeze was also mated to Samson, resulting in three champions – two in the UK and a male, Solomon the Great, in New Zealand. One champion sister, Ch. Karazan Sophia of

Honeybears, came close to catching up Golddust and won 20 CCs – her last as a veteran at Crufts.

A more recent import to the kennel has been from Peggy Helming in the USA. Ch. Pouch Coves Repeat After Me At Karazan has been a great asset to the kennel and there is no denying that 'Peter' holds a special place in Phyllis's heart. She used him carefully, first on bitches from the Karazan line, and his puppies were unmistakeable and like peas in a pod! Those first youngsters are now proving themselves in the show ring, with Ch. Karazan Loves a Risky Business, Ch. Karazan Love On A Carousel and Ch. Karazan Loves a Class Act seated firmly in the upper house, while many more are CC or RCC winners. In the show ring, 'Peter' also won a Group 2nd at Crufts 1996 and the same year won a BIS at the Newfoundland Club Championship Show.

Not content with this obviously successful recipe, Phyllis and John have newly-imported dogs from Italy where the breed is flourishing in some strength. With over twenty champions, group winners and an almost yearly title of Top Breeders, the Karazan Kennel must be destined to remain a force to be reckoned with throughout the Colgans' lifetime.

KELLIGREWS (Pat and Stewart Woolmore)
Pat and Stewart owned their first Newfies in 1982 when they bought two black sisters from Barbara Turner (Baranova). Developing an interest in showing, they turned to Karl Schmitz's famous Von Söven Kennel in Germany and imported an adult bitch, Quanda von Söven.

Quanda was to have a great influence on the British show ring and went on to produce three champions from one litter, with further generations also producing champions and CC winners. Quanda herself won two CCs and four RCCs (the first award only four weeks after coming out of quarantine), while the daughter kept by the

Ch. Kelligrews Terre Neuve with Seaquaybear and litter sister Ch. Kelligrews Nyamza.

Woolmores, Ch. Kelligrews Nyamza, collected 6 CCs.

Another champion from the kennel, Ch. Kelligrews Eagle at Tidesoak, after winning his UK title, moved to the US with his owners, where he also enjoyed success in the show ring. Eagle's brief stud career in Britain had far-reaching effects, with champion descendants in Ireland and Canada. Another Kelligrews bitch won CCs for the Kubear Kennel, while Kelligrews Mecatina Vandalia (a CC winner) was kept by the Woolmores.

Although there have been five Kelligrews BIS winners (Open level), the Woolmores' proudest moment was when Ch. Kelligrews Terre Neuve with Seaquaybear won BIS at the Newfoundland Club Champions Show, with his mother, Quanda, winning Best Veteran Bitch at the same event. Breeding has been put on hold at the moment, but the seven or so black Newfoundlands continue to enjoy family life at Kelligrews.

LISKARN (Gordon Bridges)
The early Liskarn foundation bitches were mainly from the Harratons line, with some Littlegrange, Portadurn and Caladh influence. A Millthorpe-bred bitch followed later, but the lines today are based more on Karazan and Pouch Cove blood.

The Bridges family's first success in the show ring with a Newfoundland was with Harratons Black Turmoil who won 2 CCs. Although Turmoil did not gain his title, he

Ch. and Irish Ch. Liskarn Wanda.

proved a useful sire by producing the Ch. Harratons Black Algoma, a particularly sound and free-moving dog. Turmoil also threw CC winners to Harratons and Portadurn bitches – Liskarn Gamblers Chip and Liskarn Celebrity – the latter being extremely unlucky in amassing 6 RCCs at a time when the dog competition was fierce.

Turmoil's dam was a Canadian import, Morycis Omega of Harratons, a RCC winner who was later owned by the Bridges and gave them their first homebred champion, Ch. Liskarn Ashley (by Harratons Black Piper). In an earlier litter she also produced CC winners for the Sigroc and Regelsie Kennels while still in Mr Frost's ownership.

An interest in all three colours means that winning Liskarn stock are not restricted to black. Today, the upstanding landseer, Checkmate of Liskarn, can be seen in the ring, while earlier dogs like the RCC-winning, Liskarn Katy Did, carried the landseer gene. Liskarn Leroy Brown was the first of his colour to win RCCs for the kennel. Later, Gordon used the brown German import Seebar von Drachenfels by Yaffles on a half-Danish bitch to create another line of brown recessives. In this litter was the black Ch. and Irish Ch. Liskarn Wanda, who won exceptionally well during 1993 and won her last CC when nearly a veteran.

Another brown recessive was the American Ch. Schooner Aaron of Spillway at Liskarn, imported by Gordon. Aaron attained a CC and a RCC in the show ring and produced fresh bloodlines for the Liskarn Kennel and also for others, such as Wanitopa, Harratons and Coxbrook.

These days the handling is done by daughter Lisa (remembered by older exhibitors as a capable junior handler), who is developing a reputation for her skill and is sought-after at home and abroad by owners of other breeds as well as Newfoundlands.

The Liskarn Kennel is not limited to Newfoundlands and many would argue that involvement in other breeds prevents tunnel vision or acceptance of faults. In common with other progressive kennels, Liskarn often has promising youngsters about to make their debuts and likes to keep an eye on the future.

MERCHIEN
(Roy, David and Sarah Meakin)
Even those with the most sparse understanding of the French language could not fail to see why the Meakin family chose 'Merchien' as their kennel name. Not only is the name born out of the legendary feats of the Newfoundland, but a natural working instinct and steady temperament is equally important to the image of the breed at Merchien.

The family's first show winner, purchased in 1978 from Mike and Audrey Ludlow's Mapleopal Kennels, was Mapleopal Black Velvet. She was sired by the well-known Ch. Stormsail Matterhorn and won several RCCs.

Velvet was also their foundation bitch and, when mated to Shermead High Flyer, produced Ch. Merchien Sea Jewel (who in turn threw some excellent stock for the Nutbrook Kennel), and a RCC winner, Merchien Sea Princess. For her second litter, Velvet was put to Ch. Shermead Half as Lucky, resulting in Ch. Merchien Barney

Bear who, although he gained his title young, also collected a daunting 11 RCCs on the way!

The Meakin family has also successfully shown a landseer – Sea Rambler of Merchien – a RCC winner and a particularly eye-catching sound mover. Rambler's markings and overall type won him the Newfoundland Club's landseer trophy on many occasions.

In recent years, the Meakin family and their dogs have moved to France, but contact with British dogs will be maintained as Roy is an approved championship show judge in the UK. Once young stock have been established, Merchien dogs will also be seen in the French show ring.

MERRYBEAR
(Gordon Cutts and Patrick Galvin)
Merrybear is an affix which has become synonymous with show ring success, both in Britain and overseas. Nearly a quarter of a century has passed since the first Merrybear Newfoundland crossed the threshold. That first dog, Hambledown Seafarer, won 2 CCs and a Club BIS and set a trend that still exists today.

The first Merrybear champion – Camiyou, a brown – was a landmark, being the first brown bitch champion in the UK. She also broke new ground by being the first brown to win BoB at Crufts and at a Club Open show. Her RBIS at the Club Centenary show was also an historic occasion. She was sired by the one-time breed record holder, Ch. Wellfont Admiral, as was her younger brother, Ch. Merrybear Dunhill (brown). Her litter brother Merrybear Charlie Brown at Mixbury was also a CC winner.

Since then there have been other brown champions earning their titles for the Sheridel, Truesparta and Nutbrook Kennels with the latest brown, Ch. Merrybear Carrie, staying with Gordon and Patrick and winning Top Bitch in 1996.

The champion blacks have also made a name for themselves, the best-known

probably being the BIS-winning Ch. Merrybear Luigi (sire of Chs. Carrie, Q'pid and the CC-winning Penny Farthing and Chianti), a giant of a dog whose exuberant showmanship was well-known around the ringsides. His dam, Ch. Wellfont Natashquan Nakina of Merrybear, was one of three Wellfont champions who won well for the kennel. Merrybear dogs have also gained their titles in other countries, with two Australian and one New Zealand champion to date.

New bloodlines are important to the kennel and an early importation was of the brown bitch Valborg of Merrybear (first brown to win BoB at Championship level). She also became the dam of three Merrybear champions. Latter-day imports, also from Denmark, were the black brother and sister Ch. Newfhouse Scandinavian Warrior for Merrybear (Top Newfoundland 1995, 1996 and a consistent Group Winner) and Ch. Newfhouse Scandinavian Princess for Merrybear, who was runner-up to her brother in 1995. Both have produced well for Merrybear, with several top winning youngsters now making their mark. Another two imports from Manlio Massa's Cayuga Kennel in Italy will also be shown in due course.

Despite its great success, the Merrybear Kennel is not a commercial breeding venture and retired 'oldies' can be found living out their days in the lap of luxury. Both partners are championship show judges both in the UK and abroad, and their cautious optimism is shared with fellow exhibitors, judges and pet owners alike. The Newfoundland is renowned for its dignity, sensitivity and strength – all attributes which could be applied to the Merrybear partnership.

MILLTHORPE (Anne Springthorpe)
Anne's first Newfoundland was bought in 1980 as a pet from the well-known Harratons kennels. When the puppy was around ten months old, Anne decided to

Millthorpe Noble Fir.   Photo: Bull.

attend a few shows and the following year Harratons Lady Olivia won the first RCC for the Millthorpe kennel. The earlier years were confined to mainly white and black dogs, Anne's first love. She was successful with the CC-winning import, Joey van Bellandseer at Harraton, and also the particularly well-marked Harratons Sea Christobelle, who probably won every award possible for a landseer. Anne felt that the future of landseers in the show ring was somewhat limited at that time and began to concentrate on the blacks instead. Concentrating on the black Harratons and Karazan lines worked well, with CC-winning dogs such as Thomas Tank, Santa Rosa and Noble Fir being produced. Browns were also bred, with one in particular, Ch. Chocolate Sundae of Karazan, winning Joint Top Bitch in her best year.

More recent matings have been to the Danish imports, Chs. Topsy's Oliver Twist and Offenbach, with RCC winning offspring. Pouch Cove breeding has also been introduced via the Karazan Kennel and some promising youngsters are likely to make their show ring debut. As well as 'Joey', Anne has owned other imports. Both were from the US – the black bitch Riptides Miss England for Millthorpe (dam of Sundae and Rosa) and the brown male Ebontides

Atlantic Crossing at Millthorpe (son of Am. Ch. Kendian Cadbury). Despite the judicious collating of bloodlines, Millthorpe dogs are primarily family pets and include veterans who are retired from showing.

NUTBROOK (Anne Merrick)
Nutbrook Newfoundlands was founded as a small, select kennel in 1978. The name was officially registered as an affix in 1984 when the black Newfoundland bitch, Tranquil Waters, earned the affix at her first Championship show. (This system has now been changed in the UK.) Tranquil was from the very first litter and was by La Bellas Winston, who was imported from Denmark in 1982 specifically to be mated to her dam, Ch. Merchien Sea Jewel. A littermate, Nutbrook Thomas Telford, was Best Puppy in Show at the Working Breeds of Wales Championship Show. Winston continued his success story by winning *Our Dogs* Top Stud dog 1986, having along the way sired Ch. Nutbrook Navigator of Karatarn, the CC winners Nutbrook Chalico and Nutbrook Cressy, and the RCC-winning Nutbrook Miller Mundy and Nutbrook Kit Crewbucket, all from Ch. Stormsail Maumee of Swanpool.

Nutbrook Chalico and Ch. Stormsail Maumee of Swanpool – two of the senior residents at Nutbrook.

Photo: John Hartley.

A litter by a La Bellas Winston son, Shermead Argy Bargee for Nutbrook JW (CC and RCC winner, *Our Dogs* Top Puppy 1986 and Newfoundland Club Top Puppy 1986), to Champion Merchien Sea Jewel produced Nutbrook Willow Wren JW, *Our Dogs* and Newfoundland Club Top Puppy 1987.

Further generations of Nutbrook breeding produced a consistent stream of Junior Warrant, Stud Book and Top Puppy winners, as well as Ch. Nutbrook Dudley Tunnel and NZ Ch. Nutbrook Montgomery Canal.

Following a break from showing and breeding, during which time Anne concentrated on judging Newfoundlands at championship shows both at home and abroad, another Winston son, Bouderee Romani Rokra of Nutbrook, was mated to Ch. Merrybear Q'pid of Truespata. A brown bitch was taken in lieu of stud fee. She went on to win her 3rd CC at Crufts 1996, becoming Ch. Merrybear Ariadne Nutbrook who is, together with her littermate Merrybear Armanie Nutbrook, the new foundation bitch for Nutbrook – the Nutbrook line having been continued through the male line to this point.

Having judged the Danish Newfoundland Club Show, the 'Gold Cup', in 1994, Anne imported a black bitch, Braendegardens Streethay Nutbrook, who won her class at Crufts 1996. Also imported at the same time was New-Fuur-Lands Russell Newbery Nutbrook (Int. Ch. New-Fuur-Lands Blockbuster x Int. Ch. Biserka vom Riesrand). This male is already a CC and RCC winner, as well as winning RBISs at Club shows and Best Puppy in Show at the Newfoundland Club Championship Show.

Nutbrook is currently in partnership with Cayuga Newfoundlands of Italy, campaigning a Canadian-bred landseer male, Hollibrooke Maverick St. Cayuga, who is certain to hold great promise for the future, together with the other youngsters.

Ch. Kelligrews Terre Neuve With Seaquaybear: A winner in the UK and in Germany.
Photo: Gascoigne.

SEAQUAYBEAR
(Richard and Valerie Scothern)
Val and Richard were living in Germany when they first became interested in the breed in the late 1970s. Several visits to shows introduced them to the famous Ferro von Söven. When Ferro was mated to Golda von Söven, the Scotherns were fortunate to own one of the resulting puppies – Quay von Söven.

A few years later, the Scotherns returned to Britain with Quay and began to show him at Championship Shows. Quay not only gained his title (the first German import to do so) but also became a successful, though selectively used, stud dog. His best-known litter was to Attimore Crows Nest of Mapleopal, owned by the Startrek Kennel, which produced five champions. Further champions were produced for the Kelligrews and Stormsail Kennels, with a further CC winner for the Karazan Kennel. Having appreciated the benefits of the von Söven line to improve coats and hips within the breed, the Scotherns bought in another male of similar breeding – Kelligrews Terre Neuve With Seaquaybear (Ch. Samson von Söven of Swanpool x Quanda von Söven) – and he too gained his UK title, as well as BIS, at the Newfoundland Club show. As a result of work commitments, the Scotherns again returned to Germany where they also showed both dogs to a BIS win at Braunschweig (Quay) and CAC, CACIB and Res VDH awards (Terre Neuve) – putting them in a unique position as British exhibitors. A final return to Britain heralded the first Seaquaybear litter from Kelligrews Catalina with Seaquaybear, from which a young RCC-winning male was kept (prior to this, they also owned Ch. Wellfont Natashquan Nakina before she was transferred to the Merrybear Kennel).

Other young stock at Seaquaybear currently include two offspring of the Danish Import Ch. Topsy's Offenbach (out of a daughter of Terre Neuve) and one already has a RCC to her credit. Val and Richard prefer black Newfoundlands, but dream of owning a glamorous white and black in the future.

SHERIDEL (Hedd and Del Richards)
After spending the latter part of the 1970s researching the most successful breeders, we bought our first Newfoundland, a landseer bitch, from the Mapleopal Kennel of Mike and Audrey Ludlow. Mapleopal Sea Maiden was a great family companion with a wonderful temperament and we were captivated by the breed. She gave us a good start in the Newfoundland show ring, winning a Best Puppy in Breed and, later, a RCC. Sadly, she died young before producing any progeny.

In the meantime, our Newfoundland population had increased with another bitch of similar breeding and a young, unregistered, rescued bitch. (We have never been without a 'rescue' since.)

A turning point came in 1984 when we bought a male puppy from Graham and Sue Birch (Wellfont). He became Ch. Wellfont Macillon and won Top Male in 1988, as well

as Top Stud several years in succession – siring eight UK Champions.

Later, we acquired the Danish import bitch, Wooddales Louise of Wellfont, who, together with Macillon, was the making of the Sheridel line. Their first litter together was the kind that all breeders dream of. The five puppies who were shown all won CCs – Carizma with 2 CCs and Captivation with one CC – but the three males all became champions. Ch. Sheridel Crakerjak also gained his Canadian title when his owners moved out there; Ch. Sheridel Chieftain stayed in the UK; Ch. and Irish Ch. Sheridel Crawford became a legend by winning 39 CCs, Groups and BISs, together with every award possible for a Newfoundland. He is still the breed record holder today.

We later repeated this mating to produce our Ch. Sheridel Elouisa of Swanpool. Following wins by the 'C' and 'E' litter, Louise won Top Brood Bitch All Breeds and we won Top Breeders. (Louise was also in the Top Ten the following year.)

Keeping breeding to a minimum meant that we often campaigned Newfies bred by someone else but sired by Sheridel stud dogs. Macillon sired our Ch. Krystalcove Kouros of Sheridel, who was himself the sire of our Ch. Dingro Enchantress of Sheridel (daughter of Captivation and Joint Top Bitch 1994). Macillon also sired the dual CC winner, Leumasleiloc Limara of Sheridel (a litter which contained two other major award winners), and the RCC-winning Honeybears Babbling Book of Sheridel.

The only brown so far, Ch. Merrybear Jennah of Sheridel, was bought in but was related to Macillon through her dam. A Crawford son, Beauberry Biggles of Sheridel, became a CC winner and, when mated to Limara, produced the 'I' litter containing Ch. Sheridel Inxess of Sealake and Sheridel Imagination of Abbeydore, a RCC winner, though all are very young at the time of writing.

An addition to the kennel, whom we

Ch. Sheridel Chieftain.   *Photo: John Hartley.*

consider the best dog we have ever owned, is Ch. Ceilidh Auchentoshan of Sheridel. A Macillon grandson (out of Kouros' sister), he is by Ch. Topsy's Offenbach and is a combination of some excellent Danish lines.

Health issues are very important to us, so all breeding stock is rigorously checked for hereditary defects, especially hearts. To date, dogs owned or bred by Sheridel have won a total of 85 CCs.

SHERMEAD (Val Adey)

One of the more senior, active kennels in Britain, the first Shermead litter was born in 1967. The earliest stock was founded on Sparry and Storytime lines, using champion dogs from the Sigroc and Littlegrange kennels. The kennel was dedicated to producing both black and landseer dogs of type and excellent temperament but, using combinations of the breeding stock, it produced the first two brown puppies born in the UK post-war. Shermead Brown Beauty features in all the brown pedigrees up to the present. Despite being classed as an 'older' kennel, Val has resisted the temptation to remain in a breeding time-warp and has introduced fresh lines by way of her own imports and those owned by other kennels.

Shermead Bijou of the Thatched Roof, who won 2 RCCs, came from Holland and

Shermead Jelly Baby.   *Photo: Derek Whitehouse.*

was a daughter of Shermead Lively Lad who himself won Best Dog at a World Championship. Lancelot of Shermead was imported from Finland, producing several champions, while La Bellas Quark and La Bellas Mischa came from Denmark. Quark won a RCC and sired Ch. Nutbrook Dudley Tunnel who is still winning CCs as a veteran. Recently Naristo's Aeneas from Norway and Shermead Chablis D'Empyree from Holland have joined Shermead.

Over the years the Shermead kennel has produced champions in all three colours. Ch. Shermead Fernando was the first post-war landseer dog champion and the landseer Ch. Shermead Fragrant Cloud of Karazan produced several champions for the Karazan kennel. The brown Ch. Shermead Coco Chanelle of Karazan was top winning brood bitch in 1996. Her sister, Shermead Zippyda Dooda, has produced excellent brown progeny at the Shermead kennels in France and both are fine examples of this colour. Ch. Shermead Half as Lucky was an illustrious sire, producing Ch. Laphroaig

Islay Mistress and Ch. Merchien Barney Bear along with several CC and RCC winners. Ch. Shermead Nuts in May was the dam of dual CC winner Shermead Argy Bargee for Nutbrook – himself the sire of Ch. Merrybear Luigi.

Today Shermead Newfoundlands can still be seen in the show ring. Ch. Shermead Mudlark is in the prime of her career, while in her day Shermead Fleur won the Bitch CC at Crufts 1995 and Shermead Fortune Cookie (also winner of 2 CCs, and Fleur's litter sister) won the Veteran Class. Fleur's sons Shermead Kadarka and Shermead Kess are successfully shown and their progeny can be seen in the ring.

Listing all the top winning Shermead dogs would be a time-consuming task and Val and her husband John (both championship show judges), are more concerned with looking to the future, to obtaining new bloodlines and to preserving the type and temperament so essential to a Newfoundland. To this end Val has merged her kennel in England with the Muscadine kennel of David and Heather Butcher, while Val and John's daughter Sharon is successfully breeding at the Shermead kennel in France. Val aims to continue producing Newfoundlands of the distinctive Shermead type.

STARTREK (Gill Barker)
The first Startrek Newfoundland, a pet landseer bitch, was chronically dysplastic, with the result that good health became a priority in Gill's breeding programme.

Startrek dogs are not numerically great as only a few litters have been bred. These have been tremendously successful, however, with the first litter producing a total of three UK and two Irish Champions, a Group Winner and one Crufts Group Finalist. Ten of the twelve littermates gained either CCs or Stud Book wins and also went on to produce well in the next generation. Ch. Little Kodiak Bear of Trinityfair produced three champions for the Trinityfair kennel and was herself Top

Members of Startrek's first litter: Ch. Startrek Trek To The Stars, Startrek Calamity Jane, Ch. Little Kodiak Bear of Trinityfair and Ch. Startrek Captain James Kirk.

Brood Bitch in 1993. Ch. Startrek Trek to the Stars sired the Irish Annual Champion Culnor Starshine Duglad on Startrek (himself a useful sire) and the landseer Marshill Davos. Startrek Calamity Jane had only one litter (to Ch. Kelligrews Carbonear of Trinityfair) which contained the Irish Ch. Startrek Uhuras Song at Riverbears and the CC winner Startrek Beam Me Up Scotty who himself produced some top winning Swanpool puppies.

Startrek Tribble Trouble, when mated to Ch. Merrybear Luigi, produced a litter of part landseers including the RCC winning Joalta Silver Skydragon. In Ireland the two original champions, Jefferson Starship and Midnight Cowboy, are now having an influence on a third generation of winners.

The combination of the von Söven line with the old Mapleopal strain appears to have worked well and Gill is particularly pleased with the landseers that are now being produced. Startrek dogs are not just pretty faces, as a few are also successful at waterwork and carting.

Gill is extremely careful when choosing homes for her puppies and rightly demands a contact with them throughout their lives. She is forthright in condemning over-breeding and over-use of stud dogs, and hopes that Startrek will be remembered for its quality not quantity.

STORMSAIL (Peter and Judy Oriani) With nearly thirty years of Newfoundland ownership, the Stormsail Kennel must be one of the most consistently successful in Britain. The Orianis' first dog, bought as a pet from Esther Denham (Attimore), demonstrated a great working instinct and won the Water Trials on two occasions. In 1972 came their first show dog in Ch. Bachalaos Bright Water of Stormsail who was also a group finalist. As a brood bitch, she was excellent, with five champions (three UK and two New Zealand) coming from one

Ch. Stormsail Mattherhorn JW (left) and Ch. Stormsail Wetterhorn JW – the first two homebred Champions of the Stormsail kennel.

litter.

Since then there have been twelve homebred Stormsail champions, with four of them winning BIS or RBIS at Club Championship Shows. Many Stormsail dogs gained their titles or CCs for the Arktikos, Ashness, Kubear, Nutbrook, Swanpool, Ursas and Wellfont kennels while others won well for novice owners – a true measure of quality dogs.

The Orianis have traditionally been known for their black and landseer line (the RCC winning Stormsail Sacred Spirit won Best Landseer at six Club Shows), but a recent addition is a brown from the Cumngo Kennel. Peter and Judy are quick to give assurances that brown and landseer lines will not be bred together.

The Stormsail kennel usually consists of fewer than thirteen dogs, both sexes, who all live in the house. Breeding is done only to maintain the lines and to retain a puppy. Health issues are most important to the Orianis and it is possible to read an eight-generation hip-scored pedigree of most of the present-day Stormsail dogs. The kennel has recently begun elbow-scoring and heart-testing with all results, as with hip-scoring, made public. To date there have been fourteen champions, ten CC winners and seven other RCC winners from this kennel.

STORYTIME (Douglas and Barbara Henry) Storytime has been registered under the name Henry since 1955. In those days it was Poodles – Toy, Miniature and Standard – and children! In the evening both children and dogs gathered for 'storytime', hence the name. The Henrys have also bred and shown English Toy Terriers and French Bulldogs, with Afghans as pets. In whatever breed they were involved, temperament and soundness were the two major factors and in 1957 they bought their first Newfoundland. The first puppy was not a show dog, but an excellent brood and within two generations came success at shows. As two of the few members of the Newfoundland Club, they put much thought into the breeding, not necessarily going for winning dogs, but breeding with care, hoping to choose the correct lines of genes to produce the perfect Newfie.

The couple had their first Champion, Storytime Whaler, in 1965 but never used him at stud. Ch. Storytime Black Pearl of Esmeduna (1967) together with Storytime Figurehead (CC), made up the basis of a very successful breeding programme for Colin and Jean Whittaker, producing many champions throughout the 1960s, 1970s and 1980s. Storytime Cachelot (Whaler's brother) went to Denmark, siring the first two Danish Champions. Two landseers went to the USA where they made a mark on the breed. In the 1960s the Henrys also sent puppies to Australia, New Zealand and South Africa. Since the 1970s, with other commitments, they have bred and shown less. Although all their males have won into the Kennel Club Stud Book, they have not

The Storytime kennel has been active for nearly 40 years.

made up a modern UK champion. In spite of this fact, in the last fifteen years they have won 4 CCs and 8 RCCs. In 1993 they sent Storytime Knot to Italy, where he quickly became a Junior CACIB winner. He has sired many quality puppies including landseers, one of whom is now winning at top level.

Storytime still goes first for temperament and soundness, not necessarily breeding from champions, but from those whose pedigrees look as if their genes will agree. The Standard is the measure when breeding, and all dogs are hip-scored and heart-tested. They endeavour to breed dogs that look like males and bitches who are pretty. The Henrys feel the expression in the Newfie tells you everything about the dog and is all-important. These dogs should look as if they can pull a cart, work in water and join all family outings. The very occasional litters are reared with the greatest care and personal attention.

SWANPOOL (Delia Sarson)
The first Swanpool Newfoundland was bought in 1974 as a pet and several show-winning companions followed. These were mainly male dogs and the first Swanpool litter was not born until 1990 – a far cry from those who plan their first litter before their puppy has received its inoculations! Delia's first major success was with the black Hambledown Flagship who won his Junior Warrant along with 2 CCs under respected breed judges and all-rounders.

In 1982 Delia imported from the well-known von Söven Kennel in Germany, a male puppy, 'Samson'. He became Ch. Samson von Söven of Swanpool, winning BIS and RBISs at Club shows and Top Winning Newfoundland in 1987. It was as a sire, however, that Samson really made his mark: he was Top Sire in 1987, 1988 and 1990, siring a total of nine UK Champions – a record by present-day standards. He also sired an Australian and New Zealand

Swanpool Sweet Shakira.

Champion as well as many other UK CC winners. Samson was particularly effective in improving hip scores and passed on his excellent bone, coat and most importantly his wonderful temperament.

In 1987 Delia bought in the bitch Sheridel Carizma of Swanpool who was related to Samson through the Ferro line. She won 2 CCs, a Club BIS and is the dam of SA Ch. Swanpool the Great Marquess of Mileoak (Top Dog All Breeds in South Africa 1992). Another littermate, Sassonia (by Bouderee Romani Rokra of Nutbrook), was eventually mated back to her grandfather, Ch. Wellfont Macillon, to produce the brown bitch Swanpool Sweet Shakira (Best Brown Bitch Club Open Show 1995).

Today, the Swanpool Kennel consists of a select few black and brown bitches who all live as house pets and include the daughter of the Danish import New-Fuur-Lands Russell Newbery Nutbrook.

TRINITYFAIR (Lindsay May)
After marriage and giving up her career, Lindsay decided to add to her canine family of one much-loved Border Collie. Her husband wanted a Dobermann and she wanted a Jack Russell, so a compromise was reached – a Newfoundland. A common denominator would have been difficult to find!

In May 1985 they chose a bitch from Gill Barker's litter by Ch. Quay von Söven Imp. x Attimore Crows Nest of Mapleopal. They

Ch. Trinityfair Cap'n Carebear: One of only three dogs to win BIS at an all-breeds Championship show in the UK.

Photo: Trafford.

called the puppy Trinity (Ch. Little Kodiak Bear of Trinityfair) after Trinityfair, a lovely big black horse owned by Lindsay – hence the affix.

They quickly became besotted with the breed and, after much success showing Trinity, decided to look for another puppy, a male, who could be linebred to Trinity. Fortunately the Woolmores were mating the imports Quanda von Söven and Ch. Samson von Söven, so the Mays became the proud owners of Barnaby – Ch. Kelligrews Carbonear of Trinityfair.

In 1987 they were delighted to welcome into their home, at the age of eighteen months, Adi – Ch. Startrek Captain James Kirk. He was a Championship Show Group Winner, RBIS Newfoundland Club Championship Show and Multiple Open Show BIS winner.

In 1988 Trinity and Barnaby produced Bear (Ch. Trinityfair Cap'n Carebear). He more than fulfilled the couple's dreams by winning many Open show BISs and gaining his Junior Warrant. At Championship level, he won a Reserve Group, a Group and BIS at Leicester City Championship Show 1992 and ended that year as Top Male Newfoundland. He was also a Pro Dogs and

Contest of Champions finalist. Two bitches out of this same litter were shown and received RCCs.

After gaining her title Trinity's second litter produced two Champions – one being Ch. Trinityfair Qualitayre with Ursas JW, who was Joint Top Winning Bitch in 1993, RBIS Newfoundland Club Championship Show, and Top Scottish Show Dog of the Year finalist, prior to her tragic death at three years of age. The other was Ch. Trinityfair Shooting Star, the first landseer champion in seven years, who is now the only living landseer champion in Great Britain. Two of his major wins were Best Opposite Sex and BIS at Club Shows. Another brother was Trinityfair Northern Dancer, 1 CC and 4 RCCs, one of which was gained at Crufts.

Through the combined winnings of Carebear and the above dogs the Mays were lucky enough to be Top Breeders in 1993, also making Trinity Top Brood Bitch 1993. They now have a second, a third and a fourth generation down from their original three Newfs, including Trinityfair Spinning Jenny (2 CCs to date) and her daughters, Trinityfair Lady Inga (1 CC) and Trinityfair Valdisaire who qualified for Pup of the Year at seven months, finishing in the top ten in the annual final. Black is their main colour, but they have a landseer male, Trinityfair Dynamo Domi, and a big brown youngster, Trinityfair Border Piper, who is already enjoying success in the ring. All their breeding stock have very creditable hip scores. Trinityfair is not a large kennel, only breeding to continue their lines. Their dogs are pets who live mainly in the house. They are all hip-scored and heart-tested and the Mays encourage all their puppy owners to do the same. They do not actively take dogs to water events, but on the one occasion that they did, Barnaby and Trinity passed the first two water tests at the age of seven years, without any training. One of Carebear's sons, Fhirabhata Tumble Brutus, has proved himself in obedience, water and carting tests.

WANITOPA (Juliet Leicester-Hope)
Juliet's Wanitopa kennel is another of the more senior kennels still active today. Her first Newfoundland in 1961, Ch. Bonnybay Jasmine, was a great representative of the breed, earning her title and winning the first Water Trials in 1964. She was the foundation of the kennel and headed the nine generation mother-to-daughter line which exists today.

The name 'Wanitopa' is a North American Indian word meaning 'sunlight over the water' and, with such connections, it will be no surprise to learn that Juliet has also owned and shown Newfoundlands in the USA, as well as in Australia.

There have been Wanitopa champions of all three colours, with Ch. Wanitopa Bistow of Wellfont being the first brown champion in the UK. Bistow also won his title in Ireland and Norway. (Wanitopa Pure Delight, Bistow's dam, was a brown and white and, while her colour was considered untypical, her overall construction, coat and type were certainly not – as she proved when she passed many of her qualities on to her son!)

Prior to breeding Bistow, Juliet had also owned Attimore Ketch, the first brown to win a CC in the UK. Also of note were the landseer champions Wanitopa Moonlight and the much-travelled and multi-titled Wanitopa Comedy who accompanied Juliet across the continents.

Among the champion blacks were Wanitopa Trudy, who won BoB at Crufts, and Wanitopa Wayward Wind of Laphroaig who was successful for Kay Gibson's kennel. Also winning Australian titles were Wanitopa Bosun Boy and Wanitopa Gentle Giant (who also won a CC in the UK).

As is to be expected from someone who has seen quality dogs in other countries, Juliet imported several dogs to Britain. Jasmine and Comedy returned home with her, but further imports were Edenglen's Born Free (USA) with Shadfields Rutherford

Wanitopa Madam Butterfly: A RCC winner at nine months.   *Photo: Alan V. Walker.*

House and Dory O's Harbour Grace, both from Canada. More recently, Juliet has imported, in joint ownership, a landseer bitch from Italy, and the resulting combination of old and new lines is eagerly awaited by this experienced breeder.

WELLFONT (Graham and Sue Birch)
Graham and Sue Birch started in Newfoundlands in 1976 with two bitches from the Mapleopal Kennel. Mapleopal Who Loves Ya Baby and Mapleopal Snow Boots were both shown with moderate success. In 1978 the couple imported a brown male, La Bellas Ibrahim, from Denmark. Who Loves Ya Baby (Lucy) had two litters to him. In Lucy's first litter were eight puppies – four of which became UK champions – a record for champions in one litter which still stands today. Ch. Wellfont Ambassador then went on to win his Australian and New Zealand titles when he went to live there. Also in the litter were Ch. Wellfont Amanda and Ch. Wellfont Angie.

The most well-known member of the 'A' litter was Ch. and Irish Ch. Wellfont Admiral with 26 CCs; he achieved many successes and surpassed the long-standing record of seventy years for the number of CCs won. His first CC and BoB was at eight and a half months old, his second CC, at Crufts, was gained at ten months and his title followed

Ch. Wellfont Napoleon: The first Newfoundland to win BIS at an all-breeds Championship Show in the UK.

shortly when he was only thirteen months old. He was Top Newfoundland for 1980, 1981 and 1982 and won BIS at the St. Patrick's Day Championship Show, as well as many Group wins in the UK and Ireland. In addition to his success in the show ring he also sired a number of top-winning and champion progeny.

The title of Top Newfoundland was won by Wellfont Kennels from 1980 to 1986 with an incredible five different Newfies:
1983 was Ch. Karazan Golddust of Wellfont (an Admiral daughter)
1984 was Ch. Irish and Nor. Ch. Wanitopa Bistow of Wellfont (son of Ambassador and first brown Champion in the UK)
1985 was the turn of Ch. Int. and Dk. Ch. Ursulas Admiral Ascot
1986 saw Ch. Wellfont Napoleon (another Admiral son) win the award. Napoleon also became the first Newfoundland to win BIS at an All Breeds Championship show in the

UK. Wellfont Newfoundlands imported several dogs and bitches who were very successful both in the show ring and as breeding stock. Many came from the famous Ursulas Kennel of Brigitte Gothen. Ursulas Brigitte, Figaro, White Sails (landseer) and Admiral Ascot all won their titles, while Ursulas Renata produced several champions, the most notable being Napoleon. Also from Denmark came the bitch Wooddales Louise, another outstanding brood bitch and the dam of five UK Champions. Most of these dogs and bitches are behind many of the top winning dogs of today. Wellfont kennels, while not actively breeding in the UK now, will be remembered for the impact made in the show ring with the results of combining the best of English bloodlines with the prime of Danish breeding.

BEST OF THE REST
To breed a champion in your first litter is quite an achievement and speaks volumes for the research that went into planning the mating. To progress from there by continuing a successful breeding programme without keeping large numbers of dogs is even more commendable. Examples of such skilful breeders are the Downes family (BEAUBERRY) who, from Wellfont lines, produced Ch. Beauberry Shimona and, from her, CC and RCC winning stock; Christine Griffiths (CASAVERDE) now living in Eire, who, prior to moving, made up the top winning Ch. Casaverde Aphrodite, as well as achieving success with her littermates and,

Ch. Casaverde Aphrodite.
Photo; John Hartley.

Ch. Kubear Flamenco.

Ch. Topsy's Offenbach. Photo: Soren Wesseltoft.

later on, her progeny and grandchildren who are winners of Res Green Stars in Ireland; Shonagh Cruikshanks (DANABJORN), who is not a breeder, but whose valuable imports from Denmark not only won titles and group placing for themselves, but also contributed greatly to many other UK kennels – a further four Danish imports contain a wealth of bloodlines which may prove equally important for future generations; David and Maxine Munday (KUBEAR), breeders of Ch. Kubear Flamenco – only one of three top winners in their first litter from their champion bitch – and of very promising youngsters from a third generation; John and Gloria Burrows (MAYOSS), breeders of Ch. Cinderelli of

Karazan, who have also had success with similarly-bred dogs. Linda Sussams (SEALCOVE), a championship show judge who has been involved in the breed since the 1970s, but who resisted the temptation to breed puppies until 1990 when Ch. Sealcove Crystal was born (from a combination of Stormsail and Karazan bloodlines) and whose young stock are already winning RCCs; and Gary and Ann Coldwell (ZENTAUR) whose CC-winning Karazan Whisper produced Ch. Zentaur Hot Gossip (in a litter which contained other CC and RCC winners), as well as making a contribution in the shape of other young RCC winners.

Beauberry Biggles of Sheridel.

Photo: Dave Freeman.

11 NEWFOUNDLANDS IN NORTH AMERICA

The status of the Newfoundland in the USA is undoubtedly at a peak as far as quality is concerned. The professionalism and pride displayed by so many breeders and exhibitors is often envied in other nations. Despite the proficient image of US breeders, few are commercially-minded and the betterment of the breed remains an enjoyable hobby.

Some 2500 puppies are registered annually with the AKC, making the Newfoundland a moderately popular breed (there are some unregistered puppies produced, but the AKC has no details of their numbers). The AKC is active in promoting dog ownership, and produces a number of brochures which answer an owner's queries, be they connected with breeding, showing, judging, training or many other specialised topics. The showing brochure describes the difference between Matches, All Breed Shows and Specialties, and highlights how a dog can win the necessary 15 points to become a champion.

Newfoundland clubs number more than twenty, and cover the whole country. The most eminent US club is the Newfoundland Club of America, which has more than 1200 members. The NCA runs the National Specialty – an event which attracts as many as 700 dogs and exhibitors from the USA,

Canada and overseas. As a result of such high entries, the NCA has devised a system of awarding 'Select' honours to those dogs and bitches worthy of special recognition. Up to five dogs and five bitches can be given this award after BOB has been presented. In 1985 the NCA also adopted a Register of Merit (ROM) system to recognise a few dogs and bitches who have proven themselves to be exceptional producers of champions, working dogs and ROMs.

The NCA also regulates working events such as water work, draft tests and tracking tests. Furthermore, a Health and Longevity Committee exists, to record information and advise when health issues need to be tackled.

Many US Newfoundlands have long and mysterious lists of letters before and after their names, so there follows a list of their meanings which new owners may find helpful:

VN – Versatile Newfoundland. To earn this award the dog must win his AKC Championship (Ch.), his WRD (NCA Water Rescue Dog), CD (AKC Companion Dog), and DD (AKC Draft Dog) titles. Additional titles are TDD (NCA Team Draft Dog), TDI (Therapy Dog Int.), CGC (Canine Good Citizen), TT (Temperament Tested), T (Tracking), UD (Utility Dog), and OTCH (Obedience Trial Champion).

Since the National Specialty became an independent event in 1967, some exceptional dogs have won BOB on more than one occasion. Such dogs include VN Ch. Shiprock Legacy Wheeler Dealer (owned by Linda Morley and Vicki Wakefield), who won two years in a row and created a precedent by being the first Specialty BOB winner to have his VN title. Coincidentally, in both those years, his BOS was the bitch Ch. Cypress Bay Can Do Cassandra.

An earlier success story was Am. Can. Ch. Edenglen's Banner, taking the award in 1967 and 1968. Banner was only one of many Specialty BOB or BOS-winning dogs from this kennel.

Another double Specialty winner was Am. Can. Ch. Seaward's Blackbeard, who not only took the award in 1982 and 1984, but created Newfoundland history by being the only one of his breed to win BIS at Westminster under the guidance of his handler Gerlinde Hockla.

Today's numerous Newfie breeders are successful in the show ring and the working arena, as well as having to overcome hurdles peculiar to the region in which they live. Many have helped to produce books and training manuals, while others actively participate in arranging the special events so beloved of Newfie owners. The rest of this chapter consists of a look at today's top kennels. Space does not allow the inclusion of many breeders and owners who deserve a place in the archives, but a very brief list would include: Connie Allison (ALLISON ACRES), Ken and Dallas Anderson (DALKEN), Lisa Allen and David Van Couvering (WHISPERBAY), Mr and Mrs David Barber (BARHARBER), Joan Bendure (BENHIL), Mr and Mrs Tom Broderick (AMITY), Barbara Finch (TUCKAMORE), Christine Griffiths-Grey (SKIPJACK), Hannah Hayman, Suzanne Jones (MOONCUSSER), Dr and Mrs Krokum (SHADYBROOK), Mary Price

(PADDLEWHEEL), Brenda and Rick Santiago (MUDDY CREEK), Alana Shirley (BRITANNIA), Elizabeth Stackhouse (STEAMBOAT), Penelope Stuckey (PEPPERTREE), and Mr and Mrs Dwight Summers (SKIMEISTER).

LEADING KENNELS IN THE USA

CALIFORNIA

EBONTIDE (Janice Kiseskey Anderson) Ebontide was established in 1980 by Janice after she had lived with Newfoundlands for almost a decade. She decided to become involved with the breed as more than just an owner and admirer. The dogs that Janice utilised to establish Ebontide are of Edenglen and Riptide lines. She liked the type and soundness of these magnificent animals. Health and longevity were also key concerns. These lines became the foundation of the kennel and throughout the years have given Ebontide everything that was expected, and more. Combined with some of the best lines in the country, they continue to add to the beauty, health and working ability of her dogs.

Janice has been careful and deliberate in planning her breeding programme. A commitment was made early on to produce quality, not quantity. Every litter is very carefully planned and, not being numerous, each maintains the best qualities within the breed. She has had success breeding both black and bronze Newfoundlands.

In the late 1970s, Janice began working in obedience with Newfoundlands owned by her family. She obtained her first title with Edenglen's Sea Mist CD, and continued to work in obedience but was intrigued by the conformation ring. In 1978, Janice obtained a Newfoundland who was co-owned by the Riptide kennel. From 'Stella's' eventual litter came two puppies that would be the start of Ebontide, Riptide's Kamakazi Kid ('KK') and Heather.

BISS Am. Ch. Pooh Bear's Stormalong,
still rated as one of the top ten producers
in the US.   *Photo: Rubin.*

BISS Am. Ch. Pooh Bear's Katie.

The Newfoundland Club of America National Specialty in 1990 was the first time Janice entered the conformation ring. It proved a thrilling experience, being placed with Kalanu's Stella of Lifebuoy and winning with 'KK' in Puppy Sweepstakes. These were the first of many dogs which would go on to obtain American and foreign championships. Janice, with the help and support of her husband Peter, has bred and shown many Newfoundlands to their championships, including working and foreign titles. She has also shown for others throughout the western states.

The exceptional qualities of Ebontide dogs have been proven in the ring, time and again. Specialty and Group Winners, plus working and Versatility titled dogs and a Number 1 Newf are among Ebontide's honour roll. Space does not allow a list of all Janice's successful dogs, but over the years their winnings have brought Janice many awards, including Top Producing Kennel, Top Breeder, Top Producing Stud Dog, Top Producing Brood Bitch and several achievement awards for the quality of her dogs, her own talents and dedication to the breed.

Janice has also judged Newfoundlands at Match and Specialty level and is applying for her judge's licence. Although a successful breeder herself, Janice still seeks input from Grant and Virginia Hoag and also from Helena Linn of Edenglen Kennels. Her loyalty to the breed is evident in her continued involvement with the NCA (a member since 1980), where she currently serves on the Health and Longevity Committee.

POOH BEAR (Shelby K. Guelich)
Pooh Bear Kennels were started in 1970 when there were very few Newfoundlands in northern California. At the time, Shelby owned Edenglen's Jonathon, a top winner, and shortly afterwards bought in another male and two bitches from the east coast. The shortage of Newfoundland kennels on the west coast meant that Pooh Bear was instrumental in promoting the breed to many potential pet and show owners.

Ch. Timhurst Sally Forth of Pooh, a large-framed bitch, was mated to Ch. Britannia's Union Jack to produce Ch. Pooh Bear's Stormalong, a highly successful sire who is still listed as one of the top ten producers in the US. Stormalong was also the first west coast-bred National Specialty winner since the 1930s. Sally's brother, Ch. Halirock Timhurst Timber, also produced well for the Pooh Bear Kennel and is the grandsire of Shelby's all-time favourite, Ch. Pooh Bear's Katie. A Group and Specialty winner, Katie has an unbeaten record on the west coast and was a wonderful character as well. Sadly, Katie's line died out when Shelby encountered some heart problems in her progeny.

Today, only one bitch is owned by the Pooh Bear Kennels, namely Ch. Seabrook

Sissy Pooh Bear bred by the Seabrook and Tabu kennels. If she is as successful in the whelping box as she is in the show ring, then this one bitch will achieve the future aims of the kennel without need for expansion. Shelby still places temperament high on her list of important Newfoundland traits. All Pooh Bear dogs have been bred to aim for soundness and temperament first, with show ring merit coming second.

TABU (Michael and Lucille Lomax)
Tabu Kennel is located in the beautiful, coastal hills near Carmel, Monterey and Salinas, California. The kennel name originated with Preston and Mary Hollander who combined the call names of their beloved Newfoundland pair, Ch. Nabu (a Beau Geste son) known as 'Boo', and Ch. Beaupre's Good Tern, known as 'Tabby'. The Hollanders bred about six litters, which resulted in a respectable number of champions, prior to 1976, when the Lomaxes inherited the kennel name.

Their Newfoundland family started out with a pet Newf, a rescue called Gawain, whom they showed to a Companion Dog title and as a result became hooked. The next arrival came from the Hollanders, a lovely bitch, Ch. Tabu's Nantucket Sleighride, and at about the same time an equally lovely bitch, from Shelby Guelich.

Pooh Bear's Paddywhack established the temperament and soundness the couple wanted in order to get their kennel going. In 1980 the first two litters at Tabu, born within twenty-four hours of each other, started the ball rolling immediately. The kennel always breeds 'to keep' and has never considered the serious and difficult art of dog breeding to be anything but an expensive hobby. With the help of many friends, all key figures throughout the years, the list of champions grows longer and longer. It includes Best in All Breed shows, Best in Specialty shows, National Specialty Winners, Group Winners and Placers,

Register of Merit (ROM) Dogs and Bitches, and one special Versatility Newf, Ch. Tabu's Pooh Berry Blossom.

Especially significant animals, for different reasons, have been Ch. Tabu's Mr Otis Regrets, Bos'n Bo Terra Nova Rhea (Minnie) and their daughter Ch. Pooh Bearabella. Belle's son, Ch. The Bombardier, has produced beautifully for Tabu and for other kennels as well. Other offspring of 'Otis' and 'Minnie' have adorned the Tabu tree with many branches. The kennel has a deep commitment to OFA numbers and heart certifications, and animals generally live long, active lives. Tabu has always been concerned with health and longevity first, and tries to breed a 'moderate' dog in order to achieve these aims.

The most important mentor for Tabu has been Shelby Guelich and, for the last few years, Kathy Griffin of Seabrook kennels, who got Belle and her progeny to all the right places. Her hard work and brilliance have opened the doors to an exciting future. The Lomaxes are working with Belle's daughters, grand-daughters and some lovely bitches from other kennels. Ch. Seabrook's Paxton for Tabu and Ch. The Noel Ursula have been linebred successfully, and have produced several youngsters who earned their championships at under eighteen months of age.

The most recent BISS winner at the Southern California National Specialty in February of 1997 was Ch. Seabrook's Don Juan of Tabu, and he joins a distinguished list of BISS winners with Tabu or Seabrook prefixes, mostly originating from the magical crosses of Otis and Minnie, Belle and Weston and, later, the half-brother/sister breedings of the Bombardier and Lola. Ch. Black Tie Optional at Tabu, Oppie, won BoB at the Northstar Specialty in December 1996 out of Veterans, while Int. and Ital. Ch. Seabrook's Headmaster at Tabu recently completed his requirements for his American Championship under the able care of Kathy.

Am. Ch. Tabu's Pooh Bearabella with the nine-week old
Am. Ch. Seabrook Sissy Pooh Bear.

COLORADO

DRYAD (Kitty and Maynard Drury with their daughter Mary Dewey)

Kitty's first dog was a Newfoundland given by her grandmother in 1923 when Kitty was seven years old. The dog was named Gyp and was, by all accounts, not a very good specimen. Her first show Newf was Ch. Harlingen Viking of Waseeka, obtained from Mrs Powers of Waseeka kennels in 1928. Kitty showed him to his championship herself.

The Drurys' foundation stock were Waseeka's Crusoe and Ch. Waseeka's Hesperus ('Nanny'). The breeding of these two produced Ch. Dryad's Fan, Ch. Dryad's Admiral, Ch. Dryad's Coastwise Gale, and the first BIS Newfoundland bitch, Ch. Dryad's Coastwise Showboat ('Chloe'). The couple bred over fifty champions, including three BIS Newfs, and produced the foundation stock of many of today's kennels. They also bred many ROMs and the dog who became the first UDT in the breed.

Their daughter, Mary Drury Dewey, was top junior handler at the NCA National Specialty in Greenwich in 1955, handling her puppy, Dryad's Lighthouse Beam. This bitch went on to win Best of Opposite Sex at the NCA National in 1959, handled by Maynard.

Mary took over the kennel in 1973 and has continued the Dryad line by producing over thirty title holders, the most outstanding of whom was Ch. Dryad's Flagship ROM, the NCA's first Top Show Dog of the Year in 1985, who was also pronounced Heroic Dog of the Year by the NCA that same year. He was a Select dog at the NCA National Specialty three years in a row, as well as being a multiple Best in Show winner.

In 1996 Dryad had three Multiple Group Placing dogs: Ch. Dryad's Seafarer of Douglas Mountain, Ch. Dryad's Royal Blue Onyx and Ch. Dryad's Royal Statesman. A nice record for a kennel that produces only one litter a year! Dryad kennel is currently located in Conifer, Colorado, in the heart of the Rocky Mountains. The Deweys have never kept more than five Newfs at any one time, but have continued to breed dogs "of dignity, devotion and disposition".

CONNECTICUT

NASHAU-AUKE (Jane and the late Ronald Thibault)

Nashau-Auke is a Mohegan name (a tribute to Jane Thibault's grandmother), and means 'between two rivers'. It is more than thirty years since the Thibaults tried to decide whether to buy a black Great Dane or a Great Pyrenees. However, a chance meeting with a Newfie settled the quandary and Little Bear's Cinderella joined the family. An interest in obedience work meant she was campaigned to her CD title before another of the Cherns' dogs, Little Bear's Dauntless, came to Nashau-Auke and became the couple's first champion.

Other foundation stock were Ch. Little Bear's Cutty Hunk (Ch. Little Bear's Hard Tack x Ch. Little Bear's Windjammer) and Shipshape's Nana of Nashau-Auke (Edenglen's Sea Clipper x Shipshape's Sea Urchin).

A dog which the Thibaults used greatly at stud was Wilma Lister's Ch. Shipshape's Cutty Sark, and the combination of Little Bear and Shipshape lines resulted in a reputation for the Thibaults that would be the envy of any serious breeder. The many

Am. Ch. Nashau-Auke Dream Catcher. *Photo: Ashbey.*

Am. Ch. Nashau-Auke Screaming Eagle.

champions produced are far too numerous to list, but a notable Newfoundland is Ch. Koki Winota de Nashau-Auke. She was a top producer for the Thibaults and, through her progeny, for many other top-quality kennels. Others deserving a mention are Ch. Kinunka de Nashau-Auke – sire of twelve champions – and Am. Can. Ch. Koko de Nashau-Auke, a dog who is held in high esteem by his breeders. A great success story, too, was Ch. Canoochee de Nashau-Auke, a BIS winner, top producer and very highly placed in the ratings at the end of his best year.

Of the many titleholders at Nashau-Auke, the great majority were homebred and a few were grey, although the Thibaults freely admit to aiming principally for blacks. Despite their great success, Nashau-Auke remains a family concern with every member caring for the twenty or so Newfoundlands owned by the kennel. Sadly, Ronald has recently passed away, and is greatly missed.

GEORGIA
HALIROCK (Joan and Roger Foster)
Joan and Roger's introduction to the breed in the 1960s was when they found themselves driving behind a station-wagon which had a huge, black tail hanging out of the window! They continued to follow the vehicle until they met the canine and human passengers, and were immediately smitten.

Their first two Newfs were from the well-known Little Bear Kennels – the first a family pet and the second their first Champion, Little Bear's Chula Vista. She was eventually mated to Can. Ch. Dryad's Bounty to produce their first homebred Champion, Halirock's Avalanche.

Work commitments meant a move to California for the family where they continued their breeding programme by using Ch. Edenglen's Beau Geste at stud on Vista. Of the resulting puppies Ch. and Can. Ch. Halirock's Boulder won BoW at a National Specialty, while his littermate, Ch. Halirock's Britannia, produced Ch. Britannia's Union Jack for the Britannia kennels.

The Fosters bought in an exceptionally fine bitch from Kitty Drury's well-known Dryad Kennels. Ch. Dryad's Anthony's Penelope proved herself in the show ring, and, when mated to Beau, produced three champion bitches in the Fosters' 'C' litter. In all, Penny was the dam of seven American and three Canadian Champions – many of them OFA certified. So impressed were the Fosters that they also bought Penny's sister, Ch. Franco Cassandra, who also produced OFA certified champions – four in all!

A move back to Vermont saw the Halirock kennel expanding and aiming even more determinedly for overall soundness in their dogs. Despite owning good males of their own, the Fosters also bought in OFA stud dogs to add new dimensions to their breeding programme. This obviously successful recipe has produced a total of fifty-seven champions over the years. Some of these hold a Mexican or Danish title, while many are both American and Canadian champions who are also OFA certified.

A group of Halirock Newfoundlands.

In 1991 breeding activities stopped when the Fosters moved to Atlanta, Georgia. However, these valuable lines are not lost but are being continued by Tyche Kennels in Buffalo, Minnesota.

HAWAII
ALII SHORES (Ursula Yee)

Ursula's love of and devotion to the Newfoundland breed began in 1970 when she purchased a male puppy from the first Newfoundland litter born in Hawaii. Unfortunately, the puppy, Leo, was dysplastic. He was neutered and lived comfortably to the age of nine.

In 1972, a black female from Pouch Cove kennels was acquired by Leo's breeder and lived with Ursula after the Hawaiian mandatory quarantine period (120 days). It was decided to breed this female to Ch. Little Bear's Breakaway and, in 1975, a litter of nine puppies was born. This was the beginning of Alii Shores Newfoundlands and, since then, other Newfs from kennels in Canada and the US were imported and have participated in the breeding programme. Outtrail's Abi Gail Adams, a lovely four-year-old black bitch, joined the kennels in 1980.

Even now, Ursula's Newfs still possess many qualities from Abi Gail, whom she considers her foundation bitch, and who passed on her superb intelligence, water abilities, whelp-nurturing, conformation, temperament and other good traits to her offspring.

Ursula's emphasis has always been to raise and keep the strongest bitches, and breed them to carefully selected stud dogs. Considering that Hawaii is a remote place for breeding Newfoundlands, her foremost concern was the health aspect of the animals, but she has successfully bred sound dogs that conformed to the Breed Standard. Her breeding stock are hip and elbow radiographed, eye and OFA-cleared, and heart-certified by a veterinarian cardiologist. Her chosen colours are black and landseer.

Among the outstanding dogs that contributed greatly to the Alii Shores breeding programme was Ch. Topmast Hi Tide O'Alii Shores, a landseer from Topmast kennels in Canada, and Ch. Black Venture HMS Alii Shores, a dominant black male who gave his offspring a lot of style and elegance in graceful motion. Black Venture was the 'play buddy' of the neighbourhood's children until his final days at twelve years of

LEFT: The Alii Shores in Hawaii.

RIGHT: Am. Ch. Alii Shores Chief Eagle Plume.

BIS Ch. Burningstar's Grand Slam.

age. Other great Newfs are Alii Shores Special Delivery ROM (an Abi Gail daughter by Tribute to Piper Alii Shores) and Ch. Alii Shores Madam Keeley.

Ch. Alii Shores Chief Eagle Plume (Linus) had an excellent show record in 1996, achieving Number 1 Newfoundland and the Number 5 Working Dog in the Hawaii system of shows. His half-brother, Shaquille, was the Number 9 Working Dog. Linus's half-sister, Ch. Alii Shores Madam Keeley, also showed well that year and took the BoB in the Newf Specialty among other awards.

As of 1996, Alii Shores kennels has thirty-two Champions and six Obedience-titled Newfoundlands on record. Newfoundlands being family dogs, are not usually kept in kennels. In order to provide proper attention and environment, Ursula limits herself to maintaining only eight adults at any time. This also includes retired dogs who have the time of their lives playing in the ocean and getting sunburnt. The upkeep of a Newf in Hawaii's warm climate is a challenge. Their coats do not grow as thick and long, and have very little undercoat. They shed twice a year, with tufts blowing in the trade winds all year long! Fleas and brown dog ticks are a continual nuisance, but fortunately newly-developed products are available to keep these pests under control.

To prepare and get a Newf into show condition means a bath every week, with exercise during the cooler morning or evening hours. Because the dogs go swimming in the ocean, Ursula makes time

for a thorough fresh-water rinse and dry. However, too much sun will burn the dogs' coats and leave a reddish tinge. She exhibits her dogs at a number of All Breed Shows and at the annual Newfoundland Specialty. There are twenty All Breed Shows each year: twelve in Honolulu, Oahu, six on Hawaii and two on Maui.

Alii Shores Newfs have travelled worldwide, from Singapore to Holland, Paris and Japan. Several have gone to Australia and New Zealand and a promising youngster now lives in Buenos Aires.

ILLINOIS
BURNINGSTAR (Rebecca and John Black) John and Rebecca and the Newfoundland breed began their life together in 1977. After years of learning to appreciate and understand the breed, they whelped their first litter in 1989 under the Burningstar kennel name.

The foundation bitch was Ch. Darbydale Burningstar Becky ROM, who was purchased in 1986 from Darbydale kennels, owned by Carol Bernard Bergmann. This bitch was bred to VN Ch. Viking's IOU Harley CD, WRD, TDD, owned by Dr and Mrs Clyde Dunphy. This litter produced five AKC champions, two of which were Versatility Newfoundlands and one of which was a Multi BIS dog. This foundation bitch (call name 'Star') earned her ROM from this litter. Star was a great influence on the breeding programme and went on to produce two more litters from different sires, and two more AKC champions with more working titles. Star's most well-known offspring is the Multi BIS dog Ch.

Am. Ch. Burning Star Lady Abanakis.   Photo: Booth.

Am. Ch. Burning Star's Dark Continent.
Photo Fox & Cook.

Burningstar's Grand Slam. He is best-known for his spectacular movement which caught the judge's eye many times and earned him an Award of Merit at two National Specialties.

Some of his littermates who were also successful include Ch. Burningstar Lady Abanakis, who finished her championship in three consecutive shows taking Winner's Bitch (WB) and Best of Opposite over bitch specials at all three shows. A dog, Ch. Burningstar's Dark Continent, was Reserve Winner's Dog at the NCA National Specialty, coming out of the bred-by exhibitor class, while another dog, VN Ch. Burningstar's Bodacious DD, WRD, CD, was a regional speciality winner.

The Blacks are involved with draught and water work, but have primarily concentrated on the conformation ring. Their daughter Aubrey has twice won Best Junior Handler at a National Specialty and handled Grand Slam to his first National Specialty when she was only twelve years of age.

Burningstar kennels has, to date, bred only black Newfoundlands. Another bitch who has played a part in the breeding programme is Ch. Darbydale's Burningstar Beri, a full sister to Star. Beri has produced AKC champions as well as working-titled offspring and a service dog who assists his wheelchair-bound owner. A Star daughter, Burningstar's Silhouette, and a Beri daughter, Ch. Burningstar's Forget Me Not, are currently being bred from at the kennels. In all, six Newfoundlands and one Pointer live at Burningstar. The dogs are mainly in the house with the family and are often caught lounging on the couch, love seat, or mantlepiece.

KENTUCKY

NIKOMA (Buddie and Karen West)
The Wests got their first Newfoundland puppy in 1980 after seeing one at a dog show and researching the breed. After falling in love with the wonderful disposition and dignity of the Newfoundland dog, they soon had two Newfies and were showing in conformation.

They established their kennel name in 1982, the year of their first litter, choosing the name Nikoma because of its Indian origins which they thought were appropriate to the history of the breed. That first litter produced the Wests' first champion, Ch. Nikoma's Reuben James, who finished his Championship at eighteen months of age.

The Wests can pinpoint the exact incident that has had the biggest influence on their breeding programme. It happened in 1981, when they were attending their first American National Specialty in Clarksville, Indiana, and saw two magnificent dogs that had an enormous impact on them. They were the winners of the Twelve to Eighteen Month dog class and the Veteran dog class. The first dog was Brunhaus Bobby of Topmast (now Am. Can. Mex. FCI, UCI, Int. Ch.), and the second was his sire, Topmast's Pied Piper (now Am. Can. Ch. and ROM). They immediately decided to have a puppy from 'Bobby', but it was not until four years later that they achieved that

Ch. Nikoma's Kayla
Eden of Shadow Bear.

ambition and purchased what became the foundation bitch of their breeding programme – Abbeyacre's Rita of Nikoma (Am. Can. Ch. Brunhaus Bobby of Topmast x Can. Ch. Topmast's Abigail Adams). She was a black/landseer recessive, and easily finished her Championship at the age of two, handled by Buddie.

At that point, the Wests started breeding landseers as well as blacks. In 1988 they acquired a beautiful landseer bitch puppy, Peppertree's Abbyacre Rosalee (out of Rita's litter sister, Ch. Abbyacre's Kati and Ch. Abbyacre's Duncan Mciver). She also finished her Championship easily at the age of two, handled by Buddie.

Since then, the Nikoma breeding programme has centred around these two beautiful bitches, producing blacks and landseers. The kennel strives to breed for soundness, balance, excellent movement and the wonderful temperament that initially drew the Wests to the breed. They started working with obedience training in 1994, subsequently achieved their first CD title the following year, and hope to continue in that direction and become more involved in the working aspect of their dogs.

The Wests are owners and/or breeders of the following titled Newfs.
Am. Ch. Nikoma's Reuben James (black)
Am. Ch. Abbyacre's Rita of Nikoma, OFA (black)
Am. Ch. Nikoma's Amos Moses, OFA (black)
Am. Ch. Peppertree's Abbyacre Rosalee, OFA (landseer)
Am. Ch. Nikoma's Kayla Eden of Shadow Bear (landseer)
Am. Ch. Nikoma's Brilliant Disguise, OFA (black)
Can. Ch. Nikoma's Norton of Moonfleet, Am. & Can. CD, DD, OFA (landseer)
Am. Ch. Nikoma's Afloat at Peppertree (landseer)
Nikoma's Maggie Mae CD, OFA (black)
Am. Ch. Nikoma's Just One Look, OFA

(black)
Am. Ch. Nikoma's Double Stuff, OFA (landseer).

Nikoma's future breeding programme revolves around four promising young bitches; two are Rosalee daughters (both landseers), one is a Rita daughter (black/landseer recessive) and one a Rita grand-daughter (black/landseer recessive).

NEW JERSEY
KILYKA (Betty McDonnell)
Betty purchased her first Newfoundland from Kitty Drury of Dryad kennels in 1964. Since that time she has been active in breeding, training and exhibiting her dogs. She does all her own training, grooming and handling, so has a self-imposed limit on numbers, never owning more than eight dogs with a lifetime average of four to six. Since Betty also competes in working events, the dogs she keeps and breeds have to be all-purpose dogs.

Good health as well as physical and mental soundness are requisites of all Kilyka Newfs. Betty expects all her dogs to live together in harmony. Her favourite Newf temperament can be described as one that is sweet and soft, yet also active and athletic. Betty feels that you do not have to compromise type for her multi-purpose demands.

Many of her dogs have measured up to expectations. Ten Newfs she has owned or bred have been designated ROM. Fifteen of her breeding have earned their Versatility titles. Betty has owned or bred over seventy-five champions and a similar number of Obedience titlists. Many have been Specialty winners. Two Kilyka Newfs were BoB at National specialities and two have been Best of Opposite Sex, while a number have won Select ratings. On the obedience side, twelve of Betty's Newfs have won High in Trial at National Specialties. Although Betty does not personally campaign her dogs, two Kilyka dogs have won All Breed BIS and

Four VN Champions owned by the Kilyka kennel.   *Photo: Weber.*

many have been rated in the top ten in the USA and Canada.

The most influential of Betty's Newfoundlands have been two bitches – both called Sibyl! Ch. Shipshape's Sibyl UDT, ROM is the US top producer as dam of fourteen champions, two ROMs and numerous obedience titlists. She is in the pedigrees of almost all of Betty's dogs and in a great majority of all top winning and producing dogs (largely because she was the dam of Pouch Cove's foundation stock). Betty's all-time favourite Newf was VN Ch. Kilyka's Sibyl UD, WRD, DD, ROM. She won Best of Opposite Sex at the 1988 National Specialty and High in Trial in both 1986 and 1987.

Betty served for eighteen years on the board of directors of the Newfoundland Club of America and was president for four years. Currently she is chairman of Judges Education. She served on the Standard Committee for three Standard revisions, and on the Illustrated Guide Committee. Since 1996, Betty has been an AKC-licenced judge of Newfoundlands. She also judges water and draught tests, as well as being co-author of two books on Newfoundlands.

POUCH COVE (Peggy and Dave Helming)
The name Pouch Cove probably commands instant attention from modern-day Newfoundland lovers in any country in the world. The reputation, success and unmistakable 'type' of Pouch Cove dogs are universally recognized and coveted.

However, this success story is a result of three decades of skilful breeding which began in 1968.

Peggy and Dave grew up with a variety of animals, so it was not a surprise that they involved themselves in the sport of purebred dogs. Their first brood bitch, Ch. Katrina of Pouch Cove, a Ch. Newton grand-daughter, was line-bred to Ch. Dryad's Yogi Bear CD, a Newton son. This combination produced Pouch Cove's first champion, Waldo of Pouch Cove CD. Waldo was BoB at the 1972 Westminster Show and BoB at the Regional Specialty Show during the same year. This was a very positive experience and the beginning of what has now become Newfoundland legend.

In 1970, the couple purchased a lovely puppy bitch, Ch. Kilyka's Jessica of Pouch Cove CD, ROM, from Betty McDonnell. Her background was based on Kitty Drury's Dryad kennel. As Jessica began to develop, they could see that she was of the type they wanted to produce themselves. Several years later they went back to Kilyka and purchased another Sibyl daughter out of a different stud dog. Ch. Kilyka's Becky Jo of Pouch Cove possessed the same type as Jessica and so gave the Helmings their foundation.

The Newfoundland that truly started what is known today as the 'Pouch Cove Type' was Ch. Pouch Cove's Gref of Newton Ark ROM. Gref produced quality puppies in almost every litter. To date, he has sired over fifty champions, many of them working titlists, and he can be found in virtually every

Am. Ch. John's Big Ben of Pouch Cove ROM – The NCA gives a ROM award to exceptional producers.

Pouch Cove pedigree throughout the world. In all, Pouch Cove has produced almost two hundred champions and working titlists. Some noteworthy Pouch Cove stock include:

Ch. Tuckamore's Dutch of Pouch Cove BIS
Ch. Season's Autumn of Pouch Cove BIS
VN Ch. Kilyka's Aphrodite of Pouch Cove ROM
Ch. Motion Carried of Pouch Cove BISS, ROM
Ch. Barharber's Rosco of Pouch Cove BISS
Ch. Mooncusser's Reef of Pouch Cove BISS, ROM
Ch. Amity's Bearfoot of Pouch Cove ROM
Ch. Highland Bear of Pouch Cove ROM
Ch. Keepsake of Pouch Cove BISS, ROM
Ch. Pouch Cove's Jacks or Better BISS
Ch. Pouch Cove's On All Fours ROM
Ch. Ad Lib of Pouch Cove ROM
Ch. Pouch Cove's Token
Ch. Pouch Cove's Midnite Bay BIS
Ch. Pouch Cove's Call of the Wild BIS
Ch. Pouch Cove's Girl Most Likely BISS
Ch. Pouch Cove Calls the Question BIS

Ch. Pouch Cove's American Maid ROM.

In Europe, Danish Ch. Yankee Peddler of Pouch Cove had a profound influence on Newfs in Denmark. Ch. Highland Skye of Pouch Cove was most influential in Italy, and UK Ch. Pouch Cove's Repeat after Me at Karazan is beginning his legacy in England.

Two of the most recent males on the scene, who have played a major role in the Newfoundland breed throughout the world, are Ch. John's Big Ben of Pouch Cove ROM and Ch. Pouch Cove's Favourite Son ROM. They are the all-time top producing sires and their legacy will continue to affect Newfoundlands worldwide for many years to come. They are true standard bearers for the breed. (Favourite Son's quality is such that many potential puppy owners request one "just like him", and his pet name 'Jake' is known internationally, even by those who have never seen him in the flesh!)

The Pouch Cove breeding programme has always tried to strike a balance between the pedigree and the phenotype of the dog. Each potential litter is worked out on paper before 'trouble-shooting' the pedigree. For Dave and Peggy, the ultimate aim is to create a combination of quality with the least risk of health problems. Most people would agree that they have achieved their ambition.

NEW YORK
JOLLY ROGER (Roger and Barbara Frey) The Freys' first Newfoundland, Can. Ch. Clarenhill Beau Brumel CD, was purchased in 1971 from Al and Jane Duffett. As is the way of newcomers to the breed, all Roger and Barbara wanted was a big, beautiful puppy that they would be able to show. Imagine their puzzlement when, attending a Newfoundland Club picnic, they were approached by a lady who first admired and then offered to buy 'Beau'. The lady turned out to be Kitty Drury of Dryad fame, and the Freys began to realize what a promising

puppy they had bought. Beau, in time, won his Canadian title and sired Roger and Barbara's first litter three years later. Another Newf arrived from the Clarenhill kennel, and the early successes of both dogs strengthened the Freys' interest in showing and breeding.

The first few litters were based on Dryad and Edenglen lines, but in the late 1970s the Outrail line was introduced. This was done almost unintentionally, as Barbara and Roger were looking after dogs from this kennel while the owner was ill. Impressed by the apparent soundness of the puppies, they kept two. Both won their titles and had the advantage of good hips. By outcrossing these lines with their existing stock and then mating the daughters back to their sire, Am. Can. Ch. The Hostage of Jolly Roger, good hip status was retained.

From then on, the Freys made a conscious effort to produce dogs who displayed above average intelligence and sound front and rear movement, together with heavy bone, a good coat and dark, well-shaped eyes. Their aim was to retain good qualities from *both* parents.

Some bitches who produced well for the Freys were Greengates Caribe Kerry (dam of two champions), her daughter The Ransom of Jolly Roger (who produced their first Specialty winner), and Greengates Jolly Rachel (dam of three champions). Ch. Sunberry's Ramblin Rose was their first landseer and also produced sound, well-marked landseers, one of whom, Ch. Jolly Roger's Beau Maverick, won his class at the 1993 National Specialty and Best of Winners at a Regional Specialty.

As well as owning and using Jolly Roger stud dogs, the Freys also went out to lines such as Topmast and Little Creek to improve on heads and leg length. The Am. Can. Ch. Aoteo's Saint Sebastian Bay was also used in an effort to return to their beloved Dryad type and the mating produced their excellent bitch Am. Can. Ch. Jolly Roger's Broadway

Am. Can. Ch. Jolly Roger's Broadway Ruby.

Am. Can. Ch. Jolly Roger's Honour Bound.
JC Photo.

Ruby – twice a Select winner at NCA Specialties.

Some fifteen champions later, the Freys are still active in the show ring and working arena and are proud of their Newfs, be they BIS winners or Therapy Dogs.

NEWFPORT (May and Jack Bernhard)
At a show in New Hampshire in 1968, May and Jack saw a Newfoundland and made the decision to own one of these big dogs. He turned out to be of pet quality, but introduced them to the world of dog

Am. Ch. Newfport's Fleet Commander.

obedience training and stimulated an interest in dog showing. Their second Newf, Ch. Hidden Lake's Cassiopeia ('Cassie'), a large, lovely bitch, sired by Ch. Little Bear's Sailor Port O' Call (one of the great Newfs of his era, from the famous kennels of Margaret and Vadim Chern), became the foundation of Newfport.

Cassie's first litter was sired by the National Specialty winner, Ch. Indigo's Fritzacker. This litter included several Group placers, two being the Multi-Group winner Ch. Newfport's Fleet Commander ('Clyde') and his litter sister Ch. Newfport's Megean, winner of the Brood Bitch and Veteran Bitch classes at the 1981 National Specialty. Clyde, in turn, sired the Multi-Group winner Ch. Newfport's Noah's Ark, and Megean produced Group winning litter-brothers, Ch. Newfport's Maximillian and the kennel's best-known home-bred Champion, Newfport's Outward Bound ('Byron'). He and Maximillian were both 'selects' at two National specialities. Byron also won the Stud Dog classes at the same Nationals and sired Int. Ch. Tarbell's Jethro.

In terms of numbers of litters bred and dogs kept, Newfport did things on a somewhat modest scale, never owning more than nine dogs. One claim to fame was longevity, with most living to twelve years of age, and one to fourteen. At one time the Bernhards had five 'senior citizens', all over the age of ten. They never bred anything but blacks until their last litter, which produced the one and only landseer, Ch. Newfport's K.C. Waterworks.

In 1986, with the support and encouragement of the late Kitty Drury, Jack took the plunge into judging and has since had the honour of judging at the 1990 National Specialty and in four European countries, Denmark, France, Germany and Italy. He now judges many other working breeds as well. May began her judging career in 1994 and judged a Regional Specialty in the following year. She, too, has had assignments in France and Italy and judged other working breeds.

OREGON
SWEETBAY (Judi and Ellis Adler)
Judi and Ellis began their Sweetbay Newfoundlands breeding programme in 1972 in the western State of Oregon. Their original goal has not changed throughout the decades: to produce a healthy, smart, instinctive Newfoundland.

Sweetbay owners work their dogs in every activity available to the breed. Those interested in these activities often choose Sweetbay dogs because they are indeed capable of doing it all, and are famous worldwide for achieving more obedience, draught (carting), water rescue, and tracking (search and rescue) titles than any other kennel in the breed's history.

In 1996 Sweetbay's Noah CD, TD, WD earned his Companion Dog (obedience) title. This is not unusual in itself, but it was the *five hundredth* title earned by a Sweetbay dog since the kennel's inception – an unlikely achievement as the kennel produces very few puppies each year – but one that gave the Adlers and owners of Sweetbay dogs much pride and pleasure.

Sweetbay dogs are known for their agility and precision and they work with joy. Each

Sweetbay's Rio– Am. Can. CD, Am. Can. TD, Am. Can. WRD, Am.Can.DD.

year, Sweetbay dogs are included in the list of top ten obedience Newfoundlands. Nanette Wiesner's very special bitch, OT Ch. Sweetbay's Gretl TD was (and still is) the only Newfoundland ever to achieve a perfect score of two hundred in obedience competition in the USA. Gretl and several other Sweetbay dogs have earned the highest-scoring Top Obedience Newfoundland (US) annual award on many occasions.

The Adlers' Newfs are also known for their extraordinary water skills. They dominate the lists of titled water dogs. One dog, Sweetbay's Briare CDX, Can. CD, TD, WRD, DD, owned by Lee Udelsman, has passed the most advanced water test level offered in the US an unprecedented nine times.

Tracking, the sport form of search and rescue work, provides Sweetbay dogs with an arena to test their instincts, determination and drive. Nearly half the titled tracking Newfs in the US carry the Sweetbay Kennel name and many possess the very difficult TDX (advanced tracking dog) title as well.

The Adlers feel that a well-rounded Newfoundland is important, and a sweet, smart, handsome dog is a joy. Thus they show not only in working events, but also in the conformation ring, and Sweetbay dogs have won dozens of American and Canadian championships over the years. Eleven Sweetbay dogs have earned the prestigious honour of gaining their Versatile Newfoundland awards.

Judi and Ellis have published many books on the Newfoundland, including the best-selling *The Newfoundland Puppy; Early Care, Early Training* manual (an invaluable aid for the new or experienced puppy owner), and they organise training workshops across the USA and Canada on all aspects of Newfoundland training and care. They judge at many levels of Newfoundland work, learning a great deal from the experience and taking much enjoyment in sharing this knowledge with others.

Sweetbay dogs are indeed known for their working abilities, and the joy and speed they exhibit when participating in these activities bring them much acclaim. But it is as family companions that the dogs truly excel. Their ability to comfort a household, bring in the daily mail, keep watch over the little ones and protect the floor from bits of food falling off the kitchen counter, is impressive!

PENNSYLVANIA
CYPRESS BAY
(Debbie and Marv Thornton)
Cypress Bay Newfoundlands was founded in Monterey, California in 1984 but relocated to Newtown, Pennsylvania, in 1987. Specialising in blacks, the kennel attempts to breed at least three and up to five litters per year, for soundness and movement. All puppies are sold via a 'wait' list to pre-qualified owners. Older dogs are sometimes available if they do not fit the kennel's breeding programme or if a selected person can give outstanding amounts of time and energy to that 'special' dog. Computerised pedigrees of any Cypress Bay dog are available upon request and a stud dog service is also provided to approved bitches. All breeding stock comes from OFA certified

*Am. Ch.
Cypress Bays
Cosette of Tabu
ROM.*

lines and is heart and health certified.

This careful approach has resulted in success in the show ring. In 1993, Cypress Bay Can Do Cassandra won WB, Best of Winners and Best of Opposite Sex at the Batavia Newfoundland National Specialty. The following year 'Cassy' again achieved Best of Opposite, at the Michigan National Specialty. Cassy's daughter, Ch. Cypress Bay's Dai of Summer, was a Select at the Wisconsin National in 1995 and a number of Cypress Bay dogs have won their class at recent nationals.

WASHINGTON

NAKISKA (Ingrid and Chris Lyden) Nakiska Newfoundlands really began when the Lydens acquired their foundation bitch, Kiska, in the spring of 1988. She was a successful show dog, going WB and Best of Winners at the 1991 NCA National Specialty. Moreover, she excelled in the working arenas of the breed and, beginning in 1990, produced two beautiful litters of pups. Unfortunately, VN Ch. Tatoosh's Huggable Nakiska CD, WRD, DD, ROM died unexpectedly after her second litter, but she left a permanent imprint on the kennel's breeding programme. Out of the thirteen

puppies that Kiska produced, seven have their American championship, with others pointed, and nine have multiple working titles. All of the Lydens' current dogs at home are either her children or grandchildren and they strive to produce dogs that possess her good qualities, while bringing in even better characteristics by carefully selecting outside stud dogs.

At the moment, the kennel is breeding on a relatively small scale of one to two litters per year, with some hopes of expanding if time permits. They breed only for black dogs, attempting to produce dogs that fit the Standard, are sound and have the charming Newfoundland temperament. Nakiska dogs are shown in the breed ring and do well, but are also expected to swim, pull carts and do obedience. The Lydens currently have living with them four Versatility Newfoundlands and a few other dogs who are close. They prefer a dog with enthusiasm for whatever the task might be but, more importantly, they want proper type. They like a strong head, solid topline, excellent angulation and good length of neck. The dogs need to move powerfully and cover ground correctly. Nakiska aims for good coats and have been selecting for this more carefully over the last few years. They want to produce dogs that are competitive wherever they step into a ring, but who possess a temperament that makes them a joy to cuddle on the couch.

Besides Kiska, important Nakiska dogs include:
VN Am. Can. Ch. Nakiska's Sir Humphrey Too CD, WRD, TDD, Can. WRD

*Am. Can. Ch.
Nakiska's Sir
Humphrey Too.
Mikron Photos.*

Am. Can. Ch. Hugybear's Chicory Chip.

Ch. Nakiska's Parting Gift WRD, DD
VN Ch. Nakiska's Touch of Magic CD, WRD, DD.

These three are all proven producers and the first two have also been quite successful in the show ring as specials. A couple of exciting young dogs are Can. Ch. Nakiska's Akvavit (already a proven producer and major-pointed at fifteen months) and Nakiska's No Choice About It (Best in Sweepstakes and reserve winner's dog from the 6-9 class, at a recent specialty). Both are out of Ch. Nakiska's Parting Gift WRD, DD. They have additional siblings that are major-pointed and the Lydens are very enthusiastic about her continued promise as a brood bitch.

WISCONSIN
HUGYBEAR (Joyce Ryan)
Hugybear Kennels was established in 1972 as a family endeavour. Health, type and temperament have always been given equal consideration. Quality show dogs, breeding stock and pets have evolved due to a continuing search for the latest information and understanding of canine genetics. Joyce Ryan's education in the field of nursing is used to make breeding decisions, nutritional evaluations and recognition of the importance of genetically related health checks. She also serves on the Health and Longevity Committee of the NCA.

Many work-titled dogs have been produced by Hugybear kennels. Currently there is one, VN Hugybear's Northern Lights – a landseer bitch. Joyce promotes the working abilities of the breed and sponsors workshops to educate and encourage handlers towards obtaining the working titles awarded by the AKC and the NCA. By titling dogs, the kennel's adherence to the standard is validated.

One of the kennel's aims is to continue to improve the type and substance of Hugybear landseers. The foundation black stud dog – Am. Can. Ch. Hugybear's Chicory Chip – contributed type, size and outstanding temperament to the breeding programme, while the landseer Am. Can. Ch. Hugybear's Georgeous George CGC has added soundness, easy athletic movement, clear coat and wonderful show attitude.

As Joyce looks to the new century she sees an exciting opportunity to exchange information more easily and make preservation of the Newfoundland Dog more possible than ever. The kennel is dedicated to assuring the best quality of life possible for its dogs and therefore their owners.

SEABROOK (Wayne and Kathy Griffin)
Nestling on twenty acres along the Chippewa River in Chippewa Falls, Wisconsin, is the home of Wayne and Kathy and Seabrook Newfoundlands. The gently-rolling hills and farmland in this part of the state provide an excellent climate in which to raise and enjoy Newfoundlands. The kennel name, Seabrook, began as something of a joke. When the Griffins purchased their first Newf, they lived in the state of New Hampshire and close-by was the Seabrook Nuclear Power plant.

The first Newfoundland came into their lives in 1981, and very shortly afterwards a second Newf came to live with them. In short, the Griffins were hooked. Following successful sires during the early days led Wayne and Kathy to Shelby Guelich of Pooh Bear Kennels, the breeder of an outstanding

Am. Ch. The Bombardier.

dog, Ch. Pooh Bear's Stormalong. Their first big break came in 1987 when Shelby and Lou Lomax of Tabu kennels sent them an outstanding young bitch, Ch. Tabu's Pooh Bearabella ROM.

'Belle' was exceptional in every way. She had abundant breed type, soundness, a wonderful temperament and that 'something extra' that made her a great show dog. She was Best of Opposite Sex at the NCA National Specialty in 1990 and 1991, and was also the NCA's Top WB in the same year.

The Griffins would have been happy just to have enjoyed sharing their lives with this wonderful bitch and cheering her on in the show ring, but Belle proved to be just as exciting as a brood bitch. She became the NCA's Top Producing Dam in 1993 and then had a son and a daughter earn NCA recognition as Top Sire and Top Dam in 1995 – Ch. The Bombardier ROM and Ch. Tabu Seabrook Nobelle Prize DD, ROM. A litter sister to Nobelle Prize, Ch. Tabu's Belle Fleur Seabrook, is one of the NCA's Top Dams for 1996.

Although Belle passed away in 1995, she has left a legacy to the Griffins in the sons, daughters and grandchildren that surround them at Seabrook.

CANADA

Surprisingly, although Canada is the alleged birthplace of the breed, the Newfoundland is not one of the most numerically popular breeds in this country. However, a glance through The Newfoundland Club of Canada's *Newf News* magazine reveals numerous dedicated breeders across the country's whole enormous expanse. The NDCC also has several regional breed clubs, namely Alberta, British Columbia, Central Ontario, Manitoba, Northern Ontario, Saskatchewan and South Eastern Ontario. These clubs usually run one Regional Speciality Show each per year.

Although Canada has similar practices to the USA, it has its own definite identity in many ways. The Canadian Kennel Club accepts Newfoundland puppies for registration if they are any one of the following colours: black; bronze with white markings; grey with white markings; grey with black markings; white and black; bronze; bronze with black markings; grey, black and white; and black with white markings.

In the Canadian show ring, however, only black or landseer may be shown, although black with white markings or a heavier-marked landseer may be accepted. (In 1972, a horrified Premier of St John's passed an order-in-council that the government would be totally opposed to their official Animal Emblem being depicted as anything other than the traditional black or landseer colour.)

Anyone owing a CKC-registered Newfoundland in any of these colours may use their dog at stud or breed a litter from their bitch. The only exception to this rule is if the Newf in question was registered as a 'non-breeding' animal. The Non-Breeding

Agreement, a proviso initiated by the dog's breeder, may cover the dog for life or, following mutual consent, be removed after the relevant CKC form is signed and submitted.

Canadian breeders are also very aware of inherited defects such as hip and elbow dysplasia, heart conditions and eye problems. Many dogs have OFA numbers and CERF gradings before being included in a breeding programme.

Many Canadian Newfoundlands are also shown in the USA and have both titles. As well as show ring awards, Newfoundlands can also win titles for Draught, Water and Tracking Work.

Canadian Newfoundland lovers enjoyed a special year in 1997 as the Cabot Anniversary was celebrated. In 1497, King Henry VII commissioned an Italian sailor, Giovanni Caboto, to sail forth and claim new lands for England. John Cabot, as he was later known, aboard his 15th century caravelle, *The Matthew*, unexpectedly discovered the 'New Founde Lande' and its related continent.

A replica of *The Matthew* was built in Britain to sail from Bristol to London and then on to Newfoundland to honour the success and courage of Cabot. The Newfoundland breed was chosen as the ship's mascot and six North American Newfoundlands were nominated to be present on the vessel for the ceremonies. (The British dogs who boarded the ship for the first leg of its journey were unable to sail to Newfoundland because of quarantine regulations.) The day was completed by the presence of a multitude of Newfs and their owners waiting to greet *The Matthew* at Newfoundland.

LEADING CANADIAN KENNELS
CASTANEWF KENNELS
 (Denise and Marc Castonguay)
CastaNewf Kennels was established in 1985 by Denise and Marc Castonguay. Denise has

been a dog fancier for most of her life – her mother bred Smooth Fox Terriers. The Newf line was based primarily on Kilyka and Pouch Cove stock and has incorporated Shadybrook and, more recently, European bloodlines.

CastaNewf Kennels practises limited and selective breeding of black Newfoundlands. The goal is to produce a 'whole dog', that is, one who is physically and mentally sound, healthy, naturally instinctive and conforms to the Standard. Denise is a strong advocate of the natural rearing method of raising dogs. Her philosophy is to produce sound, healthy puppies whose personalities match those of their owners. She prides herself on being available to her puppy buyers to provide advice and answer questions.

Denise is not only active in the breed ring but also in the working arena. She participates in water trials, draught tests and the obedience ring. CastaNewf dogs do well in conformation, and also list numerous working titles after their names. Some of the CastaNewf clan include, along with numerous other champions and working title holders:

Am. Can. Ch. Kilyka's Premier of CastaNewf, Am. Can. CD, Am. Can. DD, Am. WD, Can. WRD, a National Speciality and Regional Speciality Class winner.
Am. Can. Ch. CastaNewf's Witch 'O Wadin, Am. Can. CD, Am. Can. DD, a Regional Speciality Class and Best of Opposite Sex winner.
VN Am. Can. Ch. CastaNewf's Curtain Call, Am. CD, Am. DD, Am. WD, Am. WRD, Can. WRD, a National Speciality Class winner and Pet Therapy dog.
Can. Ch. CastaNewf's Mister November, a National Speciality and Regional Speciality Class winner.
Can. Ch. CastaNewf's So To Speak, a Regional Speciality Class winner.

Denise is also no stranger to breed involvement from behind a desk. She is, at the time of writing, president of the Newfoundland Dog Club of Canada (British Columbia Region), the 2nd vice president of the Newfoundland Dog Club of Canada, and currently sits on the Working Dog Committee of the NDCC. Denise has served on nearly every working event committee of the NDCC-BC Region for the past eight years and has judged water and draught work in Canada and the United States. Marc is more a 'behind the scenes' person, but has also served a term as president of the NDCC-BC Region and titled a few CastaNewf dogs along the way.

The philosophy of CastaNewf Kennels is to produce Newfoundlands who are not only typical examples of the breed in appearance but retain their natural working instinct as well.

CINALI KENNEL (Biljana Garland)
Cinali was established in 1978 and permanently registered in 1989. Its foundation bitch from the Bearbrook Kennel, Ch. Bearbrook Little Sheiba, proved not only to be an excellent companion, but also a super brood. Her second litter produced Biljana's first home-bred BIS winner. To date, Cinali has to its credit eighteen champions, and twenty All-Breed Championship BISs won by five different dogs. They are:
Can. Am. Ch. Cinali's Lucky Strike
Can. Am. Ch. Cinali's Power Play
Can. Ch. Bearbrook's Talisman of Cinali
Can. Ch. Cinali's Custom Made
Can. Ch. Cinali's Fortune Teller.

A few of the kennel's dogs also have championship points in the USA. Cinali dogs have always been black, until the last couple of years which produced a few landseer puppies, from black recessive parents. The co-operation with the Bearbrook Kennel has been exceptionally beneficial and helped incorporate some of the top Canadian and American bloodlines.

Cinali puppies have been sold all over Canada, the USA and South America. Dogs of superb temperament and intelligence, good health and conformation – that has always been the aim of the kennel.

GREER NEWFOUNDLANDS (Robert J. and Fay L. Greer)
In 1970, Fay acquired a Newfie puppy of dubious descent. Her dam was large, black and shaggy, but Fay loved her size and appearance and when she was grown another followed and the Greers were hooked!

Their first involvement and commitment to the breed was obedience work. One Companion Dog (CD) title was followed by another, and scores were always high enough to place Greer Newfs in the top three, during their individual competitions. The couple bred their obedience-titled Newf, and from her initial litter came their first real show dogs. A dog and bitch were kept and shown by a handler friend.

That first dog show presented the kennel with a Best Puppy in the Working Group (during the time when the Herding and Working Groups were still combined). The puppy, as well as her brother, went on easily to earn Canadian championships with Group placements along the way. Sadly, the Greers lost the bitch to bloat before they were able to include her in their breeding programme.

Fay and Robert do not consider themselves major breeders, and their desire is to match dogs who are sound in body and mind. They breed with the intention of keeping something, which means each mating is carefully thought out. During the

Can. Ch. Greer's Lucky Oreo Dream.

last twenty years, they have bred a total of twenty-seven litters. From those litters have come thirty-five Newfs who became Champions in Canada. Twenty of those Canadian Champions also earned US Championships and nine of them earned Canadian or American Working titles. The Greers are also proud to announce their first US Versatility Newf, owned and trained by Metta May Sherfick. Seven Newfs were purchased by the kennel over the years, who were also titled in Canada or the US, including three Register of Merits (USA ROM). During 1991, Greer produced both the Number Two Newf in Canada and the Number Three Newf in the USA. This was rather special, as both Newfs were handled exclusively by their owners in their respective countries. Am. Can. Ch. Greer's Tyler of Blackgold was shown in Canada by Terry Ann Lambert and Am. Can. Ch. Greer's Special Export was shown in the US by Richard and Sandy Donnay. Other diligent owners have taken their Greer Newfs to titles in Conformation, Obedience, Draught and Water Work.

Two Newfs from the kennel are active participants in Canada's Super Dogs, who travel around the country performing agility for huge crowds of people. Greer breeds only for blacks and landseers, as these are the only acceptable colours for show in Canada. New blood is always important to breeders and the Greers were keen to have something from the young black male, Ch. Kelligrews Eagle at Tidesoak, whom Fay had seen in England. Discovering that Lucy Stevenson (Culnor) had puppies from him and that both kennels sought new blood, they each acquired a young male from the other. With the new vigour that an outcross brings to a kennel, Fay's wish was to be able to breed the resultant youngsters back to the Greers' own dogs. In 1996, they finally achieved that goal and are very pleased with the outcome. Other breeders who purchased the initial outcross youngsters have bred back to

the Greer dogs with equally good results.

The latest Greer acquisition is from John and Mary Smith's Riverbears kennel in Ireland. This puppy bitch was sired by Fay and Robert's export to England, Greer's Canadian Trader at Culnor, out of Riverbear's Belle Star. Her grandsire is also Eng. Ch. Kelligrews Eagle at Tidesoak, which means that, even though she is an outcross, she will blend in very nicely with Greer dogs, and the new blood.

LITTLECREEK KENNELS
(Margo Brown).
The kennel name was chosen to incorporate part of their first stud dog's name. As a creek runs alongside the kennel, 'Littlecreek' was finally decided on and is now permanently registered with The Canadian Kennel Club.

The Browns bought their first Newfoundland, a bitch, in 1971, followed by a male, Can. Ch. Little Bear's HMS Challenger, who had a great influence on the Canadian and American bloodlines of today. He has produced many sound Champion progeny and was the sire of Littlecreek's foundation bitch, Can. Am. Ch. Arvals Ocean Splendor, who was Number Two Newfoundland in Canada in 1975.

The Browns have owned and bred numerous Champion and Obedience titlists, including Speciality winners and Multi BIS Winners. Among them is BIS Can. Ch. Littlecreek's Feller O' Fortune who was Top Newfoundland in Canada in 1990 and 1991 and, despite limited showing, was Number Two in Canada in 1992. His litter brother,

Can. Ch. Littlecreek's Feller O' Fortune – a multi-Group and BIS winner.

Can. Ch. Littlecreek's Buccaneer, was also a BIS winner. In addition, the kennel's bloodlines appear in some Danish dogs, as they have exported to that country.

The kennel has always endeavoured to breed sound, healthy dogs from respected Canadian/American bloodlines. It has remained a small kennel and, at the present time, has only blacks, though landseers are not ruled out in the future. The dogs have become a family hobby, and life revolves around show and club activities. The Browns' main interest is conformation, and their daughter Ann Forth is always the handler.

MOONFLEET (Ray and Donna Overman) The couple's introduction to Newfoundlands occurred in 1972, when they saw a four-month-old landseer male on their honeymoon. It was love at first sight, and they dreamed of owning the land to begin a breeding kennel.

Later that year, Shadow arrived at their home. She was a true example of what the Newfoundland character should be – loyal, dignified, hardworking, trustworthy, but, most of all, a good friend. She was never in the show or obedience ring but, in retrospect, could easily have been a champion or a high-scoring working dog.

Can. Ch. Moonfleet's Mark of Excellence.

After losing Shadow to cancer in 1981, the Overmans acquired Maggie, who had poor conformation and a strong, self-willed attitude. Maggie proved that not all Newfs are created equal. However, the Overmans learned to train any Newf to respond favourably to various situations.

The breeding aspect of Moonfleet originated with the purchase of Domino (Select Am. Can. Ch. Our Bearbrook Domino de Dourga), whose quality and soundness presaged the foundation of the Moonfleet type. Their initial bitches were from Bearbrook x Dulrick lines. Although these bitches had good movement and body type, they lacked the heads the couple were looking for. By introducing BIS Ch. Topmast Thunder Bolt TD, they incorporated his lovely dominant head, his outgoing personality and length of coat, and began seeing vastly improved heads in their litters.

In 1989, they bought Indy (Am. Can. BIS Ch. Haweneyu's Mood Indigo, OFA, CERF). Although Indy is the result of an outcross breeding (Topmast x Thunder Bay), he has proven himself to be dominant for his virtues – size, soundness and temperament. His sons and daughters are proving themselves in the breed and obedience rings, as well as in their progeny.

Great success has come from the introduction of Thunder's inbred son, Norton (Ch. Nikoma's Norton of Moonfleet), into an established bitch line. Norton, bred to Indy's daughters, sired large, heavily-boned, sound puppies with above-average working ability.

Two Indy sons, Floyd (Ch. Moonfleet's Sigmund Floyd) and Ernie (Ch. Moonfleet's Mark of Excellence), are beginning to prove themselves as stud dogs. Their first litters are now old enough to begin their show careers, and great things are expected from these puppies. Floyd and Ernie are Domino grandsons, and, like their grandfather, are Multi-Group placers/Group Winners and have working qualifications.

Moonfleet's future looks bright. In 1990, Rig (Domino's daughter) was bred to Indy. Two of the bitches from this litter were bred in different directions. Ch. Moonfleet's Dance on the Stars was bred to Ch. Bearbrook's Talisman of Cinali (a Multi BIS male). From this breeding came a lovely black bitch, Dannee (Moonfleet's Dances with Stars). A landseer bitch from the Rig/Indy litter was bred to Topmast Piper Trax. From this breeding came a landseer bitch, Eva (Moonfleet's Evening Star).

Around the same time, Dizzie was bred to Bailey (Am. Ch. Talloak's Barnum & Bailey). While Bailey is Domino's grandson, he brings in new bloodlines through both his sire and dam. Two Bailey kids, Arnold (Moonfleet's Arnold Schwartznewf) and Edith-Ann (Moonfleet's Earth Angel), are very promising puppies.

Black and landseer are the only colours in this kennel, as the CKC does not recognize bronze or grey for conformation shows. The working ability in Moonfleet Newfs is evident, as their dogs have been involved in obedience trials, draught tests, tracking trials, water work, agility, and as certified search and rescue dogs.

The Overmans believe that soundness for breeding is important in all aspects of the breed: hips, heart, structure, movement, but most important of all, a sound temperament. They require their breeding stock to meet all these requirements and argue that singling out one aspect of the breed means losing somewhere else.

Currently residing at Moonfleet are sixteen Newfoundlands ranging from senior citizens to promising puppies. Moonfleet is responsible for more than twenty title holders (USA, Canada and Germany), with many more holding a working or obedience title.

TOPMAST (Margaret Willmott)
Margaret had her first Newfoundland in 1965. When she had won her title Margaret went on to produce the first Topmast litter in 1967. The following five years brought some success but Marg's lifelong knowledge of breeding livestock told her that she was pursuing the wrong path for the type of soundness she had expected.

In 1972, Callis Shade of Black ROM joined the kennel. She was not the type of bitch that fashion favoured at the time, but she was intelligent, healthy and sound. She was bred back to the great-grandson of a dominant, typey male who was related to her maternal grandsire. It was a good recipe, with the bitch retaining her good points and the male correcting her faults. The first litter produced Ch. Can. Am. Topmast's Pied Piper ROM, a Multi BIS and Speciality winner. Two Canadian champion sisters to Piper were kept, along with a maternal half-sister. A male puppy from OFA-Excellent parents was bought in and became a Multi BIS winner. Piper's sisters were bred to him and later to two other sound males, with the resulting daughters being mated back to Piper – and the Topmast type was established. Test breedings were often carried out (brother x sister or father x daughter) to check for troublesome recessive genes and, to date, the kennel has been lucky in this respect.

In 1973 the Willmott family moved from Ontario to a ranch in Penske, Saskatchewan. Since then over 150 titles have been won, and Topmast dogs have taken sixty-four BISs! Topmast Newfoundlands can be seen in as many as eight different countries and more than 25 American states. In 1990, a Topmast dog was the all-breed top winning dog of the year in Italy. Recent exports to England are also promising and will be valuable to the breeders of landseers there. Visitors to Marg's home are amazed at the sight of over 20 Newfoundlands roaming free on the prairie in a morning pack and an afternoon pack, then coming home in time for their twice daily feed.

12 *NEWFOUNDLANDS WORLDWIDE*

AUSTRALIA AND NEW ZEALAND

How the Newfoundland came to Australia is not clear, but during the 1960s John Hughes imported two dogs – Captain Cook of Sparry (black) and Wildfields Endeavour (landseer) – and a bitch, Storytime Shenandoah, from the UK. This helped bring the Newfoundland breed from its previous standstill. From the mating of Ch. Captain Cook of Sparry to Shenandoah, a bitch was born, Seamaids Tinker Too. Tinker was mated back to Captain Cook and two top winners were produced, Ch. Seamaids Snow Shoes and Ch. Seamaids Panda (F. Wilson).

Captain Cook was a good-sized dog with excellent movement and went Runner-up in Group at Sydney Royal Show when eight years old. He was also a BIS winner prior to this. Captain Cook spent the last years of his life with Linda and Ross Windred of Majesty Kennels when John Hughes was obliged, through ill-health, to place the dogs in new homes. Ch. Seamaids Panda was the dam of approximately eighteen champions and several Speciality winners.

In 1968 Juliet Gibson (now Leicester-Hope) came to Australia from the UK and brought with her two black Newfoundlands – Wanitopa Gentle Giant and Bonnybay Jasmine. Ch. Wanitopa Gentle Giant was mated to Don and Mary McCaul's Ch. Kingfishereach Sea Wrack (Imp. UK), producing two of the most successful Newfoundlands in the Victorian rings for the next few years – Ch. Marydon Shanook (Nairobi Kennels) and Ch. Marydon Lady Giant (M. and R. Simpson). Nairobi Kennels also imported Ch. Ragtime Drunk as a Deacon (black) from the UK, and Pound of Humbugs of Ragtime (landseer).

Ch. Marydon Shanook went BoB at three Melbourne Royal Shows and at a 'Pal' International, and was a beautiful representative of the breed. Lady Giant was Challenge Bitch at two Melbourne Royals and a BoB winner at a Pal International, as well as BIS at three Victorian Specialities.

Giant's second and fourth matings were to Ch. Seamaids Panda (F. Wilson). From these two litters many champions resulted, including Ch. Planhaven Heidi (W. Ducros), Challenge winner at three Sydney Royals, and several other Royal Challenge and Best in Group winners.

Giant was also mated to Juliet Gibson's own English and Australian Ch. Bonnybay Jasmine. The best known pup from this litter would have been Ch. Wanitopa Bosun Boy (M. and D. McCaul), a BoB winner at Melbourne Royal.

The previously-mentioned Ch. Wildfields Endeavour CD sired his first and only registered litter in 1970 to Seamaids Tinker Too, owned by Majesty Kennels. From this mating, the black dog Ch. Majesty The Viking resulted. Viking, though not a large dog, excelled in coat and body and clicked extremely well with the large bitches from the Wanitopa Gentle Giant line. Endeavour spent most of his adult life with Peggy Eustace.

Over the years Australia has seen several imports, including Frances Wilson's Edenglens Born Free (Imp. USA) whose blood dominates many Newfoundlands in Australia today. The Newfoundland has made his mark, and several important kennels are producing top-quality stock. There are now Newfoundland Clubs in the States of New South Wales, Victoria, South Australia and Western Australia.

There are two Newfoundland Clubs in New Zealand. One is in the North Island: it is called The Newfoundland Club and has two branches in Auckland and Wellington. The second club is called the Southern Newfoundland Society and is in the South Island. The Newfoundland Club has a membership of approximately 500, while the Southern Newfoundland Society has a membership of about 130. Both clubs have a bi-monthly magazine, organise annual photographic competitions and also various other awards for showing and versatility achievements.

The Newfoundland Club runs one Open and two Championship Shows per year and an annual water trials event with hauling and carting competitions. The Southern Newfoundland Society holds one Open and one Championship Show per year, and also throughout each year runs a Working Dog Award for which points are accrued in obedience, carting and water work.

In recent years the growing popularity of the breed has resulted in Newfoundlands being ranked at number twenty in respect of the number of litters registered (around twenty litters or one hundred and thirty puppies). The number of breeders currently registering kennel names with the NZKC is over sixty, but some of these are at present inactive.

LEADING AUSTRALIAN KENNELS

AUSSIEBEAR KENNELS (Jenny and Trevor Schofield)

Both Jenny and Trevor have owned Newfoundlands since the early 1980s. They started with a lovely black dog, Ch. Rhovanian Chester, who was mated with Ch. Mekong Nanook to produce two sons – Ch. Aussiebear Black Duke and Aussiebear Rebel. They also purchased a daughter of Eng. NZ Aust. Ch. Wellfont Ambassador, Mekong Jentre Jedda, who was mated to Ch. Aussiebear Black Duke to produce a magnificent bitch – Ch. Aussiebear Pretty Girl. She had numerous Best in Group and BIS wins, including BIS at a Weekend Show – both Saturday's and Sunday's All Breeds Shows! Ch. Aussiebear Pretty Girl was also Runner-up BIS at a Club Show.

A second litter of Mekong Jentre Jedda and Ch. Aussiebear Black Duke produced two daughters, Ch. Aussiebear Jentre Lass and Aussiebear Khouylah. Ch. Aussiebear Jentre Lass was BIS-All Breeds also at a very early age. She has since produced offspring from Ch. Landsblak Lord Nelson, namely Aussiebear Jentre Magic and Ch. Aussiebear Commander who was Runner-up BIS-All Breeds from the Puppy class. He also went on to win an All Breeds BIS from the Junior class!

KRYSTALCOVE NEWFOUNDLANDS (Vicki and Graham Birch)

Krystalcove Newfoundlands was founded in 1987 in the UK by Vicki Carey. The foundation bitch was an import from Denmark, Ursulas Renata of Wellfont. Renata was mated to Ch. Wellfont Macillon.

Aust. Ch. Krystalcove Dark Dazzler (imp UK).

Two puppies from this litter later went on to become UK Champions, while a third won a CC and BoB.

Vicki married Graham Birch (formerly Wellfont Newfoundlands) and they emigrated to Australia in 1989, taking Krystalcove Dark Dazzler and Krystalcove Dark and Dreamy (Renata x Macillon litter) with them. Dazzler went on to become an Australian Champion, winning several Groups and a BIS All Breeds Championship Show. Dazzler has sired over ten Australian Champions.

Krystalcove Kennels has since imported Aust. Ch. Ursulas Indian Son of Dipper from Sweden and Aust. Ch. Beauberry Black Magic from the UK. Both of these have been extremely successful in the show ring. Dipper has been used extensively at stud and has produced many successful offspring throughout Australia and New Zealand including a BIS Speciality winner. Since its foundation, Krystalcove has built up a kennel of fifteen Newfoundlands, including browns and landseers, from original imports and Australian dogs.

LANDSBLAK KENNELS (Lee Wales, Jeanette Mitchel and Pam Lake)
In 1969 Ch. Planhaven Pioneer CD was purchased from Planhaven Kennels by Lee Wales, but it was not until the 1980s when Lee purchased Ch. Mekong Blazing Sun CD (landseer), her daughter Ch. Mekong Bear

Ablaze, Ch. Mekong Black Onyx CD and Ch. Mekong Lucky Lunar (a grand-daughter of Topmast Peter Pan, a Canadian import) that Landsblak Kennels was established.

Ch. Mekong Bear Ablaze was mated with Canadian import Spokinewf's Sailon to Planhaven to produce: Ch. Landsblak Lord Nelson who was Runner-up BIS at nineteen months, Ch. Landsblak Wild Lady, Best Bitch of the Year, 1991 and Ch. Landsblak Nelson's Lady. All three had Best In Group and Class BIS wins. Ch. Landsblak Nelson's Lady (Pam and Golu Lake) was mated to Ch. Planhaven Thunder Bay producing a daughter, Ch. Landsblak Lady Shadow (Best Bitch of the Year, 1993). Ch. Mekong Lucky Lunar was Best Bitch of the Year, 1987 and 1988.

In 1991 a grand-daughter of Aust. NZ Eng. Ch. Wellfont Ambassador was added to the kennels. Aussiebear Khouylah was mated to Ch. Landsblak Lord Nelson producing two litters, thus giving Landsblak both English and Canadian lines. Jeanette and Lee have integrated both Planhaven and Mekong into their lines and continue to do well in the show ring. A daughter of Khouylah, Ch. Landsblak Magic Moment, ended her career with Best in Group and has retired to be mated to a Swedish import to bring in new lines. A further addition, lovely landseer bitch Planhaven Thunderlina, will continue the Canadian and Thunder Bay lines.

MEKONG KENNELS (the late Shirley Summers and Sue Ann Miner)
Mekong Kennels began in the mid 1970s with Ch. Planhaven Presto Peta. By the end of the 1970s, Shirley had established quite a few champions and in the early 1980s Gaedheal Gargantua was added to the kennels and mated to Peta. This produced several top winning bitches including Ch. Mekong Blazing Sun CD (Lee Wales) and Ch. Mekong Midway (Sandy King), each achieving BIS and Best in Group wins. Both of these bitches were Best Bitch of the Year

Eng, NZ, Aust Ch. Wellfont Ambassador imported by the Mekong Kennels.

over a period of seven years; Ch. Mekong Blazing Sun CD, winning her first at under , eighteen months.

Gargantua and Peta also produced two litter sisters, Ch. Mekong Becky CD and Ch. Mekong Nanook (J. and T. Schofield), both having a very successful show career.

During the 1980s, together with Lee Wales, Shirley imported Eng. Ch. Wellfont Ambassador from the UK who also gained his NZ and Aust. Championships. By the end of the 1980s, Shirley added a brown bitch, Ch. Planhaven Cherry Ripe, to her kennel and from this bitch Ch. Mekong Rustic Warrior was born. With BIS, both All Breeds and Speciality shows, Rusty and his mother have more than proved that 'browns' are here to stay in Australia.

In the 1970s-80s Mekong Kennels were successful in producing 'dual achievers' in the following stock who held not only their Championship but also their Obedience titles:

Ch. Mekong Captain Bligh CD (landseer) (Lee Wales)
Ch. Mekong Ebony CD (black) (Lee Wales)
Ch. Mekong Blazing Sun CD (landseer) (Lee Wales)
Ch. Mekong Becky CD (black) (Shirley Summers)
Ch. Mekong Black Onyx CD (black) (Lee Wales, Best Bitch of the Year, 1987)

As a result of involvement, interest and dedication there are now quite a few Newfoundlands in Australia who have held this dual achievement, some going further with their Obedience to the level of CDX and UD.

In the 1990s Shirley and Sue Ann Miner entered into a partnership for Mekong and, with the addition of stock from Eng. NZ Aust. Ch. Wellfont Ambassador, continued their winning career. Shirley passed away in April 1995, and Sue Ann is continuing to keep the Mekong Newfoundlands running successfully.

PLANHAVEN KENNELS (Frances Wilson)
Planhaven Kennels was established in 1969, when a litter was produced from Ch. Seamaids Panda and Ch. Wanitopa Gentle Giant (Imp. UK). Panda had been purchased as a puppy from John Hughes who had imported three Newfoundlands from the UK.

Due to a very limited gene pool, Frances decided in 1973 to journey overseas to try and obtain a Newfoundland male to contribute to the breed in Australia. After visiting the UK and Europe, Frances eventually ended up at the Edenglens Kennel of Bill and Helena Linn in the USA, where she was lucky enough to be able to purchase Edenglens Born Free. Guiness, as he was nicknamed, came to England for his one-year quarantine, the last six months of which he spent with Juliet Gibson who used him at

Aust. Ch. Planhaven Thunder Bay: A multi BIS winner.

stud. A nice daughter from this union was produced and went BoB at Crufts. His first Australian litter was to Ch. Seamaids Panda and this resulted in Ch. Planhaven Hard Astern, who went on to be Australia's Top Winning Newfoundland of that era, scoring twenty-six BIS wins, All Breeds and Speciality.

Guiness also produced the first browns in Australia, when a daughter mated back to him produced Ch. Planhaven Bronze Eagle, a Runner-up BIS winner. Another famous son was Aust. NZ Ch. Planhaven Big Mac. He was the first Newfoundland to go BIS All Breeds in New Zealand, when he went for a visit to gain his NZ title. He later crowned his show career going BIS at Melbourne Royal, 1984, Australia's largest dog show. Mac's best known daughter was Ch. Planhaven Bonnie Belle, as she totalled BoB four times in a row at Melbourne Royal (the first time from the Puppy Class) and went Runner-up BoB to her sire at the Melbourne Royal, 1984.

Big Mac was a top sire like his father and his progeny are too numerous to mention. He was a true gentleman and lived to the ripe old age of fourteen and a half years. He, like his sire, produced litters at twelve years

of age. (Guiness survived, in good health, until he was fifteen years old.)

The other dog in the same era as Edenglens Born Free, who influenced Planhaven Kennels strongly, was the homebred landseer Ch. Planhaven Presto Teddy. He was a top show dog and was rated by a number of overseas judges as one of the world's best landseers. Kitty Drury, of Dryads fame, was particularly taken by him and awarded him top honours in the breed. Teddy produced extremely well and, with Edenglens Born Free, was rated one of the top sires in the breed, having over twenty champion progeny, including Ch. Planhaven Bonanza (landseer), the first Australian-bred Newfoundland to go BIS in Australia, All Breeds.

Ch. Planhaven Olde Salt (Roger and Sandy Howell) was a Royal winner and Multi BIS winner and produced a sound brown line in Ch. Planhaven Cinnamon (line-bred to Born Free). This line normally lives to between fourteen and fifteen years and are generally hip-scored as normal, which is an additional bonus.

Many other champion and BIS winners were sired by Guiness and he had a major influence on the breed by adding movement and improving top-lines in his progeny.

A son of Big Mac, Ch. Planhaven Thunder Bay, had beautiful conformation and was a joy to watch moving in the ring. He won Specialities in New South Wales and was a multi BIS All Breeds winner. A great sire, he produced top winners in the breed and was dominant in throwing good movement.

Thunder Bay produced the record-breaking Ch. Planhaven Thunder Dome who won fifty-two BIS, both All Breeds and Speciality shows. He was National Dog of the Year in 1991 and 1993 – Australia's Top Scoring BIS Dog, All Breeds – and so far is the only dog to have been Top Dog twice. He won numerous contests for BIS Winning Dogs. A once-in-a-lifetime dog. Thunder Dome was retired at the relatively young age of six after winning the New South Wales Speciality.

Introduced into Planhaven during 1986 were Sailor and Aloha, a brother and sister pair from Spokinewfs Kennels in Canada, who were welcome additions to the kennel. Sailor was dominant in improving head, dentition and eye colour. His most famous daughter was Ch. Planhaven Kontiki, a Best Opposite in Show winner at Sydney Royal.

Sailor produced some other good winners, including Ch. Landsblak Wild Lady, Ch. Landsblak Lord Nelson, Ch. Planhaven Aquamarine, Ch. Planhaven Call Me Sam, the good-producing Planhaven Storm Duke and Planhaven HMAS Curlew.

Aloha, mated to Thunder Dome (Sailor's son), produced the landseer Ch. Planhaven Brand Nu Teddy, a multi BIG Class in Show winner and the resident dog at Planhaven, ruling the house.

A brood bitch worthy of note was Planhaven Patchouli who was awarded BIS, judged by Kitty Drury, and produced many champions, plus Royal and Speciality winners, when mated to Presto Teddy. Gaedheal Bonnie Bear was another, producing champions in Ch. Planhaven Teddy Bear, Ch. Planhaven Teddy Junior and Ch. Planhaven Tedwena.

Planhaven Kennels, being situated in the Southern Highlands, is quite a cold area in the winter, with occasional snow, so the climate is ideal for Newfs. Frances also breeds Chow Chows, Shih Tzus and, until recently, Irish Wolfhounds, but Newfoundlands are still her main love.

LEADING NEW ZEALAND KENNELS

ALPENLIED KENNELS
(Fern and Kerry Norton)
In 1980 Fern purchased her first Newfoundland, Ch. Sea Nymph of Matthias and whelped her first litter two years later. In 1987 she imported Regine Sail Away from Australia (out of Spokinewfs Sail On to Planhaven), and in 1989 campaigned Aust. NZ Ch. Regine Mr Magic to his New Zealand title before he returned to Australia.

There have been a number of Alpenlied champions, including BIS Speciality winners Ch. Alpenlied Café Royal and Ch. Alpenlied Dark Raider CDX. The Alpenlied breeding programme to date has concentrated on UK lines from Wellfont, Australian lines from NZ Ch. Seafell Caniz James, and also Waterbear breeding. Fern has in the past served on the Committee of the Southern Newfoundland Society.

BJORN (Mopsy and Paul Blake)
Mopsy was part of the Trinity Bay Newfoundlands which was established in 1980. Mopsy remarried and together with her husband Paul set up Bjorn Newfoundlands in 1989 with the importation of NZ Ch. Planhaven Hollylea, Planhaven the Pacer and Planhaven Redfire, all from Australia.

Ch. Bjorn Race Bearfoot and Ch. Bjorn Edenglens Hylo are litter mates from Holly and Pacer, and have both won Group awards at All Breed Championship shows. Hylo is also a BIS Speciality winner. Mopsy and Paul imported NZ Ch. Planhaven Misha in 1994, and to date the Bjorn breeding programme has concentrated on the introduction of Planhaven lines from Australia.

BONAVISTA (Eve and Graham Walker)
Bonavista are currently the longest-established breeders of Newfoundlands in New Zealand. From 1974 to 1978, the prefix was registered with Alan and Eve Hooper, but was re-registered with Graham and Eve when they married. Bonavista commenced in 1974 with the purchase of Midnight Lass Quinabbey (produced by mating two Planhaven imports from Australia).

The following year Bonavista imported two Newfoundlands from England, NZ Ch. Stormsail Wildhorn and NZ Ch. Stormsail

Bonavista Lighthouse – one of the browns from this successful kennel.

Rothorn. They were littermates from Ch. Attimore Royal Sovereign and Ch. Bachalaos Brightwater of Stormsail. Wildhorn sired one litter before his accidental death, but progeny from this litter, and also from litters produced by Ch. Stormsail Rothorn, became the foundation lines for Bonavista. Lines from both these dogs also became the foundation breeding stock for other New Zealand kennels and today many New Zealand-bred Newfoundlands have some Bonavista ancestry behind them.

The Bonavista breeding programme has involved using the above lines in combination with Planhaven and with litters sired by NZ Grand Ch. Wellfont Ironside (Imp. UK), Topsail's Skipper (Imp. Denmark), Edenglens Born Free (Imp. USA) and NZ Ch. Seafell Caniz James (Imp. Aust.). Bonavista have produced thirty champions, including In Group and In Show winners, and Newfoundland Club working title achievers, as well as two CDX titlists.

GENTLE-BEAR (Anne and Bevan Rogers) Anne and Bevan purchased their first Newfoundland, Alpenlied Dark Angel, in 1983. NZ Ch. Karazan Hot Chocolate, their first import from the UK, arrived in 1985. 'Nushka' was only the second brown New Zealand Champion. The following year,

NZ Ch. Gentle-Bear Perle D'or.

their second import arrived, Aust. NZ Ch. Karazan Solomon the Great (Imp. UK). Nushka whelped a litter to newly-imported Eng. NZ Ch. Ursulas Figaro of Wellfont (Imp. Denmark) during 1987 and this litter produced five champions and included the following progeny:
Ch. Gentle-Bear Aviosa, Speciality BIS winner, Group Open Show winner and In Group All Breeds Championship Show winner
Ch. Gentle-Bear Fidelio, Reserve in Show and Multi In Group All Breeds Championship Show winner
Ch. Gentle-Bear High Society, Speciality BIS winner
Ch. Gentle-Bear Deep Secret, BIS Speciality winner
Ch. Gentle-Bear Grande Amore, Multi In Group All Breeds Championship Show winner.

Solomon was campaigned in 1989 to his title in Australia, and while there sired several litters including Aust. Ch. Mekong Sweet Revenge. In the same year, Anne and Bevan imported Karazan Huggybear from the UK, and in the November, Nushka became the first brown Newfoundland to win a New Zealand Speciality Championship Show. (One of her daughters won Reserve in Show at the same show.)

A litter in 1990 between Ch. Gentle-Bear Aviosa and Solomon produced four champions including Multi In Group winner Ch. Gentle-Bear Iceburg who has so far won

NZ Ch. Kristagale Tempa Tantrim.

five Speciality shows. In 1991, NZ Ch. Ursulas Olympus was imported from Sweden and has already won a Speciality Show as well as being an In Group and In Show All Breeds Championship Show winner.

The Gentle-Bear breeding programme has to date involved the use of UK and Danish lines – Ursulas, Karazan, Wellfont and Merrybear. Anne is a past secretary of the Southern Newfoundland Society and served as president for four years.

KRISTAGALE (John and Anne Nightingill, with Anne's children Robbie, Pam and Jenny McDonald)
Kristagale began their substantial involvement in the Newfoundland breed in 1988 with the importation of NZ Grand Ch. Waterbear Xavier (Imp. Aust.) as a two year old. Show successes for 'Elliot' included four All Breed Championship BIS and two Speciality BIS, along with many In Group and In Show awards. He also won New Zealand's Supreme All Breed Dog Award in 1990.

Anne and John imported, in 1989, NZ Ch. Planhaven Sea Urchin (Imp. Aust.) in whelp to Aust. Ch. Waterbear Dan Ruff. The arrival of this litter marked the beginning of the Kristagale breeding programme. In the same year Kristagale also imported NZ Grand Ch. Waterbear Winchester (Imp. Aust.). Winchester has now amassed five All Breed Championship BIS wins along with many In Group and In Show awards and six BIS Speciality wins, and has also won Runner-up in the 1993 New Zealand Top Dog competition.

In 1989 NZ Ch. Waterbear Temptress (Imp. Aust.) was imported, and in 1990 a litter from her and Winchester produced two winning landseers, Ch. Kristagale Tiz Tempting and Ch. Kristagale Tempa Tantr'm, both of whom have each won an All Breed Championship Show and a BIS Speciality. Tantr'm also won New Zealand's 'Pal' Puppy of the Year (1992).

Kristagale imported NZ Ch. Waterbear Akbar (Imp. Aust.) and NZ Ch. Waterbear Dozer (Imp. Aust.) in 1990 and the following year added NZ Ch. Waterbear Beauty (Imp. Aust.) to the kennels. All three have won Speciality shows.

Other especially notable Kristagale achievers are:
- Ch. Kristagale D'Screet Move
- Ch. Kristagale Shady Dreams
- Ch. Kristagale Brown Bear
- Ch. Kristagale Temptation
- Ch. Kristagale Bogart.

All have achieved many In Group and In Show awards. In 1993 Kristagale campaigned Am. NZ Aust. Ch. Spillways Caleb (Imp. USA) to his New Zealand title before he went on to Australian breeders Alan and Denise Robins (Waterbear Newfoundlands).

More recently (1996) Aust. Ch. Waterbear Abraham, sired by Caleb, was imported to Kristagale and has already won a Group BIS. The considerable effort and investment put into the importing and breeding programmes, together with superb presentation and handling skills, have produced an outstanding record of show wins.

NZ Ch. Newfhaven Black Beauty.

NEWFHAVEN (Ellen and Mick Dabner)
Ellen and Mick's association with the Newfoundland breed began in 1983 with the purchase of their first Newfoundland, NZ Ch. Alpenlied Dark Raider CDX. 'Khan' has won two Speciality BIS, is well known in the local Canterbury area for his abilities in obedience, water work and carting, and is behind most of the litters and champions bred by Newfhaven.

In 1987 Ellen and Mick purchased their first import from Australia, NZ Ch. Planhaven Oceana Roll out of Spokinewf Sail On To Planhaven. From this bitch came Newfhaven's most successful show winner so far, NZ Ch. Newfhaven Black Beauty, who has taken In Group and one In Show award at All Breed Championship shows and has won a Speciality BIS. A second Australian import arrived in 1994, NZ Ch. Waterbear Vic'Torious, who has already taken some Group wins.

The Newfhaven breeding programme has been based on a combination of Alpenlied/Kristagale (NZ) and Planhaven/Waterbear (Aust.) lines with an

UK & NZ Ch. Ursulas Figaro of Wellfont imported by the Seal Cove kennel.

American influence from Am. NZ Aust. Ch. Spillways Caleb, who is the sire of two of their Newfoundlands.

Ellen and Mick have contributed a great deal to the Newfoundland breed in the South Island, through faithful and determined advocacy of the working abilities of the breed, and have also succeeded in obedience, water and draught work, as well as encouraging newcomers to participate in these activities.

SEAL COVE (Matt Damm and Gabrielle Barnett)
Matt and Gabrielle saw the beginning of a very strong association with the Newfoundland breed in 1976 with the purchase of their first Newfoundland, Ch. Davyhulme Moksiis (whelped in New Zealand out of Australian-bred parents), who produced the kennel's first litter in 1980 to an Australian-bred sire.

Their first import arrived in 1981, NZ Ch. Nairobi Caniz Belami, followed in 1982 by Nairobi Caniz Seiger. Both came from Australia and both were sired by Topsails Skipper (Imp. Denmark). The next year, two further imports from Australia arrived, namely NZ Ch. Mekong Royal Envoy (BIS Speciality winner) and NZ Ch. Mekong Royal Tradition, both sired by Eng. Aust. NZ Ch. Wellfont Ambassador. During the same year their first import from England arrived, NZ Grand Ch. Wellfont Ironside (by Eng. Ch. Ursulas Figaro of Wellfont and Wanitopa Sepia of Wellfont). 'Ferro' was the first Newfoundland to consistently win in

the All Breeds show ring and won the highest number of BIS All Breed Championship shows that a Newfoundland has won to date in New Zealand. He is New Zealand's first Grand Champion, accruing along the way seven All Breed Championship show wins, over seventy Group and In Show awards and five BIS Speciality wins.

In 1984 Matt and Gabrielle imported NZ Ch. Seafell Caniz James from Australia and also campaigned Eng. Aust. NZ Ch. Wellfont Ambassador (Imp. UK) to his New Zealand title. During 1985, Ferro's sire, NZ Eng. Ch. Ursulas Figaro of Wellfont (Imp. Denmark), arrived from England and during his campaign to his New Zealand title won a BIS and three Reserve BIS at All Breed Championship shows and two Speciality shows.

All the imports jointly contributed much to the New Zealand gene pool through their use at stud, or in the litters and subsequent champion offspring produced by Seal Cove throughout the 1980s. Seal Cove is not breeding or showing at the time of going to press, but the significant contribution to the breed through their showing successes, presentation and handling skills in the show ring, and the numerous hours of club involvement at all levels, deserves acknowledgement.

SCANDINAVIA

In recent years the Scandinavian countries, and Denmark in particular, have been considered something of a mecca by Newfoundland fanciers in Britain. Many breeders felt that the combination of old and new bloodlines, together with a definitive 'type', were essential to the future of British dogs.

Today the Danish Newfoundland Club has roughly one thousand members. There are approximately fifty Newfoundland kennels, and about five hundred puppies are registered annually. The club has nine regions which organise some of their own events such as Obedience training, fun matches, Agility and seminars. One region has even begun water trials based on the rules of the Newfoundland Club of America.

Up until 1970, the Danish Newfoundland was heavily influenced by Swedish, Dutch, German and English dogs, but since then there has been a greater American influence. The first American import, Little Bears Royal Top Gallant, purchased by the Caniz Major kennel, was an important factor in shaping the destiny of Scandinavian breeding. 'Gallant's' son, Int. Dk. Ch. Caniz Major Skibber, became one of the most important show and stud dogs in the history of Danish Newfoundlands; according to the late Mrs Maynard K. Drury he was one of the three best Newfoundlands in the world! This bloodline, together with US and Canadian breeding, ensures that Scandinavia still has some of the best Newfoundlands in Europe.

LEADING KENNELS IN DENMARK
BJORNEBANDEN
(Winne and Soren Wesseltoft)
The kennel was established in 1977 by Winne and Soren. Their first litter was out of Ch. Ursulas Mrs Macmillan by Caniz Major Muntanus. Putting aside any 'kennel blindness', the Wesseltofts looked to the USA for Newfies to import and bought in a bitch – Birkegardens Andrea Chern – who, although born in Denmark, was from a mating which had taken place in America. Shortly afterwards they also imported Edenglens Olivia Newfy John from the USA. By now they were happy with their type of heads, but felt that they could improve upon necks, topline, hind angulation and overall balance.

After visiting the well-known American Pouch Cove kennels in New Jersey they felt that here was the right type of Newfie, and the following year the dog who became Dk.

Dk. Ch. Yankee Peddler of Pouch Cove, founder of the Bjornebanden line.

Photo: Soren Wesseltoft.

Ch. Yankee Peddler of Pouch Cove made his way to Denmark. Not only were they impressed with his type and balance, but he also proved to be an influential stud dog, particularly when used on powerful-looking bitches. In all he produced thirteen champions, mostly males. At the time of writing, Yankee had just celebrated his twelfth birthday with hardly a grey hair!

In recent years the Bjornebanden Kennel has slightly curtailed its breeding activities due to other commitments such as judging. (Soren is also a much-sought-after Newfie photographer.) However, they hope to keep carrying on the line from their two young bitches, Pouch Cove's Good News and Cayuga's When You Are Smiling.

CANNONBEAR (Einar Paulsen)
The Cannonbear Kennel was founded in Norway in 1980, before moving to Denmark in 1991. Despite changing countries, however, the Cannonbear aim has always been to produce Newfoundlands of good construction and characteristic temperament. The foundation bitches, Ch. Larissimas Edith Piaf (Scandinavian lines) and Ch. Bubbelinas Dekanawida Squaw (Canadian/American lines), were good producers. Mating their offspring together was a successful recipe for putting Cannonbears on the map, and champions were made up in Norway, Sweden, Denmark and Finland. There were also several CC winners in other European countries.

Using the well-known Ch. Yankee Peddler of Pouch Cove (Bjornebanden kennel) on Ch. Bubbelinas Dekanawida Squaw produced a notable litter containing three BIS winners. Ch. Bjornebanden's Try For An Oscar is one of them.

The same year that the Cannonbears moved to Denmark, 'Oscar' was Newfoundland of the Year and No. 6 Dog of the Year, All Breeds. In 1992 he continued his successful run by winning Male of the Year at the Danish Newfoundland Club. His daughter, Ch. Cannonbear's Cotton Top was No. 1 Bitch in 1993 – a feat which was repeated in 1994 by her half-sister, Ch. Cannonbear's Entering the Ring.

The new addition to the kennel is the US import Pouch Cove's Windwagon Whaler, already a CC-winner in two countries. His soundness and excellent temperament combined with his pedigree should mean that he will blend well with the Cannonbear lines.

JEHAJ (Ebba Roed and Jørn Knudsen)
The Jehaj Kennel was established in 1980, with a black bitch called Miranigra. Since then, a union between Newfhouse Estralita and Fjordblinks Haakon produced the kennel's foundation bitch, Jehaj Vilhelmina. She was a very large bitch and, in her first litter, produced some well-known dogs such as Jehaj Albert and Jehaj Athena. The breeding programme then, as at present,

Ch. Cannonbears Cotton Top, Ch. Bjornebandens Try For An Oscar, Ch. Cannonbears Entering The Ring.

Photo: Soren Wesseltoft.

Dk & Int. Ch. Jehaj Rikard, a multi-title winner.

concentrates on producing heavy-boned and good-moving dogs. Breeding stock is selected from first impressions and not when the eye has familiarised itself with the dog's faults. This intuition has proved successful in breeding a total of seventeen Jehaj champions. Despite this the Knudsens still consider themselves small breeders who enjoy their hobby, and are most concerned that their puppies are well cared for in good homes.

Vilhelmina and Athena have been the top producing bitches in Denmark for the past seven years, while their breeder has received a total of eleven Gold, eight Silver and five Bronze medals for her efforts. The Jehaj line is particularly strong in producing good males (twelve champions), and Albert was the winner at the German Centenary Show. Some of the other best known Jehaj males are Herluf, Ludvig and Rikard, together with Albert's sire, Fjordblinks Haakon. Both Ludvig and Rikard have offspring in England, with Rikard being top stud dog in the UK in 1995. Eight of the Jehaj champions have also won their titles in countries other than Denmark. All Jehaj dogs are black, but carry the brown gene.

LA BELLAS (Birthe and Palle Moller Hansen)
When Birthe and Palle got married in 1962 they went to a rescue centre where they

found a bitch that was apparently half-Newfoundland. A few weeks after taking her home, she produced two puppies of indeterminate breed. From this traumatic introduction to Newfoundlands *and* breeding, their dog destiny was decided!

They began to show an adult dog and found it an enjoyable hobby. Following advice, the next step was to import one bitch from Finland – La Bella of Ros-Loge (who also decided them on their kennel name, La Bellas) and another from Holland. She became Dk. Ch. Black Beauty v.d. Papenhof, and was sired by the well-known brown, Int. Ch. Duke v.d. Zeepardje.

In 1967 a black male, Ian v. St. Florian, was brought in from Germany. Black Beauty was mated to him the following year and the resulting litter was the first in Denmark to contain brown puppies. From this line came Dk. and Int. Ch. La Bellas Dodo, Dk. and Int. Ch. La Bellas Faust and Swedish Ch. La Bellas Goliath. These can be seen in numerous pedigrees in many European lines today.

In 1978, they exported a brown dog, La Bellas Ibrahim, to Graham and Sue Birch's Wellfont Kennel in England. He sired the famous breed record holder Ch. and Irish Ch. Wellfont Admiral, as well as three other champions in that litter. Other exports to England include La Bellas Winston to Ann Merrick's Nutbrook Kennel, La Bellas Quark to Val Adey's Shermead Kennel, and the brown bitch, La Bellas Abba, to Phyllis and

Dk. Ch. La Bellas Dolittle.
Photo: Soren Wesseltoft.

Dk. Ch. Newfhouse Ready Teddy.

John Colgan's Karazan Kennel. All produced champions.

Other champions to be owned by Birthe and Palle were Dk. Ch. La Bellas Dolittle (black) and Dk. Ch. Kreon v. Porte Amarre, whom they imported from Holland in the early 1980s. Today, the Moller Hansens' busy judging schedule means only the occasional litter is born. Their present dogs are black, brown, and black and white originating from Norway, Germany and Denmark. A little of the first La Bellas litter still exists in some of their dogs, but new bloodlines have also been integrated into the line.

All La Bellas dogs are rigorously checked for hip dysplasia, plus eye and heart defects. Above all, the Moller Hansens are very careful to keep the good temperament.

NEWFHOUSE (Inge Artsoe)
Inge Artsoe was given her first Newfoundland in 1970 as a birthday present from her late husband, Peter. He was a wonderful pet, but not a show dog. However, the breed had endeared itself to her and the following year a bitch, Caniz Major Rosa Danica, came to Newfhouse. She had been sired by the first American import to Denmark – Little Bears Royal Top Gallant. 'Rosa' was bred to the famous Int. Dk. Ch. Caniz Major Skibber and the first Newfhouse litter was born in 1973. Later on she was also mated to the second American import, Little Bears Two If By Sea, and a grand-daughter from this line, Newfhouse Estrelita, became the foundation bitch for the Jehaj Kennel.

Striving for type, soundness and temperament, the Newfhouse Kennel imported dogs from America and Canada, and in 1978 was part of a 'five-family' importation of the Canadian dog, Topmast Hannibal.

In 1986 Inge purchased the puppy Napsigals Rozanne. Dogs have to be two years old before they win their championship titles in Denmark. However, in those first two years, Rozanne wasted no time and won an impressive nine Certificates, five BoB, BIG 2 and Top Bitch 1988! She eventually succumbed to the call of the whelping box at six years old and went on to have three litters.

The first (by Int. Multi Ch. New-Fuur-Land's Block Buster) produced Newfhouse Roly Poly Ursula, a Danish and Swedish Champion. Her litter brother Dk. Ch. Newfhouse Ready Teddy was Top Dog 1995 with four BoBs, a BIG 1 and BIS 4.

The second litter (by Dk. Ch. Jehaj Rikard) was also very successful. A litter brother and sister went to the Merrybear Kennels in England: Newfhouse Scandinavian Warrior and Newfhouse Scandinavian Princess soon won their English titles, ending 1995 as Top Dog and Top Bitch, placing Newfhouse as Top Breeders in the UK.

Newfhouse Sweet Savannah stayed in Denmark where she won a CC as well as being very successful in Norway and Sweden – no mean feat for a kennel who breed as a hobby to maintain the breed's characteristics and who show their dogs for fun.

NEW-FUUR-LAND
(Dorte and Aage Kvols)
It is more than forty years since Dorte Kvols grew up with two Newfoundlands, who were imported by an uncle who had lived in Newfoundland. Aage was introduced to the breed in the early 1970s and bought his first

Multi-champion New-Fuur-Land's Block Buster.
Photo: Soren Wesseltoft.

Newfoundland in 1975. Together with Dorte, on the small island of Fuur, they started the New-Fuur-Land Kennel in 1987 with a combination of Canadian, American and European lines.

Their second litter was a great success (Dk. Ch. Jehaj Albert x Black Dome's Handle With Care) as it contained the well-known Multi Ch. New-Fuur-Land's Block Buster. He won his first BoB under an American judge at the prestigious Gold Cup Show! Since then he has amassed a total of twenty BoBs, six Best in Group and four times BIS at International Shows. 'Buster' has also been nominated top producing sire by the Danish Newfoundland Club – five of his progeny gained their titles in 1995. Also during that year he was Number Two (All Breeds) on the Danish Kennel Club Winners' list of progeny producers.

Of the other dogs produced at New-Fuur-Land, the most notable are Multi Ch. New-Fuur-Land's Eros, who was sold to Germany (making a name for himself as a stud dog there) and Dk. Ch. New-Fuur-Land's Easy Rider, the only brown champion in Denmark for over twelve years.

Other dogs owned or bred by the Kvols have also made a contribution to the German show ring, and New-Fuur-Lands breeding can be seen in many countries such as Holland, Switzerland, Slovenia, Japan, Mexico, Israel, Great Britain and many more European destinations.

URSULAS (Birgitte Gothen)
The Ursulas Newfoundlands were

established in 1961, making this breeding the oldest in Denmark today. At first the dogs were based on Danish, Swedish and German stock. Later the breeding programme was strongly based on English and American lines.

The use of American/Int. Ch. Caniz Major Skibber resulted in several winners. The most famous was Int. Swedish, Norwegian and Nordic Ch. Ursulas Mac Mortensen. He was a Multi-Group and BIS winner and sired many champions in Finland, Norway and Sweden. He was sold as a puppy to Gass Cohn Kennels in Sweden. His two litter sisters gained their titles, namely Ch. Ursulas Mrs Macmillan and the well-known Int. Dk. NL Ch. Ursulas and Mary's Dream. She became the dam of Eng. Ch. Ursulas Brigitte of Wellfont.

Another illustrious dog from the Ursulas Kennel was the magnificent landseer, Int. Dk. Ch. Ursulas Captain Cook (Topmast Hannibal x Ch. Roydsrook Star Maiden). 'Cook' won the Danish Speciality in a huge entry in 1981 at only twelve months old. He went on to win several BIS in Denmark, BIS in Torino (Italy) and in Monaco, as well as winning the Champion of Champions competition.

Several exports in the 1980s to the British Wellfont Kennel proved to be successful, including the landseer English Ch. Ursulas White Sails, the black male Int. Dk. and English Ch. Ursulas Admiral Ascot and English Ch. Ursulas Figaro of Wellfont.

Ch. Tuckamores Big Dipper:
Sire of over 30 champions.
Photo: Soren Wesseltoft.

SUCH Karilands Sebelon.

Figaro later went to New Zealand, where he was also an influential stud dog.

Meanwhile at home, Ascot's sister, Int. Dk. Ch. Ursulas Alexandra, a speciality BIS winner, produced Ursulas Renata who also went to the Wellfont Kennel in England and, in turn, was dam to several champions. Also at this time the Ursulas Kennels imported Tuckamores Big Dipper from America. He was to be a great supplement to the line in Denmark. He won his Danish, Swedish, Finnish and International titles as well as Groups in Finland and several Specialities in Denmark. He was an excellent stud dog, siring more than thirty champions and remaining fertile up until his eleventh year. A son from one of his last litters was exported to the Krystalcove Kennels in Australia where he quickly gained his title.

Another Ursulas youngster, Black Nestor, was imported by Willie Dobbin (Ireland) and has notched up some impressive wins. With a splendid total of thirty-four champions so far, Ursulas Newfoundlands are still active and, at the moment, there are nine dogs sharing the home of their owner and breeder, Birgitte Gothen.

LEADING KENNELS IN SWEDEN

KARILANDS (Karin and Erland Thorander)
Before the Thoranders purchased their first Newfoundland puppy in 1962, their involvement with the German Shepherd and the Swedish Foundry Dog Association created their belief that a dog must be sound and able to function correctly. The male puppy, West Side Rocco, was a successful show dog who gained his International and Nordic (Scandinavian) titles. At that time the breed in Sweden was varied in type, and 'Rocco's' sire had come from Finland (where the breed had many features lacking in Swedish dogs). A Rocco daughter and her half-sister were brought in. Both were out of the Swiss import Int. Nord. Ch. Zara de Novai and had been X-rayed free of hip dysplasia. These three Newfoundlands were the base for the Karilands line. Rocco proved to be an influential sire, producing an excellent brood bitch in Int. Nord. Ch. Klovagardens Lonaja, who went on to produce several International champions from different sires. The most well-known Rocco son was probably Int. Nord. Ch. Karilands Harpo, who sired more than twenty-five champions in Sweden and Norway. 'Harpo' was used on Int. Nord. Ch. Klovagarden's Eboli (half sister to Lonaja) to produce SUCH Karilands Pilar, dam of SUCH Karilands Ystra Yosephine, one of the most successful bitches of the 1980s. 'Pilar' was also the dam of the first Newfoundland Obedience Champion in Sweden, Karilands Odenick.

In 1981 the Hamilton Plaquette was awarded to the Thoranders in recognition of their improvement of the breed. This award, from the Swedish Kennel Club, is probably the highest honour a breeder can receive in Sweden and is presented every two years.

A significant addition to the Kariland's Kennel in 1988 was the Danish Gold Cup Winner, Borghojs Drummer of America. In spite of the demanding quarantine regulations, the Thoranders had no hesitation in purchasing him. This proved to be a wise choice, as 'Drummer' soon won his Swedish and International titles along with BIS and Group wins. Drummer passed on his size, elegance and excellent movement, and founded a very strong bitch line in his daughters. When mated to SUCH Top Bear's Colette-Canada he produced SUCH and NUCH Karilands Kalahari and his sister

SUCH Lotgardens Petra van Emigrant.

SUCH Karilands Karamba. The present-day Karilands males, SUCH and NUCH Karilands Navajo Nick, SUCH Karilands Sebelon and Sir Sampo are all sons of Karamba.

Although the lines are now into their ninth generation and contain more Danish and American blood, the old foundations are still present and are cherished by the Thoranders. To date the kennel has owned or bred approximately sixty champions, thirteen of which have been International Champions.

LOTGARDENS (Ann-Chatrin Holmkvist) The first Lotgardens litter was bred in 1977 from the black bitch SUCH Karilands Jawa, and sired by Int. Nord. Ch. Karilands Harpo. A black bitch was retained – Lotgardens Alicia-Klyka – who became a Swedish and Finnish Champion, as well as the foundation bitch for the Lotgardens line.

Since then the Lotgardens' breeding programme has continued to aim for broad backs and well-developed forechests. Ann-Chatrin often says: "You should be able to set a table for four people on the broad back of a Newfoundland!".

Many Lotgardens champions and CC winners can be found in Sweden, Norway and Finland. One of the most important dogs of this kennel is Int. Nord. Ch. Lotgardens Bommeboll (SUCH Ben-Carlow x SUCH, SFUCH Lotgardens Alicia-Klyka), a top winning dog himself and also proving to be an influential sire. Some other notable winners were SUCH, NUCH Lotgardens X-tina (Int. Nord. Ch. Framnasgarden's Eskil x SUCH, SFUCH Lotgardens Petra van Emigrant), her daughter Int. Ch. Lotgardens Q-riosa, and a son of 'Petra' (by NUCH, SUCH Spokinewfs Cariboo Cowboy) SUCH Lotgardens Lord van Cowboy.

In 1993 the kennel's most successful dog SUCH, NUCH Lotgardens Wotan van Aussie Bear (Int. Ch. Sikandi Aussie Bear x SUCH Lotgardens Lea Loa Lonaja) was the beginning of an involvement with white/black Newfoundlands. Sikandi Aussie Bear had been imported to Norway from Australia and had many followers. At the time, the lack of stud dogs made it difficult to breed this colour, but the recent opening of the borders to Europe may see the use of new and interesting bloodlines. 'Wotan' also produced the Int. Ch. Lotgardens Grodan Boll (out of Amoradas Invisible Touch).

Today the Lotgardens Kennel looks forward to be able to broaden their breeding by incorporating lines not previously available to them. Two promising youngsters are already setting this trend, being from American lines through Int. Nord. Ch. Tuckamores Big Dipper and Pouch Cove's Patriot of Cayuga.

QASHIWAS (Kerstin Einarsson) Of the three first bitches owned by Kerstin, SUCH Miklagarden's Dancing Queen, Int. S. NUCH Phantons Byronic Melancoly and Int. S. NUCH Ominmacs Qashiwa (brown), it was the last one who became the foundation for the kennel (and gave it the chosen name!). Her descendants are still important in the show ring and breeding programmes in Sweden today.

The Danish import SUCH Bjornebanden's Roy Rogers combined with the Qashiwa line produced well, and had a considerable influence on the kennel. 'Qashiwa' herself was top winning bitch in Sweden and Norway in 1985 before being mated to the Danish dog, NUCH Wooddales Lord Nelson. This litter produced Qashiwas Chiquitita and her

181

A group of four Qashiwas International Champions winning a Breeders Group.

brothers Int. S. NUCH Qashiwas Cassanova and Int. S. NUCH Qashiwas Chalabolic (the latter making a show ring comeback at eight years old to win nine Groups and ten other Group placings!). Chalabolic's daughter, Ch. Qashiwas Kiss Me Quick, was top winning bitch in Sweden, while one of Cassanova's sons was Top Winning Newfoundland in Finland in 1990 and 1993, before winning BIS at Monte Carlo and the World Winners' Show at Barcelona.

Chiquitita, although she was not a show dog, mated to Roy Rogers produced three International Qashiwas Champions, namely Johnny Walker (BIS Morokulien), Jackpot and Jasmine. All three were BIS winners and have an impressive list of BoB and Group wins. Another brother, Ch. Qashiwas Joyful Jack, had a strong influence in Finland where he won a Stud Dog of the Year title. These dogs were the only offspring of Roy Rogers left to the Qashiwas Kennel, as he was unfortunately killed in a car accident at a young age. However, he produced about twenty champions in all and the kennel has made use of his bloodlines through the dogs produced by other breeders. In particular, a son of Roy Rogers, Int. S. N. Dk. Ch. Riaborgen's Dipper Man, mated to Chiquitita, produced some first-class dogs

who are still active at Qashiwas Kennel.

Since the first Qashiwas litter in 1984 (containing the well known winner NORDUCH Qashiwas Apple Jack) there have been more than thirty champions, six being International title holders, and many more certificate winners. Although there have been certificate winners in *every litter* born at the kennel, Kerstin does not believe in repeating a mating. It is her aim to go *forward* in the breed, so each mating is planned with this philosophy in mind. Now that Sweden does not have closed borders, Qashiwas Newfoundlands can be seen in other countries, as it is not so important to keep the best dogs in Sweden.

Even though Qashiwas is synonymous with show dogs, when the first water trial tests were held in Sweden in 1995, several of this breeding attended and were successful. Soundness has remained an important aim for the kennel and Kerstin is understandably proud of the numbers of Qashiwas Newfoundlands who are free from HD – 78per cent to date.

During the late 1980s some white/black puppies were produced, but this line was not continued. The original black-carrying brown line, however, remains successful and of great use to many other Swedish breeders.

NSUCH Birkorella's Fortuna.

Qashiwas dogs are still no strangers to BIS wins, with Kerstin's Riaborgen's Dipper Man taking this award at Morokulien 96, while SUCH Qashiwas Big Bubble No Trouble and Int. Ch. Qashiwas Private Collection collected the BIS 2 and BIS 4 placings. Dipper Man has also won BIS at a Kennel Club Show and is the sixth-generation BIS winner from the Qashiwas Kennel – an enviable achievement!

LEADING KENNELS IN NORWAY

BIRKORELLA
(Astrid Indrebø and Knut Gjersem)
The kennel was established in 1983 with the purchase of N. Ch. Larissima's Emorella, a lovely black puppy bred by Rigmor and Anne-Kathrine Ulstad. Emorella was not only the foundation bitch of Birkorella and their first Champion, but also their first Newfoundland. She lived until the age of twelve and had two litters; one with N. S. Ch. Nordkjerns Apollon and one with frozen sperm from Topsails Thunder-Skibber, the first known frozen-sperm litter of Newfoundlands in the world.

From Emorella's first litter, the breeders kept two puppies, Int. N. S. Ch. Birkorella's A Touch of Tatjana and Birkorella's Akantus JomJom a-ha. 'Touchi' became champion at the age of nineteen months and is to date dam of six champions, all free of HD.

From Emorella's second litter came three champion bitches, N. S. Ch. Birkorella's Emega, who at the age of only twenty months won both Certificate and BoB at the 1992 joint Norwegian-Swedish show in Morokulien (the biggest Speciality show for Newfoundlands in Scandinavia). N. Ch. Birkorella's Etotti Eureka stayed at Birkorella and is the dam of Birkorella's Magic Touch (by Twillin Gate Pharlap), already a Certificate winner at sixteen months. From this litter also came N. S. Ch. Birkorella's Ebenne Femme (bronze bitch 1993).

Birkorella's Akantus JomJom a-ha went on to produce N. S. Ch. Birkorella's Fortuna, a Certificate winner at Morokulien 1994, bronze bitch in Norway during 1994, and silver bitch in 1995. Mated to Twillin Gate Pharlap she produced nine puppies in 1994 and, more recently, using frozen sperm, had a further two to Ch. Tuckamore's Big Dipper. The two Dipper puppies have been retained, with high hopes.

From Emorella's second litter, Birkorella's Bright Sunshine O'Majo was kept. She was mated to Ursulas Gideon the Sweet and produced one puppy, N. Ch. Birkorella's Gaia, Certificate winner in Morokulien 1994 and top winning Newfoundland in Norway in the same year. Astrid and Knut sum up their breeding programme by saying: "We have great visions to combine the best of the old Scandinavian and European lines with the top American lines, producing strong, healthy and beautiful dogs with strong anatomy and movement, with the typical Newfie temperament and working ability."

FERRYLAND (Irene and Johnny Donne) Ferryland was established in 1981 with the purchase of N. SF. Ch. Sinderalla Damsgård of Cariad. She became Ferryland's foundation bitch and their first Champion. In her four litters she produced several champions and excellent breeding material. Staying at Ferrylands were dogs such as N. Ch. Ferryland's Avec Grandeur (BIS winner), N. Ch. Ferryland's Bellevue, N.

NS Ch. Kanikula's Esmeralda Chatta Chutt.

Ch. Ferryland's En Voyage and the bitch Ferryland's Aux Petite Sabina, two CCs. Sold to other kennels were the bitches N. Ch. Ferryland's Avant Douze Heures, Ferryland's Bon Matin Therese with two CCs, and Ferryland's Bobine Noire, Ferryland's Emily and Ecolette, with one CC each. All made a valuable contribution to the breed for their owners at the Gas-Cohn, Growler, Tessmira and Toppoloppo kennels.

In 1994 they imported a male puppy, N. Ch. Twillin Gate Silvermoon from Belgium (Joringel Christmas Carol x Jubilee You're the Top). He became a Champion at twenty-four months; before that he was World Junior Winner at Brussels, Junior Winner Gold Cup 1995 Denmark, BoB NNK Special 1995 at Bergen and BIS 2 NKK International Show All Breeds Konigsberg 1996. Together with the bitch Toppoloppo's Dame Edna (Ital. Ch. Pouch Cove's Patriot of Cayuga x Ferryland's Ecolette), he is expected to reach the goals at Ferryland Newfoundlands.

KANIKULA (Eva Øverlien)
The kennel was established in 1983, with the purchase of N. S. Ch. Bubbelina's Chattanooga Choo-Choo (Int. N. S. Ch. Bubbelina's Aegir Skibber x Lifebouy's Penny of Bubbelina) from Liv and Jan Fridtjofsen's Bubbelina Kennel in Norway. Prior to this, Eva had owned a few Newfoundlands as companion dogs and had bred the occasional litter without great success.

Chattanooga was her foundation bitch and first Champion, earning her title in both Norway and Sweden. She produced the 'E' litter (by Int. N. S. Ch. Top Bear's Arramac) which included N. S. Ch. Kanikula's Esmeralda Chatta Chutt (brown), N. S. Ch. Kanikula's Eldar Anorakk (brown) and N. S. Ch. Kanikula's Elmer Automat (black). Later on, mated to Ch. Bjornebanden's Roy Rogers, she also produced the 'H' litter, containing the Champions N. Ch. Kanikula's Hundred Mile Rat Race and N. S. Ch. Kanikula's Huntonitt and Rolls Royce, both black.

Eva is particularly proud of the 'E' litter. 'Elmer', with his extremely good bone size and good temperament and movement, has sired some very good Newfoundlands in Norway. Nord. Ch. Kanikula's Leonora Fjong Luftesnora and N. S. Ch. Toppoloppo's Big Mama Gøril (out of Ferryland's Ecolette) are two of his daughters kept at Kanikula. Gøril is dam of the Newfoundland of the Year in 1995, BW-95 Kanikula's Nicoline Bertinemamelukk. 'Nicoline' is owned by the Toppoloppo Kennel and won a CC at the World Show in Brussels in 1995. At the time of writing she is too young to gain her title but is well on the route to titles in Norway, Sweden and Belgium.

One of the most recent litters (from Gøril by N. S. Ch. Kanikula's Freeway Cruiser) was the 'O' litter. Two males and a bitch were kept and it is hoped that Ola Uteligger Fjodor, Oline Baertyttesvingen and Oldsmobile Fridtjof will become well-known names for the Kanikula Kennel in the future.

TOPPOLOPPO (Irene and Knut Berglie)
The couple bought their first Newfoundland

in 1981 – Betzy (Hässleholms Yambo x Blacki), who was a friend and family dog. She was taken to a few shows, with acceptable results, but she was not a winner. Irene and Knut enjoyed the shows so much that in 1982 they bought another bitch who did well at shows, but unfortunately her hips were not quite good enough for breeding. In 1984 they bought Galbybygda's Aqua (N. Ch. Larissima's Baccardi x Raelingåsen's Bessie), a very good quality bitch with sound hips and elbows, so they decided to have one litter – their first, known as the 'A' litter. The puppies were born in May 1987, but unfortunately they did not share her good characteristics so she was not bred from again.

N.S. Dk. Fin. Nord. Ch. Toppoloppo's Birdy.

With their kennel name of Toppoloppo established, the Berglies were determined to breed first-class Newfoundlands. In 1988 they found a new bitch, Ferryland's Ecolette (Ursulas Gideon The Sweet x N. Fin. Ch. Sinderella Damsgaard of Cariad). Ecolette won a CC and several Reserve CCs at shows, so they decided to try one litter again. In September 1991 the 'B' litter, sired by N. S. Ch. Kanikula's Elmer Automat, was born and produced N. S. Dk. Fin. Nord. Ch. Toppoloppo's Birdy, N. Dk. Fin. Nord. Ch. Toppoloppo's Batman, N. Ch. Toppoloppo's Bigwig, N. Ch. Toppoloppo's Bulle v. Basten and N. S. Ch. Toppoloppo's Big Mama Gøril. Five Champions in four countries from the same litter! (Birdy and Batman missed one CACIB each to become Int. Champions). All the males have offspring in Norway and, although they are still young, their quality is obvious.

A repeat mating gave the 'C' litter, a bitch from which, Toppoloppo Calotta, has produced very good puppies to males of different bloodlines.

To build upon the successful 'B' litter Toppoloppo started to co-operate with Cayuga Newfoundlands in Italy (Manlio Massa), and Toppoloppo Batman was loaned on a temporary basis. A great opportunity arose to borrow the American male Int. I. A. N. S. Dk. Fin. Nord. Ch. Pouch Cove's Patriot of Cayuga, who stayed in Norway for six months.

Following 'Patriot's' working holiday, the 'D' litter was born in May 1995 (from Pouch Cove's Patriot of Cayuga x Ferryland's Ecolette). The Berglies kept a male and a bitch, Toppoloppo Doggens and Toppoloppo Druen Diadora. At only twelve months of age Doggens won his second CC at the largest Special show in Scandinavia. Druen Diadora at the same show won her fourth and was the Best Bitch and BIS.

Toppoloppo's Dame Edna was sold to the breeders of her dam, Ferryland Newfoundlands and in December 1995, Toppoloppo's Daddy Blue left Norway with N. S. Dk. Fin. Nord. Ch. Toppoloppo's Birdy, bound for the UK to become foundation dogs for Alan and Chris Parker of Angelhouse Newfoundlands.

At the time they sold their 'C' litter Irene and Knut decided to buy a new bitch. Naturally they chose a puppy of N. S. Ch. Toppoloppo's Big Mama Gøril, sired by N. S. Ch. Kanikula's Huntonitt and Rolls Royce. N. S. Belg. W-95 Kanikula's Nicoline Bertinemamelukk started her show career in great style, winning CCs and CACIBs many times in Norway and Sweden by the time she was two years old. At the World Show in Brussels 1995, she won the CC and Belgian Winner 1995 title. Several BoBs at Norwegian shows followed, making her Top Winning Newfoundland in Norway in 1995.

Toppoloppo's aim is to produce Newfoundlands of the correct type, typical expression, good bone and, above all, of good health and exceptional temperament. The 'E' litter will come from Ferryland's Ecolette and the famous Danish male Int. Dk. S. N. Nord. Ch. Jehaj Rikard.

BEST OF THE REST
Some other influential breeders and kennels in Scandinavia have been:
BRAENDEGARDEN (Kirsten and Ingolf Larsen) whose first homebred Dk. and Swedish Ch. Braendegardens Frodo has set them on the Yankee Peddler line that they so admire.
EGEBAEK (Marianne and Karsten Baaner) who have had recent success with Dk. Ch. Egebaek's First Flame and Dk. Ch. Egebaek's Flashpoint, as well as having produced some quality blacks from this line.
KAROUSKA (Kari and Leif Jensen) who, despite keeping breeding to a minimum, are consistent in producing quality blacks and browns while maintaining health and type.
MELDGAARDEN (Uffe Søndergaard) who has been breeding Newfoundlands since 1979 and whose personal favourite must be the Gold Medal-winning Dk. Ch. Meldgaarden's Bachimini (dam of Int. Dk. Ch. Meldgaarden's Jigger Joe).
SCHIMO (Sølvi and Inge Mosand) who have bred only 32 puppies over the last ten years, but who have had phenomenal success, especially with their well-known N. S. Ch. Schimo Ciao-Ciao Chalabaiz – a real character who loves the limelight and has an impressive array of Group and BIS wins.
TOPSY (Ernst Lilleris Agerholm and the late Erling Larsen) who, prior to Erling's tragic death, dominated the Danish show ring with

a seemingly never-ending line of champions. Topsy stock have been successful in many countries and have combined well with other lines.

FRANCE
Over the last twenty years, the breed has continued to evolve to satisfy the demand for the type of dog being produced. Dog shows, of course, provide an element of attraction to those interested in the breed, but the general public awareness in France is as a result of the water tests and demonstrations organised by the French Newfoundland Club over the past two decades.

The French Newfoundland Club is the only official breed club (in France, only one club is permitted for any breed) and is responsible for the promotion of the breed. It is recognised as a public service, affiliated to the Central Canine Society and approved by the Ministry of Agriculture. The Club has an eight hundred strong membership and a dog population of about four thousand.

In recent years the dogs have been divided into approximately 80 per cent blacks, 17 per cent brown and 3 per cent black and white. General development and the use of imported bloodlines have resulted in a growing interest and quality in the minority colours.

Many of today's breeders own only a small kennel (two–ten dogs) but there remains a widespread breeding programme throughout the country. Among the senior breeders who influenced the development of the Newfoundland are La Mare Bleue, De Tiad Douar Nevez, Du Moulin De Plainville, Du Manoir De Ricquemesnil, Du Domaine Des Deux Cedres, Du Lac Aux Genets, Des Loges De Pierrefeu and DE LA PIERRE AUX COQS (the last still successfully breeding today).

Since then, many other lines have been created, the best-known being DU

MOUSTERO (Mme Segonds), LES BLANCS CAILLAUX LEZENNOIS (M. and Mme Leroy-Napoli), LA VALLEE FERON (M. and Mme Dehais) and OF SEA BIRD SANCTUARY (M. Prunier), to name but a few.

In common with other European countries, France has recently made use of American blood, and the combination, when used realistically, has had some interesting results. The efforts of French breeders are put to the test twice a year when two important shows are held, namely the Championship Show of France (which takes place in Paris every June), organised by the Central Canine Society, and the 'National Breeders', organised by the Newfoundland Club of France. Both can attract as many as three hundred dogs each year.

LEADING FRENCH KENNELS

DU MOUSTERO (Nicole Segonds)
Nicole Segonds bought her first Newfoundland in 1972 and, a few years later, also adopted a young male. In 1981 she became interested in shows when she was offered a lovely bitch, Shiva de Ricquemesnil, by the French Club. Shiva, who originated in Switzerland, was mated to Vercors de la Pierre aux Coqs and produced the superb male Breizh du Moustero (National Champion of Beauty). Soon after, Nicole bought in a bitch from Dutch lines – Colline de la Ferme de Kerdoret.

Colline, mated to Breizh, produced three champions in the first litter, namely Fest-Noz du Moustero (French Ch.), Fargo du Moustero and Feeling-Blue du Moustero (Int. and Luxembourg Ch.)

Following a trip to Finland in 1989, Nicole returned with a bitch, Larinkallion Dee Dee Tee (called E.T.). Mated to Breizh, E.T. produced the very impressive French Champion, Golfer du Moustero. A combination of E.T. and a brown German Champion, Eskapade's Bacardi, was

Int. & Lux. Ch. Feeling Blue du Moustero.

attempted on two occasions and a female, Jolie-Belle du Moustero, was retained. A litter brother was sold to the Engrands and both were successful at the same National show. E.T. and Colline are now retired, but their offspring still reside at du Moustero, including the two males, Inook and Idem (sons of Ch. Laurent VH Hoogven and Vercors respectively), Idem's sister Ioda, the British-bred Shermead Gospel (La Bellas and Karazan lines), and E.T.'s daughter, Jolie-Belle. The future of du Moustero now rests with a daughter of Golfer and one of Gospel's puppies by Idem. A recent journey to Canada will probably also result in an imported puppy. As well as her breeding activities, Nicole is kept busy with judging, with organising shows and also as vice-president of the Newfoundland Club Committee.

DE LA PIERRE AUX COQS (M. and Mme Etienne Engrand)
This kennel was established in 1968 and is the oldest active Newfoundland kennel in France. As experienced breeders, the Engrands are keen to provide comprehensive literature to potential Newfoundland owners. They advise a natural diet and the rigorous coat care which has been so successful during their time in the breed.

Pierre aux Coqs dogs have won a great array of titles over the years and the Engrands have also been honoured for their efforts. Although there are many French title

The multi-titled Ch. Vercors De La Pierre Aux Coqs.

holders from the kennel, there is an equally impressive list of International Champions. These include the British import Int. Ch. Plaisance Night Sentinel and the Danish import Int. Ch. Wooddales Fyrst Newfy, as well as the home-bred Int. Chs. Jolie-Belle and Roz-Belle de la Pierre aux Coqs.

Bloodlines from other countries have also been useful to the Engrands, and the Swedish imports Ch. Klovagardens Rudolf and Klovagardens Asa Alea were to play an important part in the kennel's history. Other old but successful bloodlines used were Birgitte Gothen's Ursulas dogs and the Broeckers' von Luxemburg line. To date, De La Pierre Aux Coqs Newfoundlands have won a total of one hundred and twelve CACIBs, fifty-two RCACIBs, one hundred and eighty CACs and seventy RCACs – an impressive total by any standards. The Engrands' aim is still to produce a sound Newfoundland with typical temperament and the soul of a rescuer.

GERMANY

In Germany, the role of the Newfoundland in the water is less important. Although there are two working groups in Germany (North and South), there are no working titles available. The practical side of working the Newfoundland poses a few problems, in that dogs are not often allowed to swim in public water. Despite this, the small band of enthusiasts continues to train its dogs.

Breeding and showing are quite strictly controlled, with the aspiring breeder having to apply to a ruling body and state his intention to produce puppies.

The organisation governing all breeds and clubs is the Verband für das Deutsche Hundwesen (VDH) and there are two official breed clubs existing under this banner, the best-known being the Deutscher Neufundländer-Klub (DNK). The other, the Neufundländer-Klub für der Kontinent, was most important to the earliest history of the breed in Germany. The VDH's strict rules regarding the breeding and welfare of dogs may seem a little harsh to breed lovers from other countries, but some members and the breed warden of the DNK feel that Newfoundlands have considerably more freedom than many other breeds!

As in many other countries, there is great discussion as to what is the 'correct' type of Newfoundland. Imports from America are becoming commonplace, with some breeders preferring the head type, heavier bone and smooth gait of these dogs. Others feel that some of the American heads are a little overdone and avoid such bloodlines. Such diversity in opinion, however, is believed to be good for the breed, as owners can then select their preferred attributes while retaining a healthy and varied gene pool from the use of unrelated dogs.

LEADING GERMAN KENNELS

MOLLY MILL'S NEWFOUNDLANDS
(Gisela M. Decken)
The kennel was registered at the German Newfoundland Club in August 1984, with the first 'A' litter whelped in May, 1985. Gisela's first Newfoundland was the stud Quercy von Söven (Ferro von Söven x Golda von Söven) who was purchased in 1981. The

Molly Mill's Dark Devil relaxing at home.

kennel's foundation bitch was Alexa vom Kyllwaldhof (Atticus vom Söhrenwald x Ria vom Kleinen Bär), a very harmoniously-built, brown bitch. She was inbred from a half-brother/sister mating. Alexa had four litters with solid black studs: Graf von Luxemburg produced the 'A' and 'B' litters; the 'C' litter was from Alf vom Reinheimer Teich; and the 'D' litter was from Jonas v. L.

With bitches from the 'B' and 'D' litters, the line continued when they were mated to the brown Baron zu Sayn-Wittgenstein (son of Enasjöns Jonatan), in order to improve the size. Blacks and brown were produced and the resulting offspring were later mated to Elton John vom Trieberg (to stabilise the size) and Whisperbay's Full Confession (to stabilise and regain the short head type while strengthening the gait).

For the same reasons Duschenka from the 'D' litter and Filly from the 'F' litter were mated to Pouch Coves Windwagon Whaler. In order to improve gait, Gisela plans to use mostly, or even exclusively, American stud dogs until she is satisfied with the result and has achieved a distinguishable type.

Only home-bred Newfoundlands are kept at Molly Mill and, at present, there are a total of eight, including five brood bitches, two veterans and a young brown male, son of Duschenka. All live in the house and garden, as Gisela does not kennel her dogs.

Health, intelligence and then beauty is her list of priorities and attending shows is not a must for Molly Mill Newfoundlands. However, the two to four litters produced per year are well-thought-out and generally good-looking. Blacks are the preferred colour, but browns are quite often produced. To date there have been no black and whites at Molly Mill.

VOM RIESRAND (Evi Grosshauser)
Evi was introduced to the Newfoundland following her marriage into a family who had kept the breed for four generations. Since 1980 her aim has remained constant: to breed friendly and healthy companions to the required Standard. The vom Riesrand line is now in its seventh generation and continues to be successful with dogs of all three colours.

In 1985, a visit to Denmark decided the standard of the dog to aim for, when Evi saw many impressive descendants of the outstanding Skibber. Lines from Black Domes Sir Coxwain and Ferro von Söven were combined, resulting in excellent specimens such as Gammel Dansk, Grand Marnier, Girl and Gollo v. Riesrand – names which can be found in the pedigrees of many successful Newfoundlands.

*A group of Vom
Riesrand
Newfoundlands.*

When the kennel turned its attention to breeding black and white dogs, it met with a problem caused by a shortage of correct breeding material. The answer was to import, from Canada, the following dogs: Moonfleet A Saint I Aint, Ch. Tip Top's Amy of Riesrand and Ch. Tip Top's Iggzakly. From these lines some black and white champions are emerging. Vom Riesrand also has an impressive record of around eighteen brown champions and most of the black dogs also carry the brown gene.

Listing all the successful vom Riesrand dogs would need more space than is available here, and Evi is understandably proud of her breeding and show ring achievements. However, even more important to her is the ability of her dogs to live harmoniously together – a result of rigorous selection of temperament.

VON SÖVEN (Karl Schmitz)
As a youngster, Karl was fascinated by the first Newfoundland dog he saw and later on was deeply impressed by the description of a Newfoundland in the novel *Kleiner Mann* by Hans Fallada. The fact that his family came from a long line of stockmen also inspired him to breed Newfoundland dogs.

The Kennel von Söven was founded in 1971 and the first litter came in 1974 from Diana vom Broichbachtal and Quintus von Brungerst, producing Antje von Söven, who became the basis of the line. Karl feels that, in order to breed high-quality dogs, theoretical knowledge, practical experience and an instinct for what makes up the type is required. To create a good-quality

Newfoundland dog needs, in his opinion, the genes from all colour varieties. His experience has convinced him that breeding for pure colour will mean that the required type will be lost or the Standard will have to be changed.

Von Söven has produced generally high-quality dogs, among them several champions. The dog closest to Karl's ideal of a typical Newfoundland was Ferro von Söven, but similarly important for the breed were Antje, Hanno, Ulrike, Larry, Quay, Quanda, Rebekka, Samson and more recently, Festa, Dino, Dasco and many more, who were successfully used for the breed in other kennels.

*Int., Dk,
VDH, DNK
Ch. Ferro
Von Soven.*

ST. LORENZ-STROM (Brigitte Greisler)
Brigitte has owned Newfoundlands since 1968 when she lived in Erzgebirge in the former East Germany. In 1972, the kennel's first litter arrived from Blacky v.d. Bernhardshöhe (HD-0, East German Junior Champion) mated to the East German Champion Bär v. Lautertal (HD-C).

The intention then, as now, was to produce 'typey' black Newfs with endearing characters and a longer life expectancy. Brigitte had some success, although breeding was often very difficult in former East Germany. A college course taught her more about the science and art of breeding and the knowledge was usefully related to the running of the kennels. Brigitte developed a reputation for her breeding ideas throughout the southern half of East Germany.

In 1971 she purchased the male Bär v. Frankental who was not only important to the kennel but was used on about seventy bitches in his lifetime with a great percentage of his offspring being HD-free. He won his East German title in 1974/75 and also his SZG soon after.

Brigitte also began to judge Newfoundlands and Landseers, as well as visiting kennels to take breeding aptitude tests. In 1984 the kennel moved to West Germany and had to adapt to new breeding techniques and rules with little knowledge of breeding in West Germany.

Despite difficulties St. Lorenz-Strom continued breeding with the male Adonis v. Grafenstein and also mated a bitch, Esther v. Kap Race (brought from East Germany) successfully to Graf v. Luxemburg. The resulting puppies were of high quality, although unfortunately few were shown but kept as loving family pets.

Brigitte also began to produce brown dogs and was approved by the VDH to judge Newfoundlands and Landseers. Today's kennel consists of two black males, one brown bitch and two black bitches.

V.D. WÄSSERNACH (Margit and Peter Krotsch)

Margit and Peter began breeding Newfoundlands in 1983 from the bitch Cora vom Sonnenburg (Ch. Ferro v. Söven x Banja v.d. Hohenhorst). Cora won her VDH, German and International title and

Zorro Von St. Lorenz-Strom.

Graf Von Luxemburg: Owned by the vd Wässernach kennel.

became the founder of the v.d. Wässernach kennel. Their greatest influence was as a result of using German, Austrian, Yugoslavian, VDH and Int. Ch. Graf von Luxemburg in their lines. Graf was a potent stud dog who stamped his type on many of his children and grandchildren, and several of them won their titles in Germany and other countries.

The first litters (from Cora and Graf) put Margit and Peter on the right track initially. Then, by importing the males Topsy's Orlowski (Denmark) and George of the Thatch Roof (Netherlands), together with the bitch Dutch, Int. and World Champion Brendy van't Durpke, they were able to widen their breeding base.

The Krotsch family also successfully used other males at stud and Ursulas Happy Hiawatha, Black Moon Jazz van d'Oultremont, Peter's Know Me, Eskapade's Campari and Whisperbays Full Confession brought them nearer to their ideal Newfoundland. Peter and Margit would rather have all high-quality puppies in their litters than one or two champions and others of below average standard. Also important to them is to produce a long-living and healthy companion.

ITALY

Interest in the Newfoundland began in Italy in 1898 when a history and description of the breed was published by the Italian Kennel Club. It was not until 1920, however, that the first Italian Newfoundland kennel was established – Eduino Colnaghi's DEL SERCHIO line. The kennel's first stud dog, Robur v. Radegast, had the most influence on the breed until around 1936, and an imported Ch. Siki offspring from England also played an important part in the breed's development.

In 1929 the Societa Italiana Terranova (SIT) was formed and other kennels such as the Dell' Agogna line of Silvio and Agnese Cipolla were founded. By the mid-1930s puppy registrations at the Italian KC had reached a total of forty-five, but many breeders and clubs were closing or losing interest. The last Italian litter during the war was in 1941 with almost a ten-year gap before the next, in 1950, from Aido v. Friedbuhl and Flora v.d. Schurz (owned by Armando Piaggio of Genova). Only the DELL' AGOGNA kennel remained active from the previous years. In the decade between 1950 and 1960, registrations rose to sixty-two and were mainly Dell' Agogna-bred puppies. In 1966 a mating between Serio Dell' Agogna and Bounty of Sparry produced the first Italian Newfoundland to gain her International and Italian title, namely Cora. She was owned by Emmy Bruno, founder of the well-known ANGELI NERI Kennel. At this time many other influential kennels came into being. For example, Luisa Bruzzo's DELLE ACQUE CELESTI, Tina Justi Raboqliatti's DEI MOICANI and Dina Laugeri Zaccone's DELLA VENARIA REALE lines all appeared during this period and registrations peaked at eighty-five with a dozen or so importations.

The 1970s saw a sharp rise in registrations to well over three hundred and fifty with more than sixty imports. Other successful kennels began their activities – the most well-known being GEMINORUM (Adrianna Griffa), DEGLI ORSI DI S. MICHELLE (Luciano Verdonesi), INCISIE (Baldovino Incisa Di Camerlana), DELLA GABANINA (Francesco Rocca), DEL LAGHETTO (Zerilli Marimo) and DELLA COMMENSURA (Daniella Cavalli Funiciello).

Following the setting up of the Club Italiano Terranova (CIT) in 1976, there has been increasing interest in the breed and registrations again continued to rise – to over three hundred and fifty during one year. The latter part of the 1980s saw even more new kennels, and the names CAYUGA (Manlio and Paola Massa), VERTIGO (Beatrice Schiatti), OWASCO (Massimo Baronti) and DEL CASTELBARCO (Fedorra Orebic Malfatti) became familiar to Newfoundland fanciers.

These days, registrations can be in excess of five hundred annually and younger kennels are a common sight. In 1993 another club was set up for the promotion and protection of the breed – the Societe Amatori Terranova (SAT), and today Italy is held in great esteem for the high quality of her Newfoundlands.